Sustainable and Green Supply Chains and Logistics Case Study Collection

Sustainable and Green Supply Chains and Logistics Case Study Collection

Edited by Ozlem Bak

KoganPage

First published in Great Britain and the United States in 2021 by Kogan Page Limited

2nd Floor, 45 Gee Street
London
EC1V 3RS
United Kingdom

122 W 27th St, 10th Floor
New York, NY 10001
USA

4737/23 Ansari Road
Daryaganj
New Delhi 110002
India

www.koganpage.com

Kogan Page books are printed on paper from sustainable forests.

ISBNs

Hardback 9781789668216
Ebook 9781789668223

British Library Cataloguing-in-Publication Data

A CIP record for this book is available from the British Library.

Library of Congress Control Number

2021946865

Typeset by Integra Software Services Pondicherry
Print production managed by Jellyfish
Printed and bound by 4edge Limited, UK

CONTENTS

PREFACE

Given the increasing significance and impact of sustainability and green practices in organizations, the purpose of *Sustainable and Green Supply Chains Logistics Case Study Collection* is to provide insights from companies and to share best practices from industry with professionals and researchers working in the field of sustainable and green supply chains as well as to educate, inform and provide an account of real-life examples. We hope that this book will provide interesting insights to supply chain executives, practitioners and students when dealing with the complex nature of decisions considering multiple stakeholders, often with conflicting objectives on what green and sustainable practices mean and to what extent they can be deployed. Becoming a sustainable and green supply chain will involve introducing a new set of rules and their relationships within/outside supply chain boundaries. The definition of the subject area covers the application of supply chain sustainability and green solutions, the diverse industrial settings that shape the supply chain settings for green and sustainable supply chain practices, and the accounts of implementation cases. Considering that both green and sustainability within the context of supply chains are complex and multifaceted across diverse industrial contexts, presenting a set of diverse cases has been challenging. With this book, an attempt was made to collect diverse cases of sustainable and green supply chains and the challenges that they are facing. This, we hope, will give the reader an understanding of the diverse nature of the industrial contexts and the impact of sustainable and green supply chains. This edited book entails rich content, from the Australian beef industry, the Finnish air compressor industry and Vietnamese SMMEs, to Chinese construction supply chains, entailing not only diverse industrial settings but also a varied geographical coverage. Hence, the contributing authors include academics as well as practitioners and sometimes a successful collaboration of both.

The general aim of this book was geared towards embedding theory and practice, which would bring the much-sought-after reference to the industry as well as standalone cases showing the implications of sustainable and green supply chains. We hope that the cases we describe will provide an understanding of cross-disciplinary issues and that this book could start a discussion of the industrial and geographical constraints, challenges and benefits of sustainable and green supply chains. Therefore, we believe that this book provides a rich picture and a cornucopia of sources with concepts, perspectives and examples which make this book suitable for both practitioners and academics. Thirty authors across eight countries have contributed to this book, which we hope provides different perspectives on sustainable and green supply applications and their impact on the supply chain.

This book has been structured over 15 chapters reflecting the impact of sustainable and green supply chains and the authors' areas of expertise. Although the authors have contributed in diverse sectors and from diverse angles, they all entailed a reflection upon:

1 the impact of sustainable and green practices in supply chain applications;
2 the benefits and implications of sustainable and green practices upon organizations;
3 the potential solutions for sustainable and green practices in supply chains; and finally
4 the learnings and discussion points raised for future implications of sustainable and green practices in supply chains.

The book chapters are structured as follows:

Chapter 1: Dr Desirée Knoppen introduces the first chapter, which involves the Spanish multinational Saica. With €3.9 billion turnover in 2019 and more than 10,000 employees, Saica is present in 10 countries across Europe and North America. The case study highlights the potential of biomethanization and its challenges and benefits, as well as exploring the supply chain that supports this renewable energy.

Chapter 2: Dr Erica Ballantyne and Dr Graeme Heron explore an organization that was looking to develop a manufacturing and distribution facility both to meet the demands of the UK market and to support the main production site on the Western European seaboard. They demonstrate how traditional location decision models no longer reflect developments in sustainable logistics planning scenarios and the dynamic routing opportunities available to logistics service providers to satisfy complex forward and reverse product and packaging/ingredients flows.

Chapter 3: Professor Kim Bryceson, Dr Mohd Mohsin and Professor Geoff Slaughter include with this case study a 'sustainability index' for an Australian beef production organization that was looking to establish a mechanism for measuring the sustainability value of their product (beef) throughout their multi-enterprise company. The company owns multiple production units (farms), a feedlot and a processor, and thus has a vertically integrated value chain.

Chapter 4: Dr Yiqing Zhao and Dr Ying Xie introduce readers to green practices in construction supply chains – how a construction company manages and coordinates its green SCM practices. The chapter discusses context-specific issues to be considered for construction supply chains and especially highlights the fact that regulations and internal factors are considered to be the source of important green SCM drivers and pressures. In particular, medium and large Chinese companies face higher regulatory pressures than small firms. The authors also indicate that, interestingly, Chinese construction companies seem to be more mature in their adoption of green procurement practices than companies in the building materials sector.

Chapter 5: Dr Tony Cragg and Dr Tom McNamara introduce readers to a leading supermarket brand's project to install mechanized zones to speed up sorting and pallet preparation in both fresh and ambient product regional distribution centres (RDCs) across France. The chapter discusses the social and environmental concerns associated with the introduction of a mechanized and automated warehouse system as well as highlighting the importance of RDCs in terms of providing reliable distribution networks and high levels of customer service.

Chapter 6: Dr Kate McLoughlin, Dr David Lascelles and Professor Sai S Nudurupati introduce a case study of a chocolate supply chain network as multiple stakeholders therein seek to multilaterally align and coordinate their activities to achieve the common goal of sustainability. This case study explores the inter-organizational business processes that integrate economic, environmental and social dimensions of sustainability. Their case also highlights how organizational orientation towards sustainability can fundamentally alter the supply chain structure.

Chapter 7: Dr Marina Papalexi introduces the UK and Greek pharmaceutical supply chains and discusses the inefficiency observed in the delivery process for pharmaceuticals employed within two diverse geographical areas. She presents potential solutions using innovative approaches for the perceived waste in this complex delivery process.

Chapter 8: Dr Nicoleta S Tipi and Dr Elias D Georgakoudis explore the role of packaging in the supply chain and its functions and focus the discussion on paper packaging and its role in sustainability. The case study involves a typical paper packaging supply chain and the authors discuss it from the point of view of sustainability and reflect on life-cycle assessment and design for end-use.

Chapter 9: Huy Q Phan, Professor Mohammed Saad and Professor Vikas Kumar discuss the case of Vietnamese enterprises, including 58 small and medium manufacturing enterprises (SMMEs) and their sustainable SCM practices. This case study highlights the key factors that affect the level of sustainability engagement among SMMEs, such as regulations, tax, finances, incentives, stakeholders and employee resistance, to mention only a few.

Chapter 10: Mira Valkjärvi and Dr Weimu You introduce readers to the integral elements of the circular economy concept and detail the issues within the field of manufacturing and specifically air compressors and their challenges, while highlighting the environmental benefits of retaining ownership of a company's products and materials.

Chapter 11: Dr Tom McNamara and Dr Irena Descubes introduce readers to a case study that highlights the importance of considering the web of interconnected stakeholders for effective decision making in a circular economy. They also discuss the importance of decision making by providing an example of multi-criteria decision making, where the criteria stem from the agendas and objectives of the stakeholders involved.

Chapter 12: Dr Daiane Mülling Neutzling, Frediano da Silva Jales and Breno Mota Fernandes from the University of Fortaleza in Brazil explore sustainable supply chain practices from the vantage point of an SME involving a small company and SME in the food sector located in the Northeast region of Brazil, namely Natvita. The study shows the company's main practices, difficulties, challenges and motivations to manage its business sustainably in the context of a sustainable supply chain, involving valuable insights from the focal company, raw material suppliers, exporters, brokers and clients.

Chapter 13: Anne Ratsimandresy and Professor Joe Miemczyk discuss how circular supply chains can involve companies belonging to different sectors and generate a win–win scenario for sustainable development and return on investment based on collaboration. Their case study involves two leading multinational companies and how sustainable development can lead to further strategic collaboration and a win–win scenario.

Chapter 14: Milan Lani, Corporate Director Product Management Contract Logistics, and Alan Zalas from cargo-partner GmbH Austria highlight the construction of cargo-partner's environmentally friendly and sustainability-driven iLogistics Centre Austria. The case study then discusses the operationalization of the iLogistics Centre and its environmental footprint and impact on social sustainability, highlighting the contribution made to local regeneration and projects to come. In a situation where there is a lack of cases covering the sustainability efforts of third-party logistics (3PLs), cargo-partner share their case to highlight how sustainability is defined and embedded in 3PLs and how environmental sustainability has shaped the choices for their iLogistics Centre Austria.

Chapter 15: Dr Minelle E Silva from Excelia Business School, France, and Dr Ana P Ferreira Alves from the Federal Institute of Education, Science and Technology of Rio Grande do Sul (IFRS), Brazil, introduce a case study of Company Alfa which has been producing rubber-based products in Brazil for over a hundred years. This case study demonstrates the importance of a strategic orientation towards supply chain sustainability. Through describing the shift in processes, the case provides a good example of changes that took place over time, focusing on non-renewable inputs, supply-chain-wide collaboration, carbon-neutral practices, import substitution, occupation and income. This in turn means that it is not only about saying that the company is sustainable; rather, it involves an effective and evolving practice of sustainability.

Future developments

As with the developments in sustainable and green supply chains and their contextual settings, trying to forecast the challenges for the supply chain in the future, and what it holds for supply chain members, is difficult. However, through the diverse lenses of the contributing authors, we have seen that there are some convergences across the following:

- **Tailorization**: The case studies highlight that sustainable and green supply chains, although similar in nature, may require individual tailoring, depending on the contextual setting, for example international legislation, government subsidies, strict governmental regulations, the industrial context and sometimes even at stakeholder level. For example, in the case of SMMEs in Vietnamese supply chains, the needs and expectations of small and medium-sized enterprises were different when compared to their larger counterparts, especially in terms of availability and access to financing, funding and resources. Although sustainability can be a source of return on investment, the long-term initial set-up and investment costs open the door to further implementation challenges, as also seen in the case of pharmaceutical supply chains as well as Chinese construction supply chains.

- **Need for standardization**: Although this point may seem contradictory, the contributors' research into the level to which sustainability is embedded and how it is defined differs across industries, company settings, regions and countries. However, creating a sustainability index can result in the amalgamation of diverse indexes, for example as presented in the Australian beef supply chain, where customizing several standardized sustainability indices and tailoring them to the company may bring about a complex process and a long list of indices for inclusion. Although some industrial and regional-level standardization exists, as presented in the Chinese and EU cases, there is still room for the development of a simplified common language and standard procedures at a higher level (ie governmental, global). The need for integration of platforms in a regional and/or global context is paramount, as there is limited impact when applications are standalone rather than integrated.
- **Understanding of ownership**: Understanding the ownership of sustainability measurements becomes an integral element in each case study, and the dissemination of relevant information, indices, processes and integration of sustainable supply chains. Where ownership has not been well understood and established across the supply chain, the cases have indicated that the challenges of implementation become difficult to overcome; see Chapter 5 on sustainable supplier management and regional distribution centres in France.
- The above themes highlight the common issues addressed within the scope of this book. This was also one of our aims: to provide cases from industry to highlight relevant applications of the sustainable and green supply chain. We hope that this book, with its academic and practitioner contributors, will contribute to the cross-disciplinary discussion of sustainable and green supply chains and their impact. It provides only a snapshot of diverse industries with diverse case studies, and our sincere hope is that it could open the gates to further discussion and generate new research inquiries in the green and sustainable supply chain arena.

ACKNOWLEDGEMENTS

As the editor, I would first like to thank our contributing authors for their collaboration and their excellent cases. Producing this edited book would not have been possible without your excellent efforts. I am especially grateful for the contributing authors' dedication, especially during such a worrying and busy time as the Covid pandemic. Thank you very much.

A special thanks goes to Kogan Page's former editor Julia Swales and current editors Amy Minshull and Adam Cox for their friendly and supportive approach throughout the process, making this book possible, and to the Kogan Page team for their kind support throughout the process.

A wholehearted thank you goes to Dr Anne Toubilic from Nottingham University Business School, Dr Sinead Roden from Trinity Business School and James Midgley from Cargo-Partner Ltd for their kind help and support. Thank you very much for stepping in when I needed a helping hand.

I would also like to acknowledge with gratitude the support and love of my family, which kept me going; without their support and encouragement this book would not have been possible.

Thank you all.

ABBREVIATIONS

3PL	third-party logistics provider
ABSF	Australian Beef Sustainability Framework
B2B	business to business
B2C	business to consumers
CDDN	customer-driven demand network
CE	circular economy
CLSC	closed-loop supply chain
CPFR	collaborative planning, forecasting and replenishment
CSC	circular supply chain
CSR	corporate social responsibility
EIA	environmental impact assessment
EMF	Ellen MacArthur Foundation
EPOP	expired packaged organic products
ERP	enterprise resource planning
F&B	food and beverage
FSSC	Food Safety System Certification
GDP	gross domestic product
GRI	Global Reporting Initiative
GRSB	Global Beef Sustainability Initiative
GSCM	green supply chain management
HACCP	hazard analysis and critical control point
IS	information system
LCA	life-cycle analysis
LSP	logistics service provider
MSME	micro, small and medium enterprise
NGO	non-governmental organization
NHS	National Health Service
OHS	occupational health & safety
PSC	pharmaceutical supply chain
RDC	regional distribution centre
RL	reverse logistics
ROI	return on investment
SAGB	sustainable agriculture guiding principles
SCM	supply chain management

SDG	sustainable development goal
SGP	supplier guiding principles
SKU	stock keeping unit
SME	small and medium-sized enterprise
SMME	small and medium-sized manufacturing enterprise
SPE	sustainability practice engagement
SRF	solid recovered fuel
SSCM	sustainable supply chain management
STP	sustainability transformation plan
TQM	total quality management
WRAP	waste and resources action programme

CONTRIBUTORS

Dr Ana P Ferreira Alves

Ana Ferreira Alves is a lecturer at the Federal Institute of Education, Science and Technology of Rio Grande do Sul (IFRS), Campus Rolante, Brazil. She is also a researcher within the Tecnologia e Ciências da Decisão Research Group and Gestão, Economia Regional e Educação (GERE) Research Group. Her research interests focus on supply chain sustainability, including stakeholder partnership, supply chain collaboration and supply chain integration. Ana is a member of the European Operations Management Association (EurOMA) and the Brazilian National Association of Postgraduation and Research in Administration (Anpad). She has published in journals focused on sustainability and operations management. ORCID: https://orcid.org/0000-0002-2040-6775

Dr Ozlem Bak

Ozlem Bak is a senior lecturer in operations management at Brunel Business School, UK. She lectures on courses in operations management, research methods and supply chain management. She received her PhD from the University of East Anglia supported by a full scholarship from the University of East Anglia Management School in the UK. Her PhD thesis received the Emerald Highly Commended Award in the field of operations management. Her current research interests and experience lie in supply chain management, particularly organizational transformation and e-business implementation in supply chains, supply chain skills, organizational transformation and industry–higher education collaboration. Ozlem's academic activities are underpinned by her industrial and commercial background, which includes experience in the automotive industry for companies such as Daimler Chrysler, Hyundai and distributors.

Dr Erica Ballantyne

Erica Ballantyne is a lecturer in operations and supply chain management at Sheffield University Management School, University of Sheffield. She has a PhD from the Institute for Transport Studies at the University of Leeds in the area of urban logistics and freight transport. Her research interests include:

sustainable logistics and freight transport operations, particularly last-mile contexts; electrified transport applications; and reverse logistics and retail returns management. The interdisciplinary and applied nature of her research has led to her involvement in various national and international research projects. Erica has previously been employed in various operational and management roles within the logistics and transport industry, including for a major European third-party logistics service provider, working mainly in the FMCG and grocery markets. Erica is an active member of the Chartered Institute of Logistics and Transport (CILT) UK.

Professor Kim Bryceson

Kim Bryceson is a professor of agribusiness technologies at The University of Queensland in Australia. She has an extensive background in industry and government research, specializing in the use of information technology in agricultural production and agribusiness. Her research expertise areas are in the use of remotely sensed data for agricultural and environmental monitoring, and in supply/value chain analysis across the whole of the agrifood industry chain, using agent-based modelling to construct supply chain risk assessment and performance management scenarios. Recent projects have been in modelling agrifood supply chains as complex systems; developing risk assessment and performance management criteria in internal business supply chains; developing a hybrid value chain framework (HVCF) as a tool for investigating economic development of agrifood chains in small-scale societies; analysing the Australian beef industry supply chain in relation to new technology development and sustainability; and in developing augmented reality apps for agricultural and environmental education.

Dr Tony Cragg

Tony Cragg obtained his PhD from the University of Westminster in 2016 for a study of SMEs and SCM. He is associate professor at the Ecole Supérieure de Logistique Industrielle in Redon, France. He also teaches at Audencia Business School in Nantes and Excelia Business School in La Rochelle. He has published research articles in leading academic journals, including the *Journal of Small Business and Enterprise Development*, *Supply Chain Forum* and *International Journal of Procurement Management*. His research interests cover green logistics, warehousing, distribution, process automation, acceleration, worker autonomy and the human factor.

Dr Irena Descubes

Irena Descubes is an assistant professor of marketing and manager of the Executive Program of Corporate Social Responsibility and Transition at the ESC Rennes School of Business. Her research is driven by an interest in societal change and sustainable economic transition. She holds a PhD from the University of Economics and Business in Prague, Czech Republic and is currently a visiting professor there, and is a former visiting lecturer at the French National Military Academy at Saint-Cyr, Coëtquidan, France.

Breno Mota Fernandes

Breno Mota Fernandes is a Master's student in global supply chain and operations management at Berlin School of Economics and Law. He holds a Bachelor's degree in foreign trade from the University of Fortaleza (UNIFOR) and a double degree in business and entrepreneurship from Novancia Business School Paris. He works at Carl Zeiss Meditec as a working student in strategic procurement. His research interests include sustainable logistics and the global supply chain, particularly with regard to small to medium-sized enterprises. Breno previously worked for *Somos Um*, a social business based in Brazil that aims to reduce poverty and increase the well-being of low-income citizens through entrepreneurship.

Elias D Georgakoudis

Elias D Georgakoudis is a project and logistics manager in Multi-Pack S.A. His research interests are in the area of packaging design and innovation. He has a PhD from the University of Huddersfield (UK), Transport and Logistics Research Group, School of Applied Science and an MSc in logistics and supply chain management from the University of Sheffield.

Dr Graeme Heron

Graeme Heron lectures on operations management, supply chains, research methods and manufacturing systems. As part of his civic activities Graeme sits on the Awarding Panel of the Department of Education's Institute for Apprenticeships & Technical Education's Logistics and Supply Chain Board. Graeme is also a trustee of a charity which re-provisions surplus food from the UK's food manufacturing and retail systems to alleviate food insecurity and food poverty. Graeme has many years of experience across manufacturing sectors as both an engineer and supply chain manager. His research interests include sustainable supply chains, food supply chains, data commoditization to reduce food wastes and impacts, freight transport systems and applied theory of constraints development. Graeme is also an active member of the Chartered Institute of Logistics and Transport (CILT) UK.

Frediano da Silva Jales

Frediano da Silva Jales is a Master's student in business administration at the University of Fortaleza (UNIFOR) in the operations and marketing research area. He holds a scholarship from FUNCAP (The Ceará Foundation for the Scientific Support and Technological Development). He is a member of the Centre for Strategy and Sustainability Studies (NESS/UNIFOR) and has a Bachelor's degree in business administration from Potiguar University, Brazil (2012). His dissertation is focused on understanding how inter-organizational relationships in supply chains of small and medium-sized enterprises in the food sector have contributed to the adoption of sustainable practices.

Dr Desirée Knoppen

Desirée Knoppen holds a PhD in management science from ESADE Business School (Barcelona, Spain) and an MSc in industrial engineering and management science from the Eindhoven University of Technology (Netherlands). She is a professor in operations and supply chain management at EADA Business School. Her research focuses on learning capabilities and sustainability-driven innovation within supply chains and networks. She has published her research in international peer-reviewed journals such as *Journal of Supply Chain Management*, *International Journal of Production and Operations Management* and *Management Learning*. Desirée has ample consulting experience in a wide range of sectors and in different countries (Netherlands, Spain, Colombia, Mexico).

Professor Vikas Kumar

Vikas Kumar is a professor of operations and supply chain management and director of research at Bristol Business School, University of the West of England (UWE), UK. He is also a visiting professor at the Faculty of Accounting, Ton Duc Thang University, Vietnam. He holds a PhD in management studies from Exeter Business School, UK, and a Bachelor of Technology (first-class distinction) in metallurgy and material engineering from the National Institute of Foundry and Forge Technology (NIFFT), India. He has published more than 200 articles in leading international journals and international conferences, including the *International Journal of*

Production Research, *Supply Chain Management*, *Expert System with Applications*, *Journal of Business Research*, *Computers & Industrial Engineering* and *Production Planning & Control*. He also serves on the editorial boards of several international journals. He has successfully secured funding in excess of £1 million from various research agencies such as EPSRC, Innovate UK, British Academy, Newton Fund, Royal Academy of Engineering and the British Council. His current research interests include sustainability, Industry 4.0, circular economy, food supply chains and operational excellence.

Milan Lani, MSc

Milan Lani works as a corporate director product management contract logistics at cargo-partner. He is globally responsible for all contract logistics sites as well as for development of new logistics products. With his 20 years of industry experience he supports cargo-partner's goals to become a well-recognized global 3PL provider. In recent years he has been working closely with real-estate developers to define standards and requirements for logistics facilities and warehouses. He received his Master's degree in economy of road transportation from the University of Žilina, Slovakia, and his post-Master's degree in logistics management systems from the Technical University Eindhoven, Netherlands.

Dr David Lascelles

David Lascelles is a senior lecturer in supply chain management at Manchester Metropolitan Business School, Manchester, UK, where he is programme leader for the MSc in logistics and supply chain management. He is a Fellow of the UK Higher Education Academy. David is a Chartered Member of the Chartered Institute of Logistics and Transport, where he serves on the North West Policy Committee. His research interests include the development of sustainable supply chain strategy as a dynamic capability; the application of service-dominant logic to determine value co-creation within supply chains; and the utilization of temporal fault-tree analysis to simulate supply chain risk scenarios. He has successfully guided nine PhD students as a co-supervisor. Prior to returning to academia in 2011, David worked with a number of multinational companies, as both a senior executive and a management consultant.

Dr Kate McLoughlin

Kate McLoughlin is a lecturer in supply chain management in the Department of Operations, Technology, Events and Hospitality Management at MMU. Kate joined MMU in 2015 from a 15-year career in rural enterprise development, where she specialized in strategic enterprise development and multi-stakeholder clusters. Her research focuses on sustainability, inter-organizational relationships, social network analysis, critical discourse analysis and critical management studies. She is interested in political and power discourses in the field, particularly in relation to sustainability and inter-organizational relationships. Kate is a member of EurOMA, with a particular interest in the Sustainable Operations and Supply Chains Forum, the British Academy of Management, with a position on the Operations, Logistics and Supply Chain Management SIG, and the Chartered Institute of Logistics and Transport. Besides this, Kate reviews for the *European Management Journal*, *International Journal of Management Reviews*, *Journal of Business Ethics*, *Journal of Business Research* and *Journal of Supply Chain Management*.

Dr Tom McNamara

Tom McNamara is an assistant professor with the Department of Supply Chain Management at the Rennes School of Business, France, and a former visiting lecturer at the French National Military Academy at Saint-Cyr, Coëtquidan, France. He received a PhD in operations management from the Open University, UK, and had a career that spanned three decades at a Fortune 500 energy company before deciding to enter higher education. His current research interests include issues and trends in operations management

Professor Joe Miemczyk

Joe Miemczyk is professor of supply chain management at ESCP Business School. He researches sustainable and circular supply chains in a number of sectors, publishing in a variety of supply chain and operations journals.

Dr Mohd Mohsin

Mohd Mohsin is a post-doctoral research fellow in farm and agribusiness at the University of Southern Queensland (USQ), Australia. He holds a PhD in farm, rural management and agribusiness with Master's and Bachelor's degrees in business administration, specializing in finance and banking. His current research in agribusiness involves projects investigating the financial feasibility of rural irrigation systems, the financial feasibility of clonal tissue culture in avocado, and a Macadamia nut industry financial benchmarking project. He has previously been involved in the development of farmer business skills in the dairy industry, and in economic diversification projects in the Murray Darling Basin.

Mohsin has also been a sessional teaching staff member at the School of Business, USQ for the past five years, while before joining USQ he worked as an assistant professor and lecturer in finance for eight years (2006–2014) overseas. He teaches courses in investment and portfolio analysis, financial management, capital budgeting and managerial accounting. He has co-authored many industry reports and academic papers in agribusiness.

Dr Daiane Mülling Neutzling

Daiane Mülling Neutzling is an assistant professor at the Post-Graduate Program in Business Administration, University of Fortaleza (UNIFOR), Brazil. She teaches on courses in sustainability management, supply chain management and research methods. She is the leader of a research group in strategy and sustainability at UNIFOR. She received her PhD from the Federal University of Rio Grande do Sul (UFRGS) (Brazil). She is also a visiting PhD student at the University of Kassel (Germany) in the Supply Chain Management Department. Her current research interests lie in sustainable supply chain management (SSCM), alternative food networks (AFNs) and social enterprises. She is also working in mentoring startups in social entrepreneurship programmes and with local governments in open innovation projects related to sustainable public transportation systems.

Professor Sai S Nudurupati

Professor Sai S Nudurupati gained his MSc and PhD from the University of Strathclyde, UK. He received an outstanding doctoral award from EFMD and Emerald. He is currently leading research and development activity in the Gandhi Institute of Technology and Management (GITAM) by increasing scholarly activity and outputs and is currently working on two major research projects worth £60K. Prior to joining GITAM, Sai worked for 11 years at Manchester Metropolitan University, Exeter University and Strathclyde University in various capacities. During this period, he worked on various projects with clients including Pirelli Tyres Ltd, British Aerospace Systems, Mastclimbers, Allied Distillers Ltd and Daks Simpson. He has also published over 28 papers in reputed international journals and magazines (listed on the Australian Business Deans Council Journal list and the

Chartered Association of Business Schools Academic Journal Guide) and received two best-paper awards from Emerald and the Institute of Engineering Technology respectively. Sai is currently serving on a number of editorial boards of international journals. Prior to taking up his academic roles, he spent five years in SGB, UK, implementing continuous improvement projects. He gained Lean Six Sigma Transactional Black Belt certification with the British Standards Institute.

Dr Marina Papalexi

Marina Papalexi is a lecturer in operations and project management at Manchester Metropolitan University Business School. She has published articles in highly rated international journals and has been the author of a number of book chapters. Her research area is related to operations management improvement strategies, supply chain optimization, and innovation. Her research has contributed to academic literature as it adds more theoretical and empirical insights to innovative delivery processes, especially those that have been characterized as highly complex. She has also been involved in research on quality management, sport management, knowledge transfer and social media.

Huy Q Phan

Huy Q Phan is currently a PhD candidate at Bristol Business School. His PhD research topic is 'Measuring sustainability performance of SMEs in a developing country – a study of Southern Vietnam'.

Anne Ratsimandresy

Anne Ratsimandresy is a PhD candidate at ESCP Business School. Her research interests are sustainable operations and circular, collaborative supply chains.

Professor Mohammed Saad

Mohammed Saad is a professor of innovation and technology management at Bristol Business School. He is increasingly focusing his research on the key determinants of the process of knowledge exchange and the vital role of the university within a system of innovation. His research track record includes more than 150 publications, including many international quality refereed journal articles and three successful research books. He has an outstanding record in generating funded research, with leadership and involvement in projects worth £1 million since he joined BBS in 1999. From April 2015 to April 2018, he was involved in a European-funded research project whose objective was to investigate innovation in sustainable public procurement (Horizon 2020). His research activity spans several fields – mainstream operations management, innovation and technology management and more global policy-related issues of knowledge development, transfer and institutional collaborative learning. He leads a very active research team working on systems of innovation. He is the co-founder and co-editor of the *International Journal of Technology Management and Sustainable Development*. He also founded the COSINUS network, and he has organized five international conferences on the role of universities within their systems of innovation.

Dr Minelle E Silva

Minelle Silva is an associate professor in supply chain sustainability in the Supply, Purchasing and Project Management Department at Excelia Business School, France. He is also a researcher within the Research Centre in Managerial Intelligence and Innovation (CERIIM). His research interests mainly concern supply chain sustainability, including sustainable purchasing and sustainability practices and learning. Minelle is a member of the European Operations Management Association (EurOMA) and he has published in journals focused on sustainability and operations management. Currently, Minelle works as guest-editor of various special issues. ORCID: https://orcid.org/0000-0003-2074-6478

Professor Geoff Slaughter

Geoff Slaughter is associate dean academic and professor of business in the Business, Education, Law and Arts Faculty at the University of Southern Queensland in Australia. His research expertise is in the financial management of agribusinesses including on farms, agrifood value chains and benchmarking of best practice management. His principal interest is in ensuring, through modelling, analysis and education, financially viable and environmentally sustainable agriculture. Other interests include the use of agribusiness technologies and the commercialization of agribusiness innovations.

Dr Nicoleta S Tipi

Nicoleta Tipi is a senior lecturer in operations and supply chain at the Faculty of Business and Law, The Open University Business School (UK).

Her area of research includes topics in: supply chain analytics and modelling; supply chain performance measurement systems; and sustainable supply chain systems. She has a PhD from the University of Sheffield (UK), Department of Automatic Control and System Engineering, in the area of supply chain systems modelling, and an MA in professional development (Higher Education Practice) from the University of Huddersfield.

Mira Valkjärvi, MSc

Mira Valkjärvi is a doctoral researcher in the field of management and organization at the University of Turku and a project researcher at the University of Eastern Finland. She is also a researcher within the CICAT2025 research consortium funded by the Academy of Finland. Her research interests include the circular economy, service-dominant logic, agency, culture and narratives.

Dr Ying Xie

Ying Xie received her PhD degree in 2004 from the School of Computing and Information System, Coventry University. Currently she is the head of school in economics, finance and law, Anglia Ruskin University. Ying is also the director of the Research Centre of Intelligent Supply Chains at Anglia Ruskin University. Ying's research interests cover machine learning, big data analytics, modelling and simulation, forecasting, decision support systems and fuzzy sets theory. She specializes in healthcare supply chains and supply chain digitalization.

Ying has successfully won and completed several Knowledge Transfer Partnership projects, including projects from Innovate UK, ERDF and industries. She is currently working with institutions from the Arc Universities Group, including the University of Cambridge, University of Oxford, Cranfield University and the University of Buckinghamshire, to build the future of sustainable aviation in the UK. Ying is leading the working package of supply chain digitalization, in collaboration with Ocado Technology and Oracle Corporation. Ying has had a significant involvement in advancing knowledge and transferring knowledge in conjunction with many industrial and government partners. She has worked with the NHS to reduce pharmaceutical waste and develop green pharmaceutical supply chains; she is involved with Essex County Council and Iotic to develop a digital-twin-enabled ecosystem for social care and healthcare; and she is also working with Felixstowe Port (UK) to improve the utilization of rail transport of containers.

Ying has published over 20 refereed papers in distinguished scientific journals and book chapters and has successfully supervised many PhDs to completion.

Dr Weimu You

Weimu You is lecturer in sustainability and global value chains at Brunel University London. His research interests include sustainability, global value chains, innovation and technology management. His work has appeared in internationally peer-reviewed academic journals such as *Critical Perspectives on International Business*, *International Journal of Management Reviews*, *Journal of Cleaner Production* and *Technological Forecasting and Social Change*.

Alan Zalas, MSc

Alan Zalas works in cargo-partner's marketing and communications department in Fischamend, Austria. After completing his studies in communication sciences at the University of Vienna in 2008 (diploma thesis on the subject of 'advertising in scene sports'), he worked in PR and marketing in various sectors. He has worked at the headquarters of the privately owned full-range info-logistics provider since 2017.

Dr Yiqing Zhao

Yiqing Zhao received his PhD degree in 2018 from Ashcroft International Business School, Anglia Ruskin University. Currently he is the programme leader of logistics management, Linyi University. Yiqing is also the director of research at the Centre of Intelligent Logistics, in Shandong Shunhe Co., Ltd, China. Yiqing has published two papers in distinguished scientific journals. His research interests include mathematical modelling, principal component analysis, longitudinal data analysis and system optimization. He specializes in logistics management and energy investment.

He is currently working with Shandong Shunhe Co., Ltd and Shandong Institute of Commerce and Logistics to build the National Logistics Hub in China. Yiqing is leading the working package of logistics standardization and digitalization, in collaboration with China Electronics Group Corporation.

Connecting supply and demand markets in a circular economy 01

The case of Saica

DR DESIRÉE KNOPPEN, EADE BUSINESS SCHOOL, BARCELONA, SPAIN

Introduction

The circular economy (CE) aims to achieve a better balance and harmony between the economy, society and natural environment, grounded upon the principles of designing out waste and pollution, keeping products and materials in use and regenerating natural systems (Ellen MacArthur foundation, 2021). In other words, it refers to a 'regenerative and restorative economic system that aims to optimize resource usage and reduce waste, and offers potential to innovate novel value creation opportunities' (Ranta *et al*, 2020: 291). Within a CE, materials can circulate in technical or biological loops of an open or closed nature. In open-loop systems, the waste of one economic actor is channelled to other kinds of supply chains whereas in closed-loop systems the waste is re-inserted into the same or similar supply chains (De Angelis *et al*, 2018). An example of an open-loop system is that citrus juice by-products are converted into fabrics and used to produce fashion items by the Italian company Orange Fiber. An example of a closed-loop system is that Jaguar Land Rover recovers its cars at end of life and recycles the aluminium for use in new vehicles. Supply chain management literature has focused on closed-loop systems, addressing for instance reverse logistics (Bernon *et al*, 2018), coordination and collaboration within the chain (Kumar and Malegeant, 2006), or inventory models for re-manufacturing (Li *et al*, 2009). On the other hand, open-loop systems are relatively under-explored through a supply chain lens.

Open systems can increase the resilience of the system given the broad variety in possible connections between demand and supply nodes. In addition, the material streams associated with open-loop systems will continue to grow in the future (Eurostat, 2020). Therefore, the study of open-loop systems is important, even more so in the context of high uncertainty in supply markets (Knight *et al*, 2015), emergence of new players in demand markets (Priyadarshini and Abhilash, 2020) and continuous adaptation of legislative frameworks (Kunz *et al*, 2018). Actors traditionally involved in the hauling of basic recycle streams (ie paper, plastic, metal, glass) are well positioned to play a central role in open-loop systems for newly identified streams.

This chapter develops the case of Saica, a company that converts an increasing number of different waste streams into feedstock – or secondary raw materials – for a series of supply chains. For each new waste stream, Saica must invest in new technology and processes, and ponder the potential interests or objections of the stakeholders involved. This case aims to describe how Saica's decision to invest in a technology to recover value from expired packaged organic products (EPOP) hinges upon the agenda and objectives of stakeholders from supply markets, demand markets and the government.

The case: Saica

The Spanish multinational Saica, with €2.8 billion turnover in 2020 and more than 10,000 employees, is present in 10 countries across Europe and North America. Born in 1943 with a paper production plant, diversification started in the 1970s through the acquisition of a comprehensive waste management plant and two cardboard packaging plants. In the years that followed, Saica expanded geographically and became the first plant in the industrial sector in Spain that integrated cogeneration for energy production. Moreover, it incorporated energy revaluation plants, plants for recycled plastic pellets from low-density polyethylene, and plants for flexible packaging (Saica, 2020).

Saica Natur – the business unit of Saica that focuses on waste management and environmental services – has a long-standing commercial relationship with several large grocery retail customers, taking care of their cardboard, plastic and pallet waste streams. In grocery retail, it had become more and more common to sell packaged organic products, for example food positioned on a tray, wrapped in plastic. Consequently, given the perishable nature of food, there is a significant volume that must be discarded when the food reaches the end of its shelf life without having been purchased by a final consumer.

Initially, EPOP was sent to landfill. Decaying organic matter, however, turns landfills into a substantial source of greenhouse gases. In addition, the packaging content of EPOP has a high energy content that is lost when sent to landfill. Alternatively, Saica could play a role in reverse logistics and subsequent transformation to transform EPOP into feedstock for biomethanization, composting or energy recovery. Figure 1.1 illustrates the potential recovery options of EPOP.

Different destinies required different technologies for transformation. Saica's investment decision in a particular technology requested an analysis of the agendas and objectives of stakeholders involved. Below, we elaborate the perspectives of the suppliers of EPOP, the customers of the transformed EPOP, the government/legislator and the internal stakeholders of Saica.

The supply market of waste

The supply market of EPOP consists of multiple players:

- food industry;
- food distribution;

Figure 1.1 The potential recovery options of EPOP

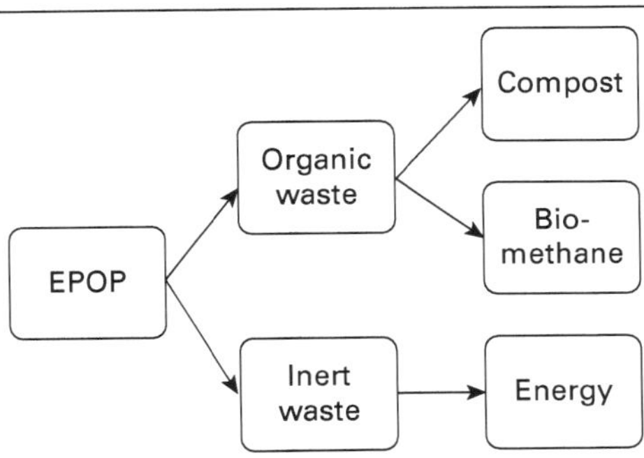

- shopping centres;
- hospitals;
- catering services;
- hotel chains;
- supermarkets/hypermarkets and other markets.

In supermarkets, the waste problem is clearly visible to the public and thus gains attention. Moreover, supermarkets concentrate large quantities of waste at a few physical locations, which offers possibilities of collecting the waste for repurposing (Porat *et al*, 2018). Consequently, the corporate social responsibility of retailers implies putting the issue on the agenda.

Alcampo, a subsidiary of the French Auchan that has 310 retail centres (hypermarkets and supermarkets) in Spain, was among the first players in Spain to move towards a solution. In line with CE principles, the aim was first to avoid products becoming residuals. Forecasting and inventory management techniques are key in that regard, but demand uncertainty made it difficult to fully eradicate expiration of products. Therefore, additional actions were to donate to food banks or to sell at a discounted price when the expiration date came close, collaborating with the platform Too Good to Go (https://toogoodtogo.es) with clear data on the expiration date of a particular product. Second, for the management of EPOP, Alcampo had chosen to work with Saica, given their price and service performance. A key issue in implementation of the initiative was correct segregation at the source of the different waste streams – separating organic waste from inert waste (which is neither chemically nor biologically reactive and will not decompose or only very slowly, for example plastics) and controlling for the amount of glass and liquids – which implied training of the employees involved and installation of storage equipment by Saica. An initial pilot project was successful and the initiative was then rolled out across the country.

As a result of the collaboration, Alcampo drastically reduced the residuals sent to landfill. In addition, in 2020 Alcampo launched its own brand of universal substrate, incorporating the compost derived from its own organic waste (10 per cent of the total) and packaged in recycled materials (low-density polyethylene, 50 per cent of the total), derived from the plastic waste generated in its own centres (El periódico de Aragón, 2020).

The demand market for feedstock: overview

An alternative to landfill is energy recovery that takes place in cement, thermal and ceramic plants. Therefore, Saica enabled a segregation system in the retail centres of selected retail customers (the pilot was developed with Alcampo), consisting of pallet containers and self-compactors for organic waste and inert waste, respectively. The self-compactors, which reduce volume and thus transportation costs, were hauled to Saica to convert the inert waste using shredding and dehydrating techniques into solid recovered fuel (SRF) for energy recovery plants. As such, SRF is a substitute for fossil fuels.

Regarding the EPOP hauled in pallet containers, there was thus an opportunity to recover valuable materials from the EPOP instead of sending them to landfill. For this purpose, Saica invested in unpacking technology to split the incoming goods flow into one flow of inert waste that could become SRF for energy recovery plants, and another flow of organic material for industrial composting or biomethanization facilities. The unpacking technology required further improvement in segregation in the retail centres to ensure that: (a) the glass content in the material was less than 1 per cent; and (b) the humidity of the material was greater than 72 per cent.

Given that EPOP potentially contained meat, the material had to be sanitized (ie keeping the product at a temperature of 70 degrees Celsius for one hour) when delivered to biomethanization plants. This additional process was not necessary when delivering to industrial composters since sanitation is inherent to the biological oxidation process. Saica thus had to compare investment in technology with or without the sanitation process, and it was therefore vital to further understand the alternative demand markets.

Saica identified six industrial composting facilities within a reasonable distance. All were saturated, however. In addition, they had higher entrance fees – the fee per ton that Saica would have to pay to drop off their residuals – than biomethanization plants, and had announced that fees would increase further.

On the other hand, Saica identified 12 potential biomethanization plants within a reasonable distance, with a general interest in the quality that Saica could offer. Biomethanization takes place in an industrial anaerobic digester and refers to a microbiological fermentation process in which complex molecules of organic matter are broken down by bacteria into simpler molecules, such as alcohol, carbon dioxide and methane, in the absence of oxygen. Methane produced under such conditions is called biomethane, a renewable gas, which can be used for natural gas end-user applications (heating and cooling, power, transport, etc). Compared to other renewable sources, biomethane takes advantage of the existing infrastructure for distribution and storage of energy. The other output of anaerobic digestion is digestate, a stable organic matter rich in various nutrients (nitrogen, phosphorus and potassium) which can be used as organic fertilizer.

The demand market for feedstock: a promising customer

One promising potential customer was Biometagas la Galera, a plant designed, constructed and installed by AGF Procesos. The plant transforms residuals into biogas in a process that has two phases versus mainstream technology based on one phase. As such, the process is reduced from 40 days to 15 days. The plant received permission for 3,000 tons of biomethane per year, corresponding to an equivalent electrical power of 2.2 MW. The biomethane would be produced from approximately 100 tons/day of a wide variety of organic waste of which Saica could deliver 60 tons/day. The owner of Biometagas highlighted:

> Saica is an important supplier especially for the quality of the product ... Our raw materials must be varied, and expired organic products from supermarkets are an important complement to the proteins and fat that we receive from other suppliers ... We were all ears to the proposal of Saica in terms of volumes, fees and contract duration, because the slurry delivered by Saica has the potential to double our productivity from 5 to 10 m3 of biogas for every m3 of slurry.

The plant would generate and inject the biomethane into the existing gas network, because that would allow sales to European countries with favourable legal conditions; that is, that allow for tax reductions when renewable energy is used. The alternative destiny – vehicle fleets – would be local, pay less for the biomethane and have a lower and more variable demand. The plant, which involved an investment of more than €5 million, was expected to pay off within four years, given the two-phase technology; that is, the production of more gas in less built volume, reducing the plant's investment and allowing for profitability at a lower gas sales price. The plant would also have a positive social impact: its location in an agricultural area and digestion of local agricultural residuals (from, for example, pig production) would avoid nitrification of the soil and contamination of aquifers and thus increase human health. In addition, it would allow local olive oil farmers to get rid of their residuals and save costs in that regard.

Despite these promises, it had been difficult to obtain finance for the different stages: idea generation – prototyping – building – testing – go life – scaling up (a process of 12 years in total). Investors were hesitant to invest in this sector and there was no government aid, in contrast to other countries (eg Germany, Italy). In addition, several Spanish states lack norms that enforce separation of waste streams, therefore not guaranteeing a sufficient and constant flow of feedstock.

Ideally, biomethanization plants are located near the places where their feedstock is generated. In practice, however, long project lead-times, during which new types of feedstock emerge (such as the one offered by Saica), may lead to the location decisions of different parties along the supply chain being decoupled. Consequently, transportation costs of the slurry from Saica to the biomethanization plant would be considerable, given the transportation distance of approximately 200 km.

The government

The stakeholder 'government' operates at different levels. At the broadest level, within the realm of the United Nations, two framework agreements set the stage for the case:

- First, multiple studies led by the Food and Agriculture Organization (FAO) indicated that about a third of all food produced on the planet and about half of all fruit and vegetables are lost and/or wasted. Therefore, the goal to halve per capita global food waste by 2030 was set, adopted by the US Federal Government, the EU Parliament and many other countries. Several solutions help in this regard and are presented in a hierarchy of desirability in Figure 1.2.
- Second, the Paris 2015 agreement, ratified by more than 125 countries, aims to keep global temperature rise this century well below 2 degrees Celsius above pre-industrial levels, and to pursue efforts to limit the temperature increase even further to 1.5 degrees Celsius. Additionally, the agreement aims to increase the ability of countries to deal with the impacts of climate change, and to make finance flows consistent with a low greenhouse gas (GHG) emissions and climate-resilient pathway.

At a European level, the European Commission proposed the Circular Economy Action Plan as one of the main blocks of the European Green Deal (European Commission, 2020). The new Action Plan announces initiatives along the entire life cycle of products, targeting for example their design, promoting CE processes, fostering sustainable consumption and aiming to ensure that the resources used are kept in the EU economy for as long as possible. The focus is on the sectors that use most resources and where the

Figure 1.2 The food recovery hierarchy (Scurce: Environmental Protection Agency, 2021)

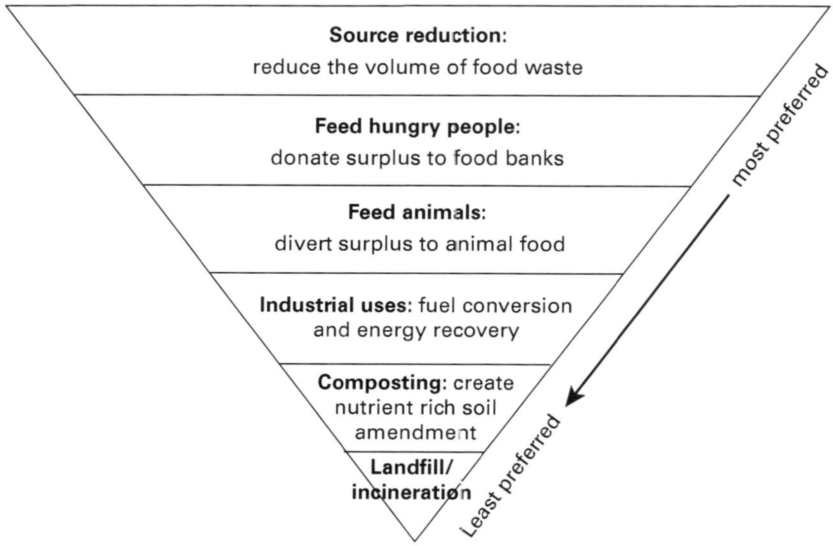

potential for circularity is high, such as: electronics and ICT; batteries and vehicles; packaging; plastics; textiles; construction and buildings; food; water and nutrients.

Aligned with the European framework, Spain has developed the plan 'Spain circular 2030', with reference years for benchmarking and specific aims for 2030 (Gobierno de España, 2020):

- Reduce national consumption of materials by 30% in relation to GDP.
- Reduce waste generation by 15%; reduce the generation of food waste in the entire food chain.
- Reduce by 50% per capita the household and retail consumption level and 20% in the production and supply chains.
- Increase reuse and preparation for reuse up to 10% of municipal waste generated.
- Improve 10% efficiency in water use.
- Reduce the emission of greenhouse gases below 10 million tons of CO_2 equivalent.

At a regional and municipal level, the governmental areas of residuals, energy and climate change converge when it comes to the case of EPOP.

Waste-to-energy is an important part of municipal waste management systems in the context of the circular economy. Traditionally, waste-to-energy has been associated with incineration. Yet, the term is much broader, and biomethanization constitutes a more intelligent alternative to incineration that should be encouraged (Malinauskaite *et al*, 2017).

The government has several instruments to influence industry and citizens' behaviour:

1. Norms refer to laws, decrees, rules, and a catalogue of residuals. The possible meat content of the packaged food implied that the material was classified as category 2 or 3 of the Sandach regulation (Boletín Oficial Del Estado, 2018), which was sharpened after the outbreak of mad cow disease and thus required an additional sanitation process in case biomethanization was the final destiny.
2. Permits refer to a particular case and must be in line with the norms. Permits are valid forever and, because the long-term destiny of the digestate was uncertain, the sanitization process became part of the government's conditions for granting a permit to Saica.
3. Subsidies refer to help in investments. They were not applicable in this case.
4. Taxes discourage undesirable behaviour and stimulate positive environmental behaviours. In that regard, landfill and incineration taxes have increased steadily for industrial waste streams, so that landfill taxes are significantly higher than incineration taxes. In addition, both landfill and incineration taxes are significantly higher than the entrance fees charged by industrial composters or anaerobic digesters.

The internal perspective

Key account management was the first area within Saica that considered the investment idea, triggered by discussions with grocery retail customers and driven by the desire to help customers solve their problems.

The business development area of Saica was also enthusiastic about the idea of converting EPOP into valuable feedstock for other supply chains, because of its alignment with Saica's mission: 'to provide sustainable solutions for the manufacture of recycled paper and packaging, as well as environmental services so that customers achieve the objectives of the circular economy, maximizing the return on available resources'.

Consequently, Saica's R+D+I department and its Production Competence Centre investigated the available technologies in the market and proposed an unpacking line that could process 25,000 tons of EPOP per year with an organic recovery volume of 88.5 per cent, 12 per cent of mixed packaging destined for energy recovery after transformation into SRF, and a rejection rate as low as 0.5 per cent. The unpacking process requires the addition of water for the separation of organic waste from the packaging materials. This added water implies a cost and also generates more tons of organic substrate and, therefore, higher transport costs and the final destination's entrance fee. The additional sanitation process, required when the destination would be biomethanization, could be achieved by heating the organic substrate to 70 °C for 1 hour.

The operations area analysed the idea and pointed to potential issues: lack of automation for reception of the waste if it arrived in formats that differed from those agreed; possible health and hygiene risks; selecting, training and retaining adequate personnel. From a financial point of view, key variables to calculate the return on investment of both alternatives were:

- estimated supply volume (average and variation, in ton);
- fee/ton paid by the retailer to Saica;
- variable production cost (eg electricity and thermic energy, water, per ton);
- fixed production cost (eg production and maintenance staff, machinery rental);
- inbound and outbound transport cost per ton;
- entrance fee/ton paid by Saica to the final destination (in sequence of increasing fee: biomethanization, composting, energy recovery, landfill);
- investment cost (equipment, civil work, engineering, and licenses, etc).

After gathering all required data and performing sensitivity analysis with the key variables impacting on the bottom-line results, it seemed that both decision alternatives, (a) unpacking technology for delivery to industrial composters and (b) unpacking and sanitation technology for delivery to industrial anaerobic digesters, promised an attractive and similar return on investment (ROI). In other words, for both alternatives, the investment could be recovered in a reasonable period, given the associated new revenue and cost structure. Outbound transportation costs had a heavy weight in the total cost structure but were similar across both alternatives.

The decision to make

Both alternatives had to be contrasted with the agendas and objectives of the stakeholders involved. Coordination across the different actors in a supply chain is key for effective change (Boons, 2002). Figure 1.3 shows the Saica supply chain, with the alternative streams related to the decision of how to deal with EPOP.

Table 1.1 provides a summary of this exercise, which explores a comparison of investment alternatives along multiple criteria for (a) supply market (waste), (b) demand market (feedstock), (c) government and (d) internal perspectives.

Learning outcomes

- This case has highlighted the importance of considering the web of interconnected stakeholders for effective decision making in a circular economy.

Figure 1.3 Saica's supply chain

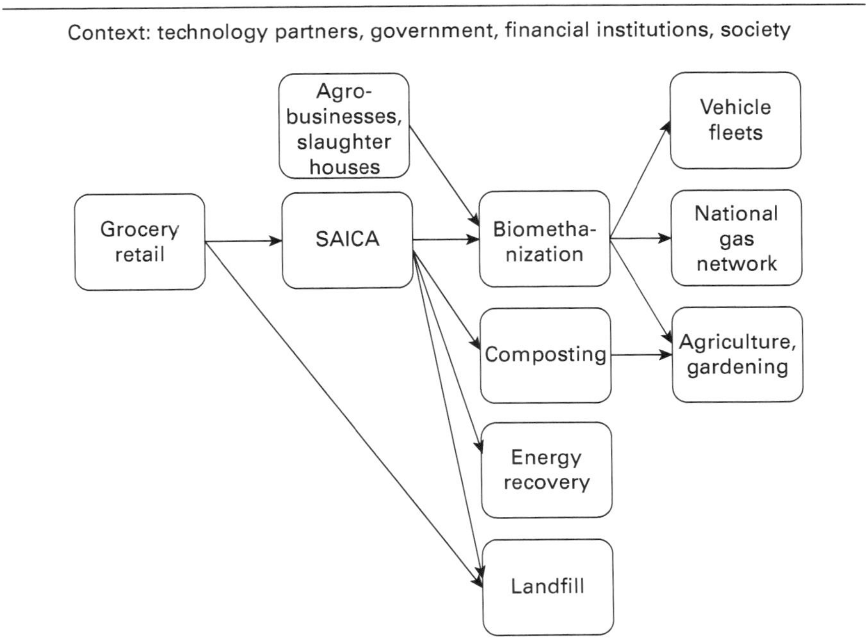

Table 1.1 Comparison of investment alternatives along multiple criteria

	Supply market (waste)	Demand market (feedstock)	Government	Internal perspective
Unpacking technology for delivery to industrial composters		Demand is limited and not growing. Entrance fees are increasing.	Permit does not require sanitation process.	Attractive ROI.
Unpacking and sanitation technology for delivery to industrial anaerobic digesters		Demand in general is growing. Demand of the quality provided by Saica is growing. Charge considerably lower entrance fees compared to composters.	Permit requires sanitation process. Biomethanization is more desirable than composting, according to the food recovery hierarchy.	ROI slightly better, compared to the previous option. Biomethanization can be vertically integrated in the future (no dependence on external parties and no outbound transport cost).
Issues applicable to both solutions	May improve CSR reporting while cutting cost on disposal. Has to correctly segregate in origin. Has to be convinced to contract this new service from Saica.	May shift to emerging competitors that pay higher fees to deliver (product with lower quality). High dependence of Saica upon energy recovery plants that have to receive the increasing flow of SRF.	May change regulatory framework, given interconnectedness of all levels (regional, national, European, global).	Add new business, in line with corporate vision/ mission and business model. Financial means are available.

Table 1.1 Continued)

	Supply market (waste)	Demand market (feedstock)	Government	Internal perspective
	May contract emerging competitors who charge less to pick up the product. May avoid this particular waste stream, eliminating packaging materials. May change the destination of their waste, in line with the food recovery hierarchy (eg donations).			Increases dependence of retailers on Saica (assuring waste streams for other business units). Availability of logistical infrastructure to support the new business.

- The case provides an example of multi-criteria decision making, where the criteria stem from the agendas and objectives of the stakeholders involved.
- The case helps readers to appreciate the importance of open-loop supply chains within the sustainability transition.
- The case highlights the potential of biomethanization and the supply chain that supports this renewable energy.

Questions

1. Saica is involved in multiple open loops within the circular economy. Explain this statement.
2. What are the challenges posed by the government for Saica's operations?
3. Looking at industrial composters and industrial anaerobic digesters as alternative destinations, are the challenges for Saica different and, if so, why?

Based on all the data (especially Table 1.1 and Figure 1.3), what would be the most appropriate decision to take regarding investment in a technology to recover value from EPOP? Discuss your decision.

References

Bernon, M, Tjahjono, B and Ripanti, E F (2018) Aligning retail reverse logistics practice with circular economy values: an exploratory framework, *Production Planning & Control*, **29** (6), pp 483–97

Boletín Oficial Del Estado (2018) [accessed 7 July 2021] Disposiciones Generales Ministerio De La Presidencia Y Para Las Administraciones Territoriales, Núm. 38, Lunes 12 de febrero de 2018 Sec. I. Pág. 16714 [Online] www.mapa.gob.es/es/ganaderia/temas/sanidad-animal-higiene-ganadera/rd50_2018sandach_controlcazamayor_tcm30-441034.pdf

Boons, F (2002) Greening products: a framework for product chain management, *Journal of Cleaner Production*, **10**, pp 495–505

De Angelis, R, Howard, M and Miemczyk, J (2018) Supply chain management and the circular economy: towards the circular supply chain, *Production Planning & Control*, **29** (6), pp 425–37

El periódico de Aragón (2020) [accessed 7 July 2021] El periodo de Aragón [Online] www.elperiodicodearagon.com/noticias/la-cronica-de-ribera-alta-del-ebro/alcampo-crea-sustrato-universal-marca-propia_1434847.html (archived at https://perma.cc/RNC8-NL5W)

European Commission (2020) [accessed 7 July 2021] EU Circular Economy Action Plan, *European Commission* [Online] https://ec.europa.eu/environment/circular-economy/ (archived at https://perma.cc/D7N2-M9YN)

Eurostat (2020) [accessed 7 July 2021] Municipal waste statistics, *Eurostat* [Online] https://ec.europa.eu/eurostat/statistics-explained/index.php/Municipal_waste_statistics (archived at https://perma.cc/894A-6N4Y)

Ellen MacArthur Foundation [accessed 7 July 2021] Ellen MacArthur Foundation [Online] www.ellenmacarthurfoundation.org/ (archived at https://perma.cc/C9ZZ-UUZR)

Environmental Protection Agency (2010) [accessed 7 July 2021] Environmental Protection Agency [Online] www.epa.gov/ (archived at https://perma.cc/DR6K-FAQS)

Gobierno de España (2020) [accessed 7 July 2021] Economía Circular, Estrategia Española, *Gobierno de España* [Online] www.miteco.gob.es/es/calidad-y-evaluacion-ambiental/temas/economia-circular/estrategia/ (archived at https://perma.cc/W4J7-QZY8)

Knight, L, Pfeiffer, A and Scott, A (2015) Supply market uncertainty: exploring consequences and responses within sustainability transitions, *Journal of Purchasing and Supply Management*, **21** (3), pp 167–77

Kumar, S and Malegeant, P (2006) Strategic alliance in a closed-loop supply chain: a case of manufacturer and eco-non-profit organization, *Technovation*, **26** (10), pp 1127–35

Kunz, N, Mayers, K and Van Wassenhove, L N (2018) Stakeholder views on extended producer responsibility and the circular economy, *California Management Review*, **60** (3), pp 45–70

Li, C *et al* (2009) A stochastic dynamic programming based model for uncertain production planning of re-manufacturing system, *International Journal of Production Research*, **47** (13), pp 3657–68

Malinauskaite, J *et al* (2017) Municipal solid waste management and waste-to-energy in the context of a circular economy and energy recycling in Europe, *Energy*, **141**, pp 2013–44

Porat, R *et al* (2018) Postharvest losses of fruit and vegetables during retail and in consumers' homes: quantifications, causes, and means of prevention, *Postharvest Biology and Technology*, **139**, pp 135–49

Priyadarshini, P and Abhilash, P C (2020) Circular economy practices within energy and waste management sectors of India: a meta-analysis, *Bioresource Technology*, **304**, 123018

Ranta, V, Keränen, J and Aarikka-Stenroos, L (2020) How B2B suppliers articulate customer value propositions in the circular economy: four innovation-driven value creation logics, *Industrial Marketing Management*, **87**, pp 291–305

Saica (2020) [accessed 7 July 2021] Saica [Online] www.saica.com/en/ (archived at https://perma.cc/3Z3K-253Q)

'You want it where?' 02

How a holistic and end-to-end sustainable logistics strategy can inform manufacturing plant location decisions

DR ERICA BALLANTYNE, SHEFFIELD UNIVERSITY MANAGEMENT SCHOOL, UNIVERSITY OF SHEFFIELD, UK

DR GRAEME HERON, SHEFFIELD UNIVERSITY MANAGEMENT SCHOOL, UNIVERSITY OF SHEFFIELD, UK

Introduction

This chapter is presented as an investigative case study undertaken by the authors, following a request by an organization (Company X) who were looking to develop a manufacturing and distribution facility to both meet the demands of the UK market and support the main production site on the Western European seaboard. Previous research conducted by the company suggested the location of a site should be a new-build facility in Northamptonshire (Site A); however, our investigation revealed several often-overlooked shortcomings arising from location decisions. In addition to Company X's perspective, we also consider other organizations potentially relocating to an alternative Site B, a 22-hectare site north of Tyneside, offering business space for manufacturing, storage and distribution environments. Site B is owned by Company Y and is a multi-tenanted brownfield site redevelopment.

Our initial investigation indicated the shortcomings, which included:

- **Continuing development of customer-driven demand networks (CDDN):** Whereby fixed assets and networks are not flexible enough to reflect rapid change as some suppliers are compelled to build buffer inventory to overcome forecast errors, supply delays and stock-outs elsewhere in the supply chain.

- **Vendor-managed inventory (VMI) and collaborative planning:** There are many opportunities to reduce overall miles travelled in Company X's supply chain and address inventory issues such as stock shortages at different geographical locations.
- **Collaborative planning, forecasting and replenishment (CPFR):** These initiatives tend to benefit large-scale multinational manufacturing operations (eg Unilever, Johnson & Johnson, Procter & Gamble) and do not scale-down well. However, locating to Site B enables a greater opportunity to reduce overall environmental impacts by reduced distances travelled and offers multi-modal opportunities.
- **Assumed supply and demand characteristics reflecting historical trends:** Introduction of an end-to-end supply chain analysis reflects a more holistic approach to sustainability and the roles of logistics service providers (LSP), allowing the supply network to develop in a more sustainable manner. A clear example of this had been the identification of a single point of distribution (Site A) within London's orbital motorway system.

Therefore, this case study adopts a 'whole chain' perspective and is based on the organizational knowledge of Company X that was provided to the research team. This included: planned volumes, current operating site locations, key raw ingredients and processing mediums required, primarily water and oats.

As a result, utilizing a site-embedded LSP can allow improved levels of service value creation that occur in the contexts of 'value' being defined in a twofold perspective: sustainable logistics system values delivering supporting stakeholder value and social capital, both in the contexts of impact and stressor reductions. Resultantly, this research allies our *a posteriori* knowledge with recently emerged practices such as vested outsourcing (Vitasek, 2016) in the development of a competitive strategy based upon the adoption of a sustainable logistics strategy.

Environmental impact can be described as the 'green' issues that surround operations' relationship with the physical environment, for example air pollution, contamination of ecological systems, and noise emissions. In this context environmental impact may be considered to have three components: first, environmental stressors such as CO_2/CO_2 equivalent pollutants, noise, or styrene-butadiene and carbon black, compounds of lead, sulphur and zinc from tyres, and iron brake dust are released in natural ecosystems, which increase stress. This is an important factor in the overall sustainability of a freight journey as Site A supplying a nominal distribution point within the M25 (the London Orbital Motorway is a major road encircling almost all of Greater London, England) is proportionally longer in a time per mile perspective, which indicates more stopping, starting and braking occurring in this journey *ceteris paribus*, thus overlooking current models for distribution to the UK multiple retail sector and major wholesale organizations.

Each tonne of goods transported places stress on the environment, and many stressors can be measured in units per tonne of goods transported. Thus, the total amount of stress placed on the environment depends on the quantity of goods and the distance they are transported; expressed in the simplest form:

$$\text{Total stress} = (\text{Quantity of goods} \times \text{Distance travelled}) \times \text{Stress per tonne}$$

The second component involves the spatial pattern of goods transported, including the transport mode used. In this case we consider sea, rail and road freight systems. The environmental impact of the total stress is determined by the nature of the receiving environment. Additionally, clean air zones and ambient characteristics, such as physical ecosystem characteristics, density of the human population affected and whether the receiving ecosystem is considered critical or includes endangered species, are also important considerations in the development of a sustainable logistics strategy.

Some environmental stressors, notably air and water pollutant emissions, are easily quantified, and clearly rise with increases in freight. Others, such as noise, increase with the number of trips made, but not with distance travelled or quantity of goods carried, which are very important factors in the development of a sustainable logistics strategy. Dirtier journeys are those of which a greater proportion of the journey occurs in urban areas and can be attributable as having a societal impact beyond the emissions themselves. In this respect of 'dirty vs clean' there is evidence of antecedent government interventions in the creation of clean air zones and the introduction of clean air corridors to support the UK Government's Clean Air Strategy (Department for Environment Food and Rural Affairs, 2019).

What is a 'sustainable' logistics strategy?

A corporate strategy exists to guide an organization towards achieving its long-term objectives (Johnson *et al*, 2008), and as companies operate within increasingly complex supply chain networks it is important to consider logistics within strategic planning. However, the introduction of a more formal logistics strategy needs also to consider the company's sustainability objectives at its core. Thus, a sustainable logistics strategy is one which encompasses an organization's concerns across its strategy timelines (see Table 2.1) in relation to reducing the impacts of emissions, environmental stressors, road presence by volume, and land/building use in relation to inventory and built environments (Grant *et al*, 2017). This aligns to the definition of green and sustainable logistics as the planning, control, management and implementation of logistics systems through advanced logistics technologies and environmental management, aiming to reduce pollutant emissions and improve logistics efficiency (Bask and Rajahonka, 2017).

Common to strategy development is a three-tier hierarchical approach: strategic, tactical and operational (Johnson *et al*, 2008), each having a feedback loop to assess fitness for purpose and to identify areas for further development and continuous improvement as summarized in Table 2.1:

- **I Strategic level**: Here the overall market service requirements and mission objectives of the organization are addressed in order to achieve the overall journey of the organization. This usually occurs at a time horizon of 5 – >5 years.
- **II Tactical level**: At this level it is common to set specific quarterly objectives, performance indicators, result areas and costings/planned expenditure in relation to the logistics function over a time horizon of 1–5 years.
- **III Operational level**: Common to a unionist or non-unionist perspective of the logistics functions is a need to develop and set realistic targets for expenses and, in the case of this research, the likelihoods of revenues related to the warehouse function at a site level, by month, for a one-year financial period.

There are several different approaches to the development of a sustainable logistics strategy. Common to them all are operations management realities linked to transport cost economics, asset efficiency, data commoditization as informational symmetry and bounded rationality.

Halldorsson *et al* (2017) support this view in that transport cost economics (TCE) provides a governance structure to be able to manage and respond to changes in volumes and operational costs such as fuel prices. TCE represents a branch of applied microeconomics and can be summarized as seeking a profit motive from the movement of goods. However, given the dynamic nature and routing complexities involved, consolidations and value-adding operational factors, many trips can be unique events. The accepted canons of market economics

Table 2.1 Sustainability aspects: transport, warehousing and inventory

Activity	Strategic level	Tactical level	Operational level
Transportation	Choosing the logistics service provider (LSP) and the transport modes/inter-modality options available.	Configuration of warehousing racking areas in relation to the needs of Company X and Site B accordingly/in support of the logistics functions.	Load planning, fill rates, route planning, minimization of vehicles and maximization of loads.
Warehousing	Selecting the operational zones and characteristics of the warehousing space and racking systems available at the site in their current configurations.	Possible redesign of warehouse layout linked to volume growth and customer requirement as a result of VMI or CPFR® initiatives.	Order picking, pack and delivery, both as internal functions in support of manufacturing, and fulfilment of customer orders: per colleague/per order/per shift.
Inventory management on supply and demand sides	Optimizing choices for modes for incoming materials, multiple-trip reverse logistics system picking and outgoing finished goods or recyclable materials, compostables, extended value by-products etc.	Supply chain risk management through dynamic adjustment of inventories in relation to lean and agile trade-offs.	Fulfilment measures based on pre-set success levels regarding on-time in-full deliveries to customers. Management of outstanding in-bound deliveries.

based upon relative scale, scope and repeatability cannot be applied (Bassett, 1974; Cowie, 2009; Grant, 2012; Stubbs, Tyson and Davli, 2017). However, a basic measure of overall profit or loss can simply be expressed as the difference between the total operating costs of the organization and the total transport charges invoiced to customers as a service commodity over a defined period of time. It can be simply stated as:

$$\text{Total revenues} - \text{Total transport cost} = \text{Profit or loss}$$

Notwithstanding these definitions, and within the context of this case, we posit that sustainable TCE can be described as an overall net value that an organization can generate in consideration of social and environmental benefits and impacts that have been taken into account as part of these transport costs. This exemplifies connecting the role and benefits of LSP provision with the triple bottom line (TBL) values and financial/optimal performance (Elkington, 1998).

Another factor in the development of a sustainable logistics strategy at site and organizational level relates to a resource-based view (RBV), indicating that an organization as a collection of resources is ultimately limited by the ability to endow resources as volumes grow. An RBV is important as it reviews and records how organizations gather and exploit organizational inputs (Wernerfelt, 1984; Barney, 1991; Lockett *et al*, 2009) dependent on contexts both of customers predisposed to scarcity and supply streams at the mercy of forecasting errors, peaks/troughs, seasonal factors and so on, whereby a lack of visibility and access impinges upon the control and optimization of logistics functions. In the context of this case an RBV can be seen as the opportunity sets available to an organization in their selection of an LSP, gaining advantage and performance over a finite period of time so that the organization can focus on its core competencies and strategy delivery.

Using an LSP therefore removes a major constraint to growth and allows the organization to concentrate on its core competencies while also benefitting from a single point of contact in relation to order fulfilments (Heron and Oglethorpe, 2013). RBV and TCE are different, but converge for the development of a sustainable logistics strategy: establishing relationships with an LSP to develop shared activities under an agreed costing mechanism leads to synergetic advantage of '1 + 1 = 3', which contemporaneously addresses sustainability issues considered by the TBL of profits, people and planet (Figure 2.1) (Elkington, 1998).

These feedback loops are important and commonplace in both total quality management (Steyn, 2002; Tool, 2005; Ross, 2017) and as stage 5 of the theory of constraints (Goldratt and Cox, 2016), in that separate interpretations and thoughts can be easily analysed and compared using a common feedback template. After all, we often incorrectly assume that everyone in a multiple stakeholder environment shares their comprehensions and understandings of how one thing affects another.

Figure 2.1 Triple bottom line influences on sustainable logistics development

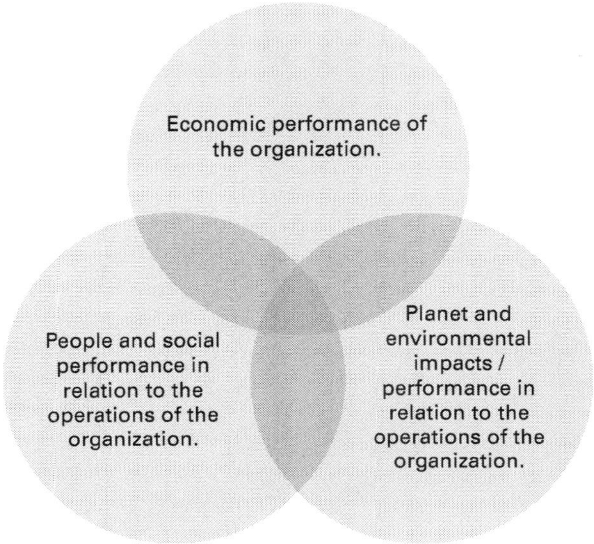

Feedback loops provide dynamic information to allow real-time measurements, which, in turn, allow those controlling the logistics functions to make the correct decisions at the correct time (Sarkis *et al*, 2010). Therefore, a sustainable logistics strategy is one that seeks to minimize traffic flows into and out of a site at an organizational level and to reduce road miles wherever possible, within the regimes of management performance indicators, operational performance indicators and environmental condition indicators.

Primary packaging components and milled oats logistics management

Packaging is currently manufactured in Lund, Sweden and delivered to the Swedish process and filling site. UK manufacturing of this packaging occurs near Chester, Cheshire. However, our analysis (Table 2.2) leads us to recommend that from environmental sustainability, supply chain risk management and Logistics 4.0 perspectives (Amr, Ezzat and Kassem, 2019) the company should continue to print the packaging in Lund for supply to the UK.

Table 2.2 Analysis of packaging trip impacts: Chester UK versus Lund SE

Trip – presuming base vehicle returning 14.49 km/4.54 litres (UK imperial gallon)	Distance	Emissions (tonnes)	Total
Lund to Landskrona	35 km road	0.029	**0.029**
Chester to Site B	322 km road	0.275	**0.275**
Lund to Site B via Malmo (SEMMA) and Port of Tyne (GBSSH) Port of Tyne to Site B	17.6 km road 1118.6 km sea freight container 13 km road	0.015 0.168 0.011	**0.194**

Here, we looked at two options based on the information available to us for the principal ingredient, oats (Avena sativa): mill availability at Crewe, Cheshire, and future possible mill availability at the Port of Tyne. With respect to the Crewe Mill we considered two options: the road option and the road → rail → road option as an intermodal opportunity to reduce impact and support the overall sustainable logistics strategy. Intermodality in this journey reduces CO_2/CO_2e emissions by 76 per cent in the movement from road to rail for most of the journey (Table 2.3).

Further leverage of the LSP relationship can be gained in relation to other items being delivered to site using a factory gating policy, lower prices can be negotiated for purchased materials, greater utilization of the LSP's fleet can be achieved and vehicle trips can be reduced.

Table 2.3 Analysis of intermodal opportunities: road and rail

Trip – presuming 30,000 ltr bulk powder container	Distance (km)	Emissions (tonnes)	Totals
Crewe to Site B	322	0.266	**0.266**
Crewe to Site B as road → rail → road journey	10 – 337 – 25	0.008 + 0.067 + 0.021= 0.096	**0.096**
Port of Tyne (South) to Site B	20.5	0.017	**0.017**

Outsourcing decisions and selection of an LSP

Outsourcing decisions relate to the concept of core competence and determining which activities, if outsourced to a third-party LSP, would provide sufficient tangible benefits and value (Grant, 2012): see Figure 2.2. An LSP is an organization which offers value-adding services beyond a simple dyadic relationship of 'you say, we send'. These additional activities typically extend to documentation management, warehousing and inventory management (receipt and despatch), packing, consolidation of components into complex orders and a single point of contact (Coyle *et al*, 1996; Panayides and So, 2005). With the onset of Logistics 4.0, a more sophisticated LSP has emerged which can deliver mutual benefit to itself and its customers through the commoditization of autonomously generated data in more interconnected supply chains (Oláh *et al*, 2018).

In support of Company X's overall strategy to minimize flows in and out of site, increase load fill rates and reduce overall road miles and their associated environmental burdens, Site B has a clear advantage related to the inherited warehousing space and racking systems. The available infrastructure lends itself well to using an LSP rather than a traditional transport company where evidence suggests that many of these relationships tend to become dyadic and do not always extend to a second or third contract, since many outsourcing partnerships sour over time (Hill, 2004; Slack *et al*, 2010; Harrison and van Hoek, 2011; Slack *et al*, 2012) and ultimately fail.

Common to LSPs are their ability to add value through additional services beyond transportation, warehousing and delivery. At a site level there is an opportunity not only for Company X, but for the wider Site B itself, to be able to use an LSP to be able to flex volume accordingly. This could help other micro, small and medium enterprises (MSME) organizations looking to move to the site to comprehend that there is an established LSP to smooth setting up and distribution, as they will benefit from:

- an ability to focus on core competencies and skills;
- reduction in non-value-adding operational requirements;
- enhanced customer confidence via a single point of access to live load updates;
- freedom from transport liabilities while contemporaneously gaining cost advantage though leveraging the LSP's economies of scale and scope;
- leveraging the ability of the LSP to host technology beyond the cost that most MSMEs can afford.

Figure 2.2 LSP decision matrix (adapted from Lynch, 2000 and Slack and Brandon-Jones, 2018)

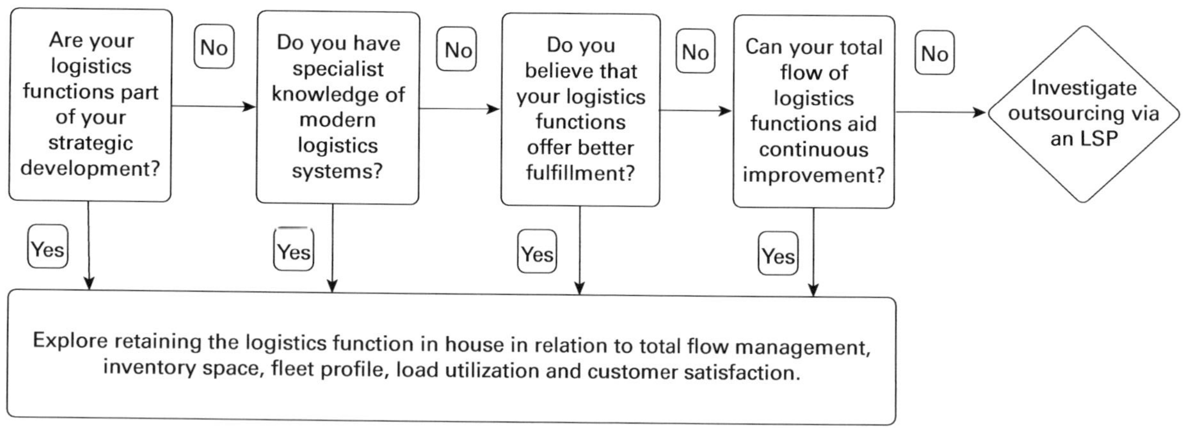

Research has revealed that successful outsourcing agreements operate differently. These agreements move away from traditional transaction-based mindsets based almost solely on lowest possible price and cheapest space/labour. Vested outsourcing represents an outcome-based business model that's based on collaboration, innovation and sharing value as well as data, to create partnerships in which the parties have a vested interest in succeeding together for the long-term win–win more closely aligned with a sustainable logistics strategy and wider sustainability objectives previously discussed: the TBL win, win, win effect. Many organizations requiring logistics services assume that if they 'buy', they should use market forces to ensure they are getting the best deal as a transactional cost. This is evident in companies on the supply side of the relationship; for instance, colleagues earn bonuses for achieving year-over-year cost savings, which rapidly reduces returns to all of parties involved in a 'zero sum' game. As organizations seek a best price, the default approach is to use a transaction-based model where a buying organization can 'test the market' by comparing prices across transactions, such as price per mile, per pallet, per kilogram and so on. Choosing an LSP with a strong cultural sustainability compatibility is an essential difference from classic ways of sourcing an LSP.

With this in mind, a 'Request for Partner' methodology is well suited when the buying organization(s) need to develop a long-term contract with an LSP for development and delivery of a sustainable logistics strategy. It is also ideal when the buying organization(s) are seeking an LSP who will play a major role in transformation or innovation, seeking high degrees of collaboration, cultural fit and a *'what's in it for us'* mindset typified by the win–win–win of the TBL and the wider sustainability agenda. In this context, Logistics 4.0 refers to 'the logistical system that enables the sustainable satisfaction of individualized customer demands without an increase in costs and supports this development in industry and trade using digital technologies' (Winkelhaus and Grosse, 2020: 20). Logistics 4.0 represents a reality that manufacturing organizations and their customers can be negatively impacted upon when logistics phases do not reflect manufacturing phases under Industry 4.0, whether these be internal flows, business-to-business flows or business-to-customer flows (Szymańska *et al*, 2017; Schmidtke *et al*, 2018). In this case, Logistics 4.0 can clearly support a sustainable logistics strategy. Benefits can include: automated and predictive delivery management, real-time item tracking, route planning, centralized and synergized data as a commodity, automated communication, artificial intelligence as multiple serving chatbots and machine learning from every trip, taking the data collected and using it to plan more efficient and sustainable future journeys.

Vendor-managed inventory is an agreement by the vendor/supplier to manage inventory in relation to the customer's needs. The customer is responsible for providing consumption data (eg what is sold and consumed in real time); this enables the supplier to balance out the customer requirements, executing goods movement directly either to the wholesaler, regional distribution centre or stores. Using an LSP allows the inventory management function, historically held by the customer, to improve supply chain visibility through adaptation of current systems or adoption of relatively low-cost technology. This enables the LSP to better 'green' the supply chain through increased trailer/container fill-rate utilization, which also reduces overall transport impacts and emissions.

Focusing on vendor-managed inventory (VMI) and collaborative planning, forecasting and replenishment (CPFR)

Both VMI and CPFR are introduced in this case study as they lend themselves well to the warehousing/racking systems infrastructure at site B. In this context the following challenges have been addressed:

- VMI is an agreement by the vendor, in this instance Company X itself using an LSP, to manage inventory in relation to their various customers' needs. Company X through their LSP would be able to balance out the customer requirements at a geographic level with their own production plans and goods movement executions. This in turn influences efficient decisions by the LSP linked to resource utilization. The LSP and Company X assume command over the inventory management function historically held by the customer base, each one with its own peculiarities. Company X and the LSP can now determine patterns and schedules of deliveries either to regional distribution centres (RDCs), DCs or direct store deliveries.
- There is a considerable amount of evidence to suggest that CPFR does not readily scale downward. Notwithstanding this current issue of scalability, both Logistics 4.0 and Web EDI are likely to overcome this, especially in the context of establishing an onsite LSP; Web EDI is readily established in a 'hub and spoke' distribution model, in which the proposed LSP as a business partner acts as the hub and other organizations locating

to Site B represent the spokes. CPFR is a natural development of VMI principles. Currently it is constrained to large companies pulling common goods through supply networks. It does away with the shifting of inventories among trading partners that sub-optimizes the logistics functions in the supply chain. This potential to lower transport costs and increase efficiencies/fill rates as a result of collaborations reduces overall inventory costs. In turn, this leads to a reduction in fuel and overall road miles, which themselves lead to less inefficient loading on incumbent transport and infrastructure systems, ultimately reducing environmental stressors.

Conclusion

The logistics network that we have described in this case as a sustainable logistics strategy is based upon other network theories and displays similar properties to them. These other 'self-organizing' network theories include wider operations management and business communications. Common themes running through these networks are short characteristic path lengths and high degrees of collaboration.

Logistics networks and network modelling have historically been represented through the construction of basic linear dependencies and dyadic buyer–seller relationships. However, this appealing and straightforward method of mapping a logistics supply network distorts the intricacies and realities of logistics as it does not readily 'weight' all of the nodes in a network correctly. For instance, the inclusion of quantifying environmental measures in network models adds complexity and conflict as companies try to adjust parameters in order to both maximize profit/minimize costs and optimize customer service (Harris *et al*, 2015). Resultantly, the other independent research, which suggested a processing and filling plant in the Northampton area, with a single point of distribution, is at best recidivist. Notwithstanding, we should not overlook that exigencies as urgent demands and immediate reactions are realities of logistics networks, so having a single LSP adds a layer of 'scale' defence. Another aspect is the adaptability of a logistics network to withstand and reshape/change as a result of unexpected impacts and neutral or negative node activity.

It is imperative in the context of this case to recognize key differences between logistics resilience and logistics adaptability; supply networks which can reconfigure connectivity to fit with new customers, products and demands are adaptable and sustainable rather than resilient. An embedded LSP should provide short characteristic paths of information flow to allow data throughout the logistics network.

Although it is conceded that environmental impact assessments (EIAs) do not always deliver optimal decision making as a result of their use, it was important to this research given the key differences between Site A and Site B (Ortolano and Shepherd, 1995; Wood, 2002; Retief, 2010; Morgan, 2012). It is more prescient than ever before to be able to assess decision processes which will impact upon society through to biophysical environments, before final decisions are made. In respect of Site A's area new-build proposition, Akbarnezhad and Xiao (2017) record that building and construction is responsible for up to 30 per cent of annual global GHG emissions, commonly reported in carbon equivalent units (CO_2e). We have indicated that the previous study, which suggested a processing and filling plant in the Northampton area, with a single point of distribution within the M25, was at best recidivist. This is a very important factor to consider in such a location decision, since a greenfield site as proposed by option A in Northampton will generate GHG emissions in the construction phase, emissions that have already been accounted for and captured at Site B. The research recommended that Company X conduct an EIA to help them consider their location decision from a more holistic perspective. This EIA should comprise a comparable data gathering and analysis in relation to the built environment factors at both sites and include the following suggested elements: air, contamination, control during works phases, ecology, flood, noise, socio-economics, waste management and wider environment.

Notwithstanding these EIA factors alone, the logistics 'golden triangle' that the Northampton area is supposed to represent (*and location for Site A*) is something of a misnomer in developing sustainable logistics networks. The historical context is that the area represents one of the first in the UK to become de-industrialized in relation to heavy engineering and mining. As such, there was a need for many jobs to be replaced, which inevitably attracted organizations by being incentivized to set up in the golden triangle area. It is now seen as a 'via', with major retail organizations reconfiguring warehousing space for efficient 'live load' cross-docking so that inventory is minimized by these organizations, but without a fall in relative demand. This initiative in turn has forced suppliers to set up inventory buffers in the area which are fed by geographically remote manufacturing plants, thus creating excessive inventories which remain a supply chain risk to the manufacturer, hence our identification of the potential for VMI or CPFR. Beyond this it is evident that Site B allows a greater degree of flexibility linked to future growth of a sustainable logistics network, offering both a backup to mainland operations and a fast time land bridge to fulfil and export to the mainland EU and to the nearby Irish market.

This case identifies that up to the point of commissioning production systems, and *ceteris paribus* in post-commissioning operational phases, Site B presents a better option from an environmental impact perspective. The refurbishment of a modern facility with existing services infrastructure is less impactful on the environment than Site A's new-build option. Critically, the product's principal ingredient by volume is water, of which availability is higher at Site B as a result of lower population density, lower business demands and higher rainfall in the geographic area. It is important to comprehend that for both site options under review, each needs to undergo a comparable and holistic EIA exercise. The proper assessment and management of potential wider impacts on human health and the ecosystem are essential in the formulation of an effective environmental policy related to Company X. We have addressed this by identifying that a move from current approaches, which are predominantly dyadic in nature, towards a more circular approach and the integration of a sustainable logistics strategy can adduce logistics factors (Navarro, Cronemyr and Huge-Brodin, 2018), therefore representing a clear opportunity for best practice and competitive advantage.

In addition, total quality management (TQM) can contribute to LSP efficiency and development through their ability to recognize a defined problem and identify the 'voice of the customer', therefore fostering continuous improvement within operational fulfilment (Ballantyne and Heron, 2020); for example, the ability to satisfy multiple customers on a single milk-round delivery without compromising others' delivery schedules while engaging with opportunities to collect goods for Site B. An embedded LSP can gain operational and sustainability benefits, ultimately leading towards meeting air quality targets, by engaging with compliance and recognition schemes, which provide access to multifaceted socio-technical approaches (eg driver education around fuel-efficient driving, enhanced vehicle maintenance, load optimization etc) (Ballantyne and Heron, 2020).

Socio-economic evidence is also important regarding the availability of and access to public transport. Such transport poverty factors are important in business location decisions, since new-build sites are often in locations that are very easily accessible from the existing road network (namely motorways and major highways) but suffer from a lack of public transport accessibility options (Lucas, 2006; Ballantyne and Genovese, 2018). These dynamics may result in poor workplace accessibility for employees, leading to recruitment difficulties for companies linked to the perceived accessibility of jobs (Ballantyne and Genovese, 2017). From a wider sustainable logistics perspective, Site B is preferable since it is located on established public transport links that provide an opportunity to reduce the associated negative socio-environmental impacts of developing a new-build site.

We base our conclusions on an end-to-end operational analysis supporting the holistic development of a sustainable logistics strategy:

- Site B should be the preferred site option as it has a lower overall environmental impact than the Site A 'new build' option, from environmental impact, embodied carbon, resource availability, logistics, and manufacturing carbon offsetting perspectives.
- Site B's infrastructure is well suited to the role of an embedded LSP, who can, in turn, develop and manage a sustainable logistics strategy for Company X.
- A sustainable logistics strategy allows clear opportunities to introduce and develop emerging sustainability practices which clearly support the core sustainability values of Company X.
- The simple 'point A to point B' logistics scenario described to Company X as an underpinning reason for the Site A 'new build' option does not reflect the current logistics network distribution models employed by the major multiple retailers and their logistics subcontractors.
- Further, the research considered an 'end-to-end' environmental analysis which evaluates opportunities for inter-modality and modal swaps which are more compelling for the Site B option.
- There is significantly less demand per head of population for water resources at the Site B location, and therefore less stress on the water system network than at Site A.

In conclusion, simple centre-of-gravity location models no longer reflect the realities of modern supply and demand fulfilment strategies. The sustainability agenda requires a much more holistic and encompassing approach that looks beyond simple metrics.

Learning outcomes

- This case highlights the importance of assessing location decisions from a wider, more holistic perspective that includes environmental impact at all stages from construction to operations, resource availability, logistics/fulfilment, and manufacturing carbon offsetting perspectives.
- The case provides an example of how a sustainable logistics strategy enables the introduction and development of emerging sustainability practices to be incorporated into strategic decision making.
- This case demonstrates how traditional location decision models no longer reflect developments in sustainable logistics planning scenarios and dynamic routing opportunities available to LSPs to satisfy complex forward and reverse product and packaging/ingredient flows.

Questions

1 This case considers an 'end-to-end' analysis which evaluates opportunities for third-party logistics provision as an LSP, offering single points of control, fulfilment as less than truck/trailer loads (LTTL) and less than pallet loads (LTPL) as customer service outcomes. List the opportunities and barriers to this scenario and how they can be addressed.

2 A sustainable logistics strategy allows clear opportunities to introduce and develop evolving sustainability practices. Discuss the future of supply chains and how they may change as a result of the sustainability agenda.

3 As a result of this case study, list the factors which you would now include in your decision processes for evaluating suitable site locations which you had not thought of previously, and why they would support a sustainable logistics strategy.

4 Referring to the discussion in the chapter on the importance of a holistic EIA, for Company X or another organization of your choosing, discuss and complete an EIA as shown in Table 2.4.

Table 2.4 Comparative analysis of Site A and Site B environmental impact assessment

Elements should include, but are not limited to:	Refurbishment of Site B	Suggested metric	Possible outcomes	New-build facility Site A option	Suggested metric	Possible outcomes
Air						
Contamination						
Control during works phases						
Ecology						
Flood						
Noise						
Socio-economics						
Waste management						
Wider environment						

References

Akbarnezhad, A and Xiao, J (2017) Estimation and minimization of embodied carbon of buildings: a review, *Buildings*, **7** (1), p 5

Amr, M, Ezzat, M and Kassem, S (2019) Logistics 4.0: definition and historical background, in *Novel Intelligent and Leading Emerging Sciences Conference (NILES)* (vol. 1, pp 46–49), IEEE.

Ballantyne, E E F and Genovese, A (2017) Transport poverty in the logistics workforce: an empirical investigation, *Proceedings of the 22nd Annual Logistics Research Network Conference*, Southampton Solent University, 6–8 September

Ballantyne, E E F and Genovese, A (2018) A comparative case study analysis of access to work in the UK logistics industry, *Proceedings of the 23rd Annual Logistics Research Network Conference*, Plymouth University, 5–7 September

Ballantyne, E E F and Heron, G (2020) Can transport operator schemes deliver regional sustainability benefits? The case of the UK Northern Powerhouse Region, *Sustainability*, **12** (4), p 1662

Barney, J (1991) Firm resources and sustained competitive advantage, *Journal of Management*, **17** (1), pp 99–120

Bask, A and Rajahonka, M (2017) The role of environmental sustainability in the freight transport mode choice, *International Journal of Physical Distribution & Logistics Management*, **47**, pp 560–602

Bassett, R G (1974) *Road Transport Management and Accounting*, Heinemann, Portsmouth, NH

Bento Pereira, N, Calejo Rodrigues, R and Fernandes Rocha, P (2016) Post-occupancy evaluation data support for planning and management of building maintenance plans, *Buildings*, **6** (4), p 45

Brander, M and Davis, G (2012) Greenhouse gases, CO_2, CO_2e, and carbon: What do all these terms mean?, *Econometrica*, White Papers

Cowie, J (2009) *The Economics of Transport: A theoretical and applied perspective*, Routledge, Abingdon

Coyle, J J, Langley, C J and Bardic, E J (1996) *The Management of Business Logistics*, West Publishing, Eagan, MN

Department for Environment, Food and Rural Affairs (2019) [accessed 7 July 2021] Clean Air Strategy, *DEFRA* [Online] www.gov.uk/government/publications/clean-air-strategy-2019/clean-air-strategy-2019-executive-summary (archived at https://perma.cc/K3M3-3MKY)

Elkington, J (1998) Partnerships from cannibals with forks: the triple bottom line of 21st-century business, *Environmental Quality Management*, **8** (1), pp 37–51

Emmi, N, Mortenson, B and Heineken, J (2016) Environmental impact assessment of a school building in Iceland using LA, including the effect of long distance transport of materials, *Buildings*, **6** (4), p 46

Goninan, K and Hasanagic, M (2018) A systematic review on drivers, barriers, and practices towards circular economy: a supply chain perspective, *International Journal of Production Research*, **56** (1–2), pp 278–311

Goldratt, E M and Cox, J (2016) *The Goal: A process of ongoing improvement*, Routledge, Abingdon

Grant, D B (2012) *Logistics Management*, Pearson Higher Education, Harlow

Grant, D B, Wong, C Y and Trautrims, A (2017) *Sustainable Logistics and Supply Chain Management: Principles and practices for sustainable operations and management*, Kogan Page, London

Gusmerotti, N M *et al* (2019) Drivers and approaches to the circular economy in manufacturing firms, *Journal of Cleaner Production*, **230**, pp 314–27

Halldorsson, A *et al* (2017) Complementary theories to supply chain management, *Supply Chain Management*, **12** (4), pp 284–96

Harris, I *et al* (2015) Restructuring road freight networks within supply chains, in *Green Logistics, 3rd edn,* ed A McKinnon *et al*, Kogan Page, London

Harrison, A and van Hoek, R (2011) *Logistics Management and Strategy: Competing through the supply chain*, 4th edn, Prentice Hall, Marlow

Heron, G and Oglethorpe, D (2013) Testing the theory of constraints in UK local food supply chains, *International Journal of Operations & Production Management*, **33** (10), 1346–67

Hill, T (2004) *Operations Management*, 2nd edn, Palgrave, London

Johnson, G, Scholes, K and Whittington, R (2008) *Exploring Corporate Strategy: Text & cases*, Pearson Education, Harlow

Kirchherr, J, Reike, D and Hekkert, M (2017) Conceptualizing the circular economy: an analysis of 114 definitions, *Resources, Conservation and Recycling*, **127**, pp 221–32

Lieder, M and Rashid, A (2016) Towards circular economy implementation: a comprehensive review in context of manufacturing industry, *Journal of Cleaner Production*, **115**, pp 36–51

Lockett, A, Thompson, S and Morgenstern, U (2009) The development of the resource-based view of the firm: a critical appraisal, *International Journal of Management Reviews*, **11** (1), pp 9–28

Lucas, K (2006) Providing transport for social inclusion within a framework for environmental justice in the UK, *Transportation Research Part A – Policy and Practice*, 40 (10), pp 801–09

Lynch, C F (2000) *Logistics Outsourcing: A management guide*, Wiley Blackwell, Oxford

Morgan, R K (2012) Environmental impact assessment: the state of the art, *Impact Assessment and Project Appraisal*, **30** (1), pp 5–14

Navarro, P, Cronemyr, P and Huge-Brodin, M (2018) Greening logistics by introducing process management – a viable tool for freight transport companies going green, *Supply Chain Forum*, **19** (3), pp 204–18

Oláh, J *et al* (2018) Information technology developments of logistics service providers in Hungary, *International Journal of Logistics Research and Applications*, **21** (3), pp 332–44

Ortolano, L and Shepherd, A (1995) Environmental impact assessment: challenges and opportunities, *Impact Assessment*, **13** (1), pp 3–30

Panayides, P M and So, M (2005) Logistics service provider–client relationships, *Transportation Research Part E: Logistics and Transportation Review*, **41** (3), pp 179–200

Pavlushko, M O and Polishchuk, V G (2019) Innovative technologies of logistics companies in Ukraine from the point of view of sustainable development

Retief, F (2010) The evolution of environmental assessment debates: critical perspectives from South Africa, *Journal of Environmental Assessment Policy and Management*, **12** (04), pp 375–97

Ross, J E (2017) *Total Quality Management: Text, cases, and readings*, Routledge, Abingdon

Sarkis, J *et al* (2010) Developing environmental supply chain performance measures, *Benchmarking*, **17** (3), pp 320–39

Schmidtke, N *et al* (2018) Technical potentials and challenges within internal Logistics 4.0, *4th International Conference on Logistics Operations Management (GOL)* (pp 1–10), IEEE

Slack, N *et al* (2012) *Operations and Process Management: Principles and practice for strategic management*, 3rd edn, Prentice Hall, Harlow

Slack, N and Brandon-Jones, A (2018) *Operations and Process Management: Principles and practice for strategic impact*, Pearson, Harlow

Steyn, H (2002) Project management applications of the theory of constraints beyond critical chain scheduling, *International Journal of Project Management*, **20** (1), pp 75–80

Stubbs, P C, Tyson, W J and Dalvi, M Q (2017) *Transport Economics* (Book 21), Routledge, Abingdon

Szymańska, O, Adamczak, M and Cyplik, P (2017) Logistics 4.0: a new paradigm or set of known solutions?, *Research in Logistics and Production*, **7** (4), pp 299–310

Vitasek, K (2016) *The Vested Outsourcing Manual: A guide for creating successful business and outsourcing agreements*, Springer, New York

Wernerfelt, B (1984) A resource-based view of the firm, *Strategic Management Journal*, **5** (2), pp 171–80

Winkelhaus, S and Grosse, E H (2020) Logistics 4.0: a systematic review towards a new logistics system, *International Journal of Production Research*, **58** (1), pp 18–43

Wood, C (2002) *Environmental Impact Assessment: A comparative review*, Routledge, Abingdon

The development of a triple bottom line sustainability index for a vertically integrated beef production company 03

PROFESSOR KIM BRYCESON, THE UNIVERSITY OF QUEENSLAND, BRISBANE, AUSTRALIA

DR MOHD MOHSIN, UNIVERSITY OF SOUTHERN QUEENSLAND, TOOWOOMBA, AUSTRALIA

PROFESSOR GEOFF SLAUGHTER, UNIVERSITY OF SOUTHERN QUEENSLAND, TOOWOOMBA, AUSTRALIA

Case study

This chapter reports on an investigative case study undertaken by the authors, following a request by an Australian beef production organization

(Company X) who were looking to establish a mechanism for measuring the sustainability value of their product (beef) throughout their multi-enterprise company (the company owns multiple production units (farms), a feedlot and a processor and thus has a vertically integrated value chain). The push for a metric addressing sustainability value came from the company's international customers through the company's marketing group.

The initial suggestion was to develop a carbon footprint (the process of quantifying greenhouse gas emissions emitted directly or indirectly by an individual, company or product (Wiedemann and Dunne, 2021)). However, as discussions with Company X progressed, it became clear that to address 'sustainability metrics' for their vertically integrated internal value chain, more than just a carbon footprint of the business was required. For example, different customers at different stages in the chain were asking for different sustainability metrics – one wanted an overall carbon footprint, another was interested in animal welfare, yet another was interested in how the company managed their land and water resources sustainably, and the company itself was also interested in how its staff were managed and nurtured. It was agreed that whatever was developed in the way of metrics should focus on a triple bottom line (TBL) approach that supported the Australian Beef Sustainability Framework (ABSF). Therefore, a brief desktop review of general sustainability literature was undertaken, with a focus on beef production systems underpinned by a TBL approach, to provide a context to creating metrics to address Company X's sustainability value requirements. A dynamic sustainability index was then developed using the extant literature as context. The methodology employed in creating the index is reported here as the case study.

Sustainability

Sustainability has always been difficult to define (Lélé, 1991) and as a result has many different meanings to many different people – in fact so much so that McKenzie (2004: 1) said: 'sustainability is now a broad multi-focal agenda, and terms such as "triple bottom line" and "sustainable development" are being used interchangeably. As a result, "sustainability" is in danger of carrying so many implications and nuances that in order for it to be properly understood it must be defined whenever it is used' – and so we do this below.

At face value, the word 'sustainability', as a noun, means 'a process or state [that has] the ability to continue or be continued for a long time'

(Oxford Dictionary, 2020). In an effort to be more precise, variants on this definition have been developed and argued over for many years, for example:

- Environmentalists see sustainability from the viewpoint of using natural products and energy without harming the environment, especially by replacing what has been used (Morelli, 2011).
- Businesses see sustainability primarily from a financial perspective, namely a business's financial ability to continue to make a profit and provide services over time with minimum risk (Zabolotnyy and Wasilewski, 2019).
- Social scientists regard sustainability as primarily about human-based activities – it is the least clearly defined of the sustainability definitions and includes a mix of human well-being and equity, access to basic needs, fair distribution of income, good working conditions and decent wages, equality of rights, inter- and intra-generational justice, access to social and health services and to education, social cohesion and inclusion, empowerment, and participation in policy making (Dainiene and Dagliene, 2015; European Union (EU), 2020).

As well as these baseline definitions, there are a number of recognized approaches to sustainability – one of which is the TBL approach. The TBL is an accounting system that includes three components of organizational performance: social, environmental and financial, or, people, planet and profits (Elkington, 1994, 1997). Savitz and Webber (2014: 8) expand on this definition as follows: '[TBL] captures the essence of sustainability by measuring the impact of an organization's activities on the world – including both its profitability and shareholders' values and its social, human and environmental capital'.

The problem, however, is not simply in defining TBL and thus sustainability but in measuring it – the more complex the situation the less useful it is to assess it across the different domains of economics, ecology, politics and culture (Magee, James and Scerri, 2012). Interestingly, Elkington (2018) discusses how TBL has been used (and abused) over the years since he coined the phrase, and requested a 'recall' of the concept to do some 'fine tuning' to bring it up to what he had intended – a more whole-of-system approach rather than simply an accounting tool.

From an agriculture and food production perspective, the main approach to sustainability has been to look at sustainable, inclusive food systems through the lens of a complex system approach (Gamboa *et al*, 2016; Ingram, 2011; Tai, 2018), which in medium to large modern organizations tends to lead to an emphasis being placed on corporate metrics that may or may not adequately describe 'sustainability', rather more addressing corporate social responsibility goals (Garriga and Mele, 2004; McGuire, Sundgren and Schneeweis, 1988; Bryceson and Ross, 2020). The beef industry, which is an extremely large agrifood industry globally with the global beef market size expected to reach USD 383.5 billion by 2025 (Grandview Research, 2019), has taken a lot of criticism around its production impacts on climate change and the environment (Cederberg *et al*, 2011; Gerber *et al*, 2013; Ogino *et al*, 2016). As a result, much research has been undertaken on how to monitor and manage sustainable beef production systems (see for example: Yapp *et al*, 2001; Bracke *et al*, 2005; Calker *et al*, 2005; Beauchemin *et al*, 2011; Capper, 2011; Lebacq, Baret and Stilmant, 2012; Herrero *et al*, 2013; Scholten *et al*, 2013; Rotz *et al*, 2015, 2019; Wiedemann *et al*, 2015; Greenwood *et al*, 2018; Maia de Souza *et al*, 2017; Asem-Hiablie *et al*, 2018).

In 2012, as a more industry-focused operational environment, a Global Roundtable for Sustainable Beef (GRSB) was established as an initiative of five main actors in the global industry supply chain: the producers and producer associations, the processing and commerce sector, retail companies, civil society (academics, non-government and non-commercial institutions) and national or regional roundtables to promote global beef sustainability initiatives (GRSB, 2017a). The core principles of producing sustainable beef that are outlined by GRSB (2017b) can be summarized under three headings that relate to the TBL approach described above:

1. Environment
   - Managing natural resources responsibly and improving and protecting the environment
   - Minimizing beef's carbon footprint
   - Water: growing more with less
2. Social/Ethics
   - Providing for the health, welfare and behavioural needs of your animals
   - Ensuring food safety and traceability
   - Respecting human and labour rights while providing a healthy workplace and fair treatment
   - Operating your business with integrity

3 Economics

- Contributing to economic sustainability
- Ensuring efficiency within the supply chain
- Contributing to global food security
- Contributing to the well-being of your local community.

Additionally, in a number of countries such as Australia (ABSF, 2017), Canada (CCSBF, 2016) and the United States (USBF, 2019) the nation-specific industry bodies have created Beef Sustainability Frameworks which identify a practical and common-sense set of criteria that can be measured in most beef production entities. Table 3.1 shows the Australian Beef Sustainability Framework referred to in this study, which was created with input from internal and external stakeholders in the Australian beef industry chain.

Table 3.2 shows a thematic comparison of the Australian, Canadian and US Frameworks as the beef production industries of the latter two countries are comparable to Australia in terms of farming practices and cultures focusing on the themes of (a) economy: yield and productivity; (b) animal welfare; (c) social: people and community environment.

As can be seen, the Australian Beef Sustainability Framework is very similar to those of the Canadian and US Frameworks and they all clearly sit within the GRSB Principles which also address the three key principles of the TBL approach (economic, social and environmental).

Creating a dynamic sustainability index for a vertically integrated beef production company: underpinning concepts

Based on extant literature, it was agreed with Company X that a more holistic sustainability index (SI) would be created to address their needs rather than just a carbon footprint – and that the SI would be developed with the view that it could be used as a practical application at enterprise level in a beef production scenario. Further, the SI would be based on TBL principles combined with attributes of the ABSF.

The main deliverable required by Company X was an accurate and dynamic SI with the integrity of data that would:

- facilitate continuous improvement;
- enable Company X to align itself with the industry framework;
- identify current energy usage across the vertically integrated company chain.

Table 3.1 Outline of key Australian Beef Sustainability Framework Themes (taken from ABSF, 2017)

Australian Beef Sustainability Framework
https://www.sustainableaustralianbeef.com.au/the-framework/

The Framework defines what 'sustainable beef production' looks like in practice and annually tracks how the industry is performing over a series of indicators. The Framework consists of 4 themes and 6 priority areas (ABSF, 2017).

Themes

Theme 1 – Animal welfare
Theme 2 – Economic resilience
Theme 3 – Environmental stewardship
Theme 4 – People and community

Priority areas

Animal husbandry techniques:
These techniques include castration, disbudding, horn removal (dehorning), branding and spaying. This priority looks at alternatives to practices (eg breeding selection for the polled gene, immune-contraceptive desexing, effective electronic identification) and, in the interim, administer pain relief when carrying out necessary but aversive husbandry procedures.

Profitability across value chain:
To be economically sustainable, the industry must generate a positive rate of return over the long term on all capital used in cattle raising and beef production. Currently this priority looks only at farm business profit due to data limitations.

Balance of tree and grass cover:
Beef production is compatible with well-managed landscapes. This priority looks at industry's care of natural resources and biodiversity, by measuring area of land managed for environmental outcomes and changes in vegetation.

Antimicrobial stewardship:
Maintaining the efficacy of antimicrobials so that infections in humans and animals remain treatable is of critical importance. This priority looks at industry use of antibiotics and surveillance programmes to detect resistance to them.

Managing climate change risk:
Greenhouse gases are emitted throughout the beef value chain, including methane produced through cattle's natural digestion. This priority looks at carbon dioxide equivalents emitted when raising and processing beef, as well as carbon sequestration.

Health and safety of people in the industry:
Working environments throughout the beef value chain, especially on-farm, expose employees and contractors to risk. This priority looks at notifiable fatalities; however, the industry recognizes that further investigation of injuries could highlight risk factors and improve work safety.

Table 3.2 A comparative thematic analysis of the Australian, Canadian and US Beef Sustainability Frameworks (adapted from US Beef Framework, 2019; Australian Beef Framework, 2017 and Canadian Beef Framework, 2016)

Themes	United States	Australia	Canada
Economic: Yield and productivity	• Long-term economic viability of Individual operation within the chain • Employee well-being and rural livelihood • Preservation and enhancement of ecosystem • Productivity and efficiency of the cattle and cow-calf sector	• Long-term profitability across the value chain (profitability across the industry) • Farm, feedlot and processor productivity and cost of production (total farm productivity) • Access to market (domestic and international) • Customer loyalty to beef market (product integrity)	• Long-term profitability in cow-calf and feedlot sector • The long-term cost of production for cow-calf and feedlot sector • Retail beef domestic demand index • International beef demand Index
Animal welfare	• Antibiotic stewardship (responsible animal treatment) • Cattle pre-conditioning before backgrounding • Holistic veterinarian–client–patient relationship • Adequate care, feed and water • Technology and best management practices	• Freedom from hunger and thirst • Freedom from discomfort • Freedom from pain, injury or disease • Freedom to express normal behaviour • Freedom from fear and distress	• Animal welfare audit • Technologies/installation for animal handling • Certified cattle worker for animal handling • Stunning and killing method

Social: People and community	• Safety policy and procedures • Risk and hazard identification • Training • Performance evaluation • Continuous improvement • Employee financial counselling • Employee benefits packages to full-time employees • Employer-sponsored retirement programme • Employees' vacation time • Employee immunization programme • Sponsoring community actions • Encouraging employees to engage with the community	• Beef as a healthy diet • Consumer food safety • Workforce capacity building • Workforce diversity • Workplace safety/notifiable fatality • Workforce emotional well-being	• Freedom of association and bargaining • Fair salary • Equal opportunities • Worker occupational health and safety • Worker social security • Consumer feedback protocol • Consumer health and safety • Community engagement • Promoting social responsibility • Contribution to the economic development of region/society

(*continued*)

Table 3.2 (Continued)

Themes	United States	Australia	Canada
Environment	• Sustainable land management • Water stewardship metrics • On-farm water use literacy to employees • Air and greenhouse gas emission • Energy use optimization strategy • Farm public reporting of CO_2e • Partnership, initiatives, or programmes for GHH emission	• Minimizing nutrient and sediment loss • Balancing trees and grass cover • Managing climate change risk • Readiness to climate change adaptation • Water efficiency in beef operations • Efficient solid waste management	• Climate change – Carbon footprint • Resource consumption – Fossil fuel depletion – Water depletion • Agricultural land occupation • Air Pollution – Terrestrial acidification – Photochemical oxidant formation • Water pollution – Marine eutrophication – Freshwater eutrophication

Figure 3.1 shows the TBL approach combined with the Australian Beef Sustainability Framework where the three key principles of TBL (economic, environmental and social issues) overlap with the ABSF identified attributes to provide a secondary set of crossover metrics that can be quantified, thus enabling a quantitative measure of overall company sustainability.

Sustainability index (SI): Developing appropriate metrics and indicators

As identified earlier, after discussion with Company X, the underlying metrics were chosen to be the three principal components or categories associated with the TBL (economic, environmental and social), with general indicators being identified as: (i) the economic viability of the internal value chain; (ii) the environmental stewardship along the internal value chain; and (iii) the socio-economic commitment of the internal value chain. These were combined with the key attributes of the Australian Beef Sustainability Framework, which included:

- Animal Welfare
  - Enhance animal well-being
  - Promoting animal health
- Economic Resilience
  - Enhance profitability and productivity
  - Optimization of market
- Environmental Stewardship
  - Improvements to land management
  - Mitigate and manage climate change (including carbon emissions)
  - Minimize waste
- People and Community
  - Produce nutritious and safe food
  - Build workplace capacity
  - Ensure health, safety and well-being of people in the industry.

Figure 3.1 Key TBL principles and crossover areas

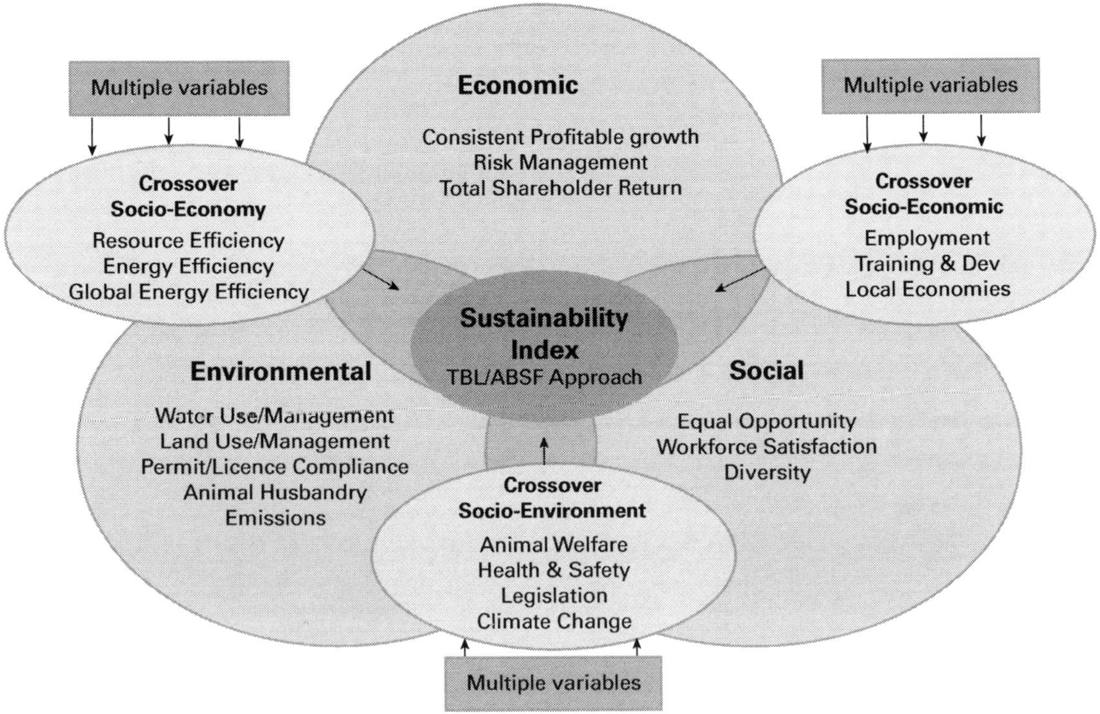

The SI indicators were developed using typologies from other research, including:

- livestock farming sustainability indicators (Lebacq *et al*, 2013);
- cattle farm sustainability indicators. beef cattle environmental footprint indicators (Rotz *et al*, 2019);
- environmental indicators (Beauchemin *et al*, 2010; Beauchemin *et al*, 2011).

The indicators were then validated against the American and Canadian Beef Sustainability Frameworks as comparable instruments. In this study, the process of developing the SI is shown diagrammatically in Figure 3.2.

A life-cycle assessment (LCA) (Rotz *et al*, 2015; Muralikrishna and Manickam, 2017) of category metric and indicator development was followed as the whole of the internal value chain of beef production needed to be addressed. To comply with the LCA approach, which involves the systematic analysis of the potential [environmental] impacts of products or services during their entire life cycle, the same indicators were identified for farm, feedlot and processor. The precise indicators agreed to by Company X were arrived at on the basis of what and how they contributed to the overall index and the availability of appropriate data. Any assumptions related to the data were clarified at the start in order for the final indicators and associated metrics to be created. Table 3.3 shows TBL categories and associated ABSF themes with general indicators and agreed-to indicators as used in the case study.

The categories and their associated indicators were put into MS Excel spreadsheets to enable a linked, dynamic and updateable measure of the sustainability index to be created that could be used for multiple purposes – including, but not limited to, internal continuous improvement and external marketing. Table 3.4 shows the Economic/Economic Resilience category with indicators. including measures used for quantifying them, worked through in full detail for each component of the chain (farm, feedlot, and processor).

The indicator calculation process used for the calculation of each category's sustainability indices is detailed in Figure 3.3.

Figure 3.2 Process involved in developing the sustainability index

Table 3.3 ABSF themes, TBL categories and associated indicators

TBL Categoy (ABSF)	General Indicator	Case Study Indicator	Case Study Sub-Indicator
Economic (Economic Resilience)	Profitability	Profitability across value chain	Operating return
			Capital retum
			Cost ratio (enterprise cost plus overhead cost)
		Financials	Equity ratio
			Net worth
	Productivity	Productivity across value chain	Total productivity
		Yield efficiency	Cattle performance
			Feed conversion
	Market optimization	Market resilience	Access market
			Market reach: omni-channel strategy
	Economic value to Australia	N/A	N/A
	Risk management	Risk resilence	Production risk
			Business Risk
	Other financial measures	N/A	N/A

Environmental (Environmental Footprint)	Land management practices	Land management practices	Soil health
			Pasture management
			Bio-diversity
			Deforestation
		Water footprint	Water efficiency in raising beef cattle (Cow-Calf/ ML)
			No of watering points
			Use of recycled water
	Climate change management & mitigation	Climate readiness	Land management drought (destocking)
			Rainfall drought (irrigation infrastructure)
	Carbon footprint	Emission management	Carbon footprint: CO_2e
			Fossil fuel usage
			Refrigeration
	Waste minimization	Waste management	Solid waste recycling to compost
			Solid waste recycling to landfill
		(Social)	N/A
	Animal welfare permit compliance	Permit types	Production
			Animal Welfare
			Health and Safety
			Export

(continued)

Table 3.3 (Continued)

TBL Categoy (ABSF)	General Indicator	Case Study Indicator	Case Study Sub-Indicator
Social (Social Value)	Workforce	Workforce capacity building	Employment (training diversity, staff turnover)
		Workforce health, safety and well-being'	Health, safety and well-being
	Community	Community	Community engagement
			Living tension
			Local employment
			Indigenous rights
	Nutritious and safe food production	Consumers	Health and safety
			Transparency
			Feedback
			End-of-life responsibility
		Animal welfare	Livestock handling/husbandry
			Meat processing
			Export practices

Table 3.4 Detailed economic/economic resilience category with indicators worked through in full detail for each component of the chain (farm, feedlot and processor)

ABSF theme/ TBL category	Case study indicator	Sub-indicator	Description/ measurement	Units	Farm (breeding and backgrounding)	Feedlot	Processor	Total chain	Data location
Economic resilience	**EC_1: Profitability**	Operating return	Earnings before interest and taxes (EBIT) divided by total assets	%	Farm net return / On-farm total assets	Feedlot net return/ Feedlot total assets	Processor net return/ Processor total assets	Total chain net return/ Total chain capital asset	Income statement and balance sheet
		Capital return	Increase or decrease in asset value (mainly land) as % of operating asset	%	Farm return to operating assets	Feedlot return to total operating assets	Processor returns to total operating asset	Total returns to total operating assets	Balance sheet
		Cost ratio (enterprise cost plus overhead cost)	Cost of beef produced at farm level; cost of feedlot, and cost of cattle processed per head	A$/head or A$/kg	Cost per live animal/weight per live animal	Net weight gain at feedlot/ animal * cost of total grain consumed/ head	Carcass weight/ animal at abattoir * cost of processor carcass/ head	Total cost in the chain/Total sales	Income statement and balance sheet

(continued)

Table 3.4 (Continued)

ABSF theme/ TBL category	Case study indicator	Sub-indicator	Description/ measurement	Units	Farm (breeding and backgrounding)	Feedlot	Processor	Total chain	Data location
	EC_2: Financials	Equity ratio	Equity as % of total assets	%	Equity used in farm/Total assets	Equity assets used in feedlot/ Total assets	Equity assets used in processor/ Total assets	Total equity used in the chain/Total assets	Balance sheet
		Net worth	Total assets minus total liabilities (mainly change in land value)	%	Pro-rata net worth in farm	Pro-rata net worth in feedlot	Pro-rata net worth in processor	Total net worth/Total assets	Balance sheet
	EC_3: Productivity	Total productivity	Ratio of total input to total output used: Input/output model = how much input in terms of feed and the cost per kg of feed to how many kg of beef out – liveweight and dressed.	%	Total input value ($) used in farm/ Total output value ($) generated	Total input value ($) used in feedlot/Total output value ($) generated	Total input value ($) used in processor/ Total output value ($) generated	Total input value ($) used in chain/Total output value ($) in chain generated	Income statement and balance sheet

EC_4: Yield efficiency	Cattle performance	Calving rate: Calves born alive per cows bulled	%	(Calves born alive/ cows and heifers bulled) *100	n/a	n/a	Farm level only	Calving records
		Mortality rate	%	(Cow deaths/ cows and heifers bulled) *100	n/a	n/a	Processor level only	Farm stocking records
	Feed conversion	Feed efficiency	kg/head	Total grain consumed per head/Net weight gain per head	Total grain consumed per head/Net weight gain per head	n/a	Farm and feedlot level	
EC_5: Market resilience	Access market	Access to live cattle, beef market	%	Yearly market growth	n/a	Yearly market growth	Farm and processor level	Sales data
	Market reach: omni-channel strategy	Growth in market integration in retailing	%	n/a	n/a	Yearly rate on integration		Sales data

(*continued*)

Table 3.4 (Continued)

ABSF theme/ TBL category	Case study indicator	Sub-indicator	Description/ measurement	Units	Farm (breeding and backgrounding)	Feedlot	Processor	Total chain	Data location
	EC_6: Risk resilience	Production risk	Qualitative check: Does the company have a production risk shock observer in the chain?	% (converted from qual score)	Farm has production risk shock observer: 0 = Yes 1 = Developing 2 = Mature	Feedlot has production risk shock observer: 0 = Yes 1 = Developing 2 = Mature	Processor has production risk shock observer: 0 = Yes 1 = Developing 2 = Mature		Risk statement
		Business risk	Loss of market share due to input price	% (converted from qual score)	Farm has business risk shock observer: 0 = Yes 1 = Developing 2 = Mature	Feed lot has business risk shock observer: 0 = Yes 1 = Developing 2 = Mature	Feedlot has business risk shock observer: 0 = Yes1 = Developing 2 = Mature		Risk statement

Figure 3.3 Flow chart of Indicator calculation*

1. Each indicator listed in the input MS Excel Spreadsheet under its associated Category and measures for each indicator identified

2. Average timeline of data for each index intended identified (for example, 3 years, 5 years, 7 years average)

3. Data collected for each indicator for the number of years agreed

4. Base year chosen for comparison of indicator performance from a baseline in time

5. Verifiable assumptions set in addition to data for eg:
   - Weights for each index category set as well as for specific indicators covered under each category. (NB in the version described, a uniform weighting principle was applied to each category (Environment, Economics & Social) at the outset of the index development for simplicity: further complexity could be added in later versions to address real world practicalities)

6. Year specific values of indicators calculated

7. Confidence scores (reliability score of each indicator's value) set. In this version, the confidence scores were set as:
   - 100%= If data collected from farmers
   - 90%= If data is collected from stakeholders
   - 80%= if data collected from anecdotal/peer-reviewed literature

8. Normalize the favourable or unfavourable indicators by converting each indicator to a scale of 0–100 and set the ranges of values of indicators by which each indicator can be expressed from 0–100 scales

9. **Calculate Sustainability Indices for each Category using Sustainability equations**

* Weighting is an important step. In the initial development of this project, a uniform weighting principle was applied to each category at the outset of the index development for simplicity. A more detailed weighting scheme, created using expert-assigned weights to bring real-world perspectives into the index construction philosophy, could be developed to address which category was considered more important to the company concerned. For example, is the Economics category more important than Environment or Social and thus should it have a higher weighting? Or similarly, is Environment or Social more important? We contend that this is likely to be related to the stage in the value chain and is intrinsically bound up with a company's core income proposition and belief and value system.

Sustainability equations

The individual sustainability indices were developed using multiple different sources from beef and other agricultural sustainability studies as reference. These were:

- Antunes *et al* (2017). 'A holistic framework to assess the sustainability of irrigated agricultural systems.'
- Atkisson and Hatcher (2001). 'The compass index of sustainability: prototype for a comprehensive sustainability information system.'
- Cruz *et al* (2018). Methodologies for assessing sustainability in farming systems.
- Ding (2005). Developing a multi-criteria approach for the measurement of sustainable performance.
- Frater and Franks (2013). Measuring agricultural sustainability at the farm level: a pragmatic approach.
- Gan *et al* (2017). When to use what: methods for weighting and aggregating sustainability indicators.
- Gonsalves and Lopes (2014). Firm-specific determinants of agricultural financial reporting.
- Lebacq *et al* (2012). Sustainability indicators for livestock farming. A review.
- Lopez-Ridaura *et al* (2002). Evaluating the sustainability of complex socio-environmental systems. The MESMIS framework.
- Marandure *et al* (2016). Indicator-based sustainability assessment of the smallholder beef cattle production system in South Africa.
- Rivera-Huerta *et al* (2019). Social sustainability assessment in livestock production: a social life-cycle assessment approach.
- Rotz *et al* (2015). Cradle-to-farm-gate environmental footprints of beef cattle production in Kansas, Oklahoma and Texas.
- Calker *et al* (2005). Identifying and ranking attributes that determine sustainability in Dutch dairy farming.

Based on the above sources the following indices were calculated.

Economic sustainability index

$$f(EC_{SI}) = \sum_{i=1}^{n}(ECR_i * ECC_{i1}) + (ECR_j * ECW_k * ECC_k) + \\ ------(ECR_n * ECW_n * ECC_n)$$

Where,

$f(EC_{SI})$ = Economic sustainability index
ECR_i = rated scale of 1st economic indicator
ECW_{i1} = weight of 1st economic indicator
ECC_{i1} = confidence estimates of 1st economic indicator
n = nth items of economic indicators used in the economic indices

Environmental sustainability index

$$f(EV_{SI}) = \sum_{i=1}^{n}(EVR_i * EVW_i * ECVC_{i1}) + (EVR_j * EVW_k * EVC_k) \\ +------(ECVR_n * EVW_n * EVC_n)$$

Where,

$f(EV_{SI})$ = Environmental sustainability index
EVR_i = rated scale of 1st environmental indicator
EVW_{i1} = weight of 1st environmental indicator
EVC_{i1} = confidence estimates of 1st environmental indicator
n = nth items of indicators used in the environmental indices

Social sustainability index

$$f(SO_{SI}) = \sum_{i=1}^{n}(SOR_i * SOW_i * SOC_{i1}) + (SOR_K * SOR_k * SOC_k) + -----(SOR_n * SOW_n * SOC_n)$$

Where,

$f(SO_{SI})$= social sustainability index
SOR_i = rated scale of 1st social indicator
SOW_{i1} = weight of 1st social indicator
SOC_{i1} = confidence estimates of 1st social indicator
n = nth items of indicators used in the social indicators

Overall beef production sustainability index

$$f(OSI)=((f(EC_{SI})*WEC)+(f(EV_{SI})*WEV)+(f(SO_{SI})*WSO)))$$

Where,

$f(EC_{SI})$ = Economic sustainability index calculated in eq.1
WEC = weight of economic index in the whole matrix
$f(EV_{SI})$ = Environmental sustainability index calculated in eq.2
WEV = weight of environmental index in the whole matrix
$f(SO_{SI})$ = Social sustainability index calculated in eq.3
WEV = weight of social index in the whole matrix

A detailed example of the data inputs and initial economic indicator calculations as a percentage is shown in Table 3.5 and the overall economic sustainability index scoring and classification is shown in Table 3.6.

NB Risk resilience statements

1. If the company has self-sufficient capability to continue the farm operation at each level of the value chain, in the face of any natural/market risk 0 = no; 1 = yes at Developing stage = 10% (for methodological simplicity); 2 = Mature plan = 20% (for methodological simplicity).
2. If the company has a production risk shock absorber at each stage of value chain 0 = no; 1 = yes at Developing stage = 10% (for methodological simplicity); 2 = Mature plan = 20% (for methodological simplicity).
3. If the company has a business risk shock absorber at each stage of the value chain 0 = no; 1 = yes at Developing stage = 10% (for methodological simplicity); 2 = Mature plan = 20% (for methodological simplicity).

Table 3.5 Detailed economic resilience category indicator data inputs for each of the three value chain components (farm, feedlot and processor) over three years as a percentage

Years		**2017**			**2018**			**2019**			**Total beef chain (3 years average)**		
Value chain/ Economic resilience category	Units	Farm	Feedlot	Processor	Farm	Feedlot	Processor	Farm	Feedlot	Processor	Farm Avg.	Feedlot Avg.	Processor Avg.
1. Profitability indicator													
1.1 Operating return measures	%												
EBIT	A$/ Head	270	300	300	200	190	110	165	110	98	212	200	169
Total assets	A$/ Head	1000	1000	1200	1700	1100	1200	1100	1200	1100	1267	1100	1167

(*continued*)

Table 3.5 (Continued)

Years		2017			2018			2019			Total beef chain (3 years average)		
Operating return ratio	%	**27%**	**30%**	**25%**	**12%**	**17%**	**9%**	**15%**	**9%**	**9%**	**17.92%**	**19%**	**14%**
1.2 Capital return measures/ ROI	%												
EBIT	A$/Ha	200	300	300	200	190	110	165	110	98	188	200	169
Total investment	A$	10000	20000	15000	12000	11000	10000	15500	11000	11000	12500	14000	12000
Return on investment	%	**2%**	**2%**	**2%**	**2%**	**2%**	**1%**	**1%**	**1%**	**1%**	**2%**	**1%**	**1%**
1.3 Cost ratio	%												
Revenues	A$/ Head	100	150	200	200	200	200	200	200	100	167	183	167
Cost	A$/ Head	70	60	50	170	170	170	70	70	70	103	100	97

Cost to revenue ratio	**%**	**70%**	**40%**	**25%**	**85%**	**85%**	**85%**	**35%**	**35%**	**70%**	**63%**	**53%**	**60%**
2. Financial viability indicator													
2.1 Equity ratio	%												
Total equity	A$	3000	2000	4200	3300	3000	3000	3000	3000	3000	3100	2667	3400
Total capital	A$	4000	4000	5000	4000	4000	4000	4000	4000	4000	4000	4000	4333
Equity to Total Capital	**%**	**75%**	**50%**	**84%**	**83%**	**75%**	**75%**	**75%**	**75%**	**75%**	**78%**	**67%**	**78%**
3. Productivity indicator													

(continued)

Table 3.5 (Continued)

Years		2017			2018			2019			Total beef chain (3 years average)		
Productivity ratio	%												
Total input	A$	3900	3000	4800	4000	3500	3400	3000	3000	3000	3633	3167	3733
Total output	A$	4000	4000	5000	4000	4000	4000	4000	4000	4000	4000	4000	4333
Output to Input Ratio	**%**	**98%**	**75%**	**96%**	**100%**	**88%**	**85%**	**75%**	**75%**	**75%**	**91%**	**79%**	**85%**
4. Yield efficiency indicator													
4.1 Mortality rate	%	10%			15%			9%			11%		
4.2 Feed conversion efficiency													

Net weight gain	Kg/ head	120	150	170	90
Total grain consumed	kg/ head	910	810	750	573
Net Gain to Grain	%	**13%**	**19%**	**23%**	**16%**
4.3 Carcass efficiency					
Live weight	kg/ head	300	310	340	317
Dressed weight	kg/ head	210	250	210	223
Dressed weight to live weight	%	**70%**	**81%**	**62%**	**71%**

(*continued*)

Table 3.5 (Continued)

Years		2017	2018	2019	Total beef chain (3 years average)
5. Market resilience indicator					
5.1 Access to live cattle market: growth	%	5%	5%	5%	5%
5.2 Access to beef market: growth	%	6%	6%	6%	6%
5.3 Market deepening : Wholesale to retailer	%	7%	7%	7%	7%

5.4 Market reach strategy: Omni-channel approach	%			8%			8%			8%			8%
6. Risk resilience indicator													
6.1 Self-sufficiency (in times of drought)	Score	20%	10%	0	10%	20%	10%	10%	10%	10%	13%	13%	7%
6.2 Production risk	Score	10%	20%	20%	20%	0	10%	20%	10%	10%	17%	10%	13%
6.3 Business risk	Score	10%	10%	10%	10%	10%	10%	0	20%	10%	7%	13%	10%

Table 3.6a Overall beef economic sustainability performance for the farm using data over a three-year period average (*NB: values are hypothetical*)

Indicators	Three-year overall average internal beef chain economic performance	Confidence score (Estimate's reliability)	Confidence adjusted performance	Scoring (Equalizing favourable and unfavourable indicators)
Operating return	16.9%	100%	16.9%	100
Capital return	1.3%	100%	1.3%	60
Cost efficiency	58.7%	90%	52.8%	100
Net worth	74%	90%	68%	80
Productivity	85%	90%	76.5%	90
Yield mortality	11%	90%	9.9%	90
Yield feed conversion	16%	90%	14.4%	80
Yield carcass efficiency	71%	90%	63.9%	80
Market resilience	7%	80%	5.6%	80
Risk factor	12%	80%	9.6%	80
Aggregated average score				**84**
Overall economic index				**Fairly Sustainable**

(*continued*)

Table 3.6b > Keys to individual economic sustainability indicators: indicative scores & ranges in %

Indicators	Strongly sustainable (91–100)	Fairly sustainable (81–90)	Poorly sustainable (71–80)	Slightly unsustainable (61–70)	Very unsustainable (0–60)
Operating return	15%–20%	10%–15%	8%–10%	5%–7%	>=5%
Capital return	10%–12%	8%–10%	5%–8%	3%–5%	>=3%
Cost efficiency	>=60%	60%–70%	70%–80%	80%–90%	<=90%
Net worth	80%–100%	75%–80%	55%–75%	35%–55%	>=35%
Productivity	80%–100%	70%–80%	60%–70%	50%–60%	>=50%
Yield mortality	15%–20%	20%–25%	25%–30%	30%–35%	<=35%
Yield feed conversion	10%–15%	8%–10%	5%–8%	5%–7%	>=5%
Yield carcass efficiency	75%–100%	65–75%	8%–10%	5%–7%	>5%
Market resilience	15%–20%	10%–15%	5%–10%	3%–5%	>3%
Risk factor	>=5%	5%–8%	8%–10%	10%–15%	>15%

Discussion

Creating a single sustainability index as discussed with, and agreed to by, Company X, which included all three TBL categories plus components of the Australian Beef Sustainability Framework and calculated from representative indicators, is not a trivial task. The most critical part was to create appropriate indicators that could be quantified and where appropriate data were available in company datasets which are rich in data collected over the years in the financial, environmental and social TBL categories.

What has been presented in this case study is a methodology used in creating such an overarching sustainability index which appears, after preliminary checking with Company X, to be a useful measure of their beef production sustainability value. Other benefits to the company are primarily that they can tune and update such an index and its component parts interactively and easily using their existing company systems (MS Excel) and staff skills. Additionally, the index addresses their different customer information needs as well as being an internal benchmarking tool for any continuous improvement that they may wish to make. The final key benefit is that the index developed includes a strong focus on the social domain which can include availability of jobs, staff turnover and gender, age and culturally related equality indicators. All of the issues such indicators represent (individually and/or combined), when quantified, monitored and benchmarked against best practice, can have a very significant impact on the viability of local communities in rural Australia where the company is present.

There are, however, a number of limitations of the current technique which need to be addressed in later versions of the SI. These include:

- Availability of quality and reliable indicator data.
- Quality of an individual indicator's data set: data set used in the index calculation could have a confidence bias. Some data have been taken from records classified as highly reliable (from farm records), reliable (estimated or extrapolated data) and uncertain (anecdotal).
- Indicator exclusion: it has been impossible to include all the different types of indicators under each category. In this case study only representative indicators that had easily sourced data were considered.
- Category weightings: all categories in the SI as presented have been assumed to be weighted equally. But there are other ways to value the

component weights, such as using a statistical weight and/or an expert's value weighting.

- Beef chain weighting: likewise, all the business units in the internal beef chain (farm/breeding, feedlot and processor) have been assumed to be equally weighted. This assumption may not fit the company's *core* income proposition and belief and value system.
- Indicator weighting: indicator weights have been assigned at random in the version of the SI discussed in this chapter so that Company X's data remain anonymous. In real terms, assigning these weights needs to be tuned using expert farm/feedlot/processor management staff input.
- Qualitative data trade-off: for methodological uniformity and simplicity, qualitative scoring of some indicators has been expressed quantitatively in the version of the SI discussed in this chapter.
- SI index base year: the base year of the SI needs to be as 'normal' a year climatically as possible in order to ensure major disruptions (eg drought, floods) do not have a greater than expected impact on the index.
- Seasonal variation: as with the last point, seasonal variability could impact the SI value and needs to be included in weighting. However, in the version of the SI discussed here, this was not addressed.
- Greater evaluation of SI required: a more critical evaluation of the SI should be undertaken and the indicators – particularly the weightings as discussed above – 'tweaked' according to expert input.

Learning outcomes

- This case has highlighted the importance of considering and including the interconnected stakeholders in the whole chain for effective sustainability value creation in agrifood systems.
- The case provides an example of multi-criteria analysis, where the criteria stem from the agendas and objectives of the stakeholders involved.
- The case highlights the potential of quality data collection and management throughout the chain as a value-adding tool to a final product.

Questions

1 What are some issues associated with choosing indicators for an agrifood industry?

2 What alternative indicators to those identified in the text, for each of the three categories described for a beef production entity, could be used?

   a. What measures could be used to quantify these indicators – why and how? Use the economic resilience tables shown in the case study as templates for indicator development and calculation.

3 Assume that Covid-19 has distorted the supply chain of the beef farm in 2020. The company has its own calving stock, backgrounding stock and processing facilities. However, the sales department has reported it lost two overseas market orders amounting A$3 million (2% of revenue) and A$6 million (4% of future revenue) in this 2020 financial year and for the 2021 financial year.

   a. How will this event impact the economic resiliency of the farm enterprise and overall company sustainability?

   b. What measures could have prevented any potential impact on sustainability? How can this kind of future experience be avoided?

4 It has been reported in the media that 200 live cattle belonging to Company X have died while the cattle were being exported by ship to the Middle East. An independent inquiry revealed that the cattle on board were in poor health. As a regulatory reprimand, the company was fined A$2 million.

   a. What is the potential impact of this event on the company sustainability index? Hint: note that the animals could be counted as coming from either the farm or the feedlot.

   b. How can similar occurrences be avoided in future and how would this be reflected in the indicators?

5 Company X is expanding its beef operations in a nearby remote area. The company has already spent A$2 million on site construction and the preliminaries associated with the extension. However, recently, the Community Heritage Protection Platform (CHPP) found that the company's proposed extension takes its production facilities to within 500 m of a 1,000-year-old Indigenous Cultural Heritage Site – not far enough away to ensure the continued safety of the heritage site. The company was sued by local indigenous landholders as a result and the lawsuit was for A$5 million. As a strategic sustainability decision maker, how would you respond to this kind of incident?

References

ABSF (2017) [accessed 7 July 2021] Australian Beef Sustainability Framework [Online] www.sustainableaustralianbeef.com.au/ (archived at https://perma.cc/2RMU-EGP5)

Asem-Hiablie, S *et al* (2018) A life cycle assessment of the environmental impacts of a beef system in the USA, *International Journal of Life Cycle Assessment*, **24** (3), pp 441–55

Antunes, P *et al* (2017) A holistic framework to assess the sustainability of irrigated agricultural systems, *Cogent Food & Agriculture*, **3** (1), doi:10.1080/23311932.2017.1323542

Atkisson, A and Hatcher, R (2001) The compass index of sustainability: prototype for a comprehensive sustainability information system, *Journal of Environmental Assessment Policy and Management*, **3** (04), pp 509–32

Beauchemin, K A *et al* (2010) Life cycle assessment of greenhouse gas emissions from beef production in western Canada: a case study, *Agricultural Systems*, **103** (6), pp 371–79

Beauchemin, K A *et al* (2011) Mitigation of greenhouse gas emissions from beef production in western Canada: evaluation using farm-based life cycle assessment, *Animal Feed Science and Technology*, pp 166–67, 663–77

Bracke, M, De Greef, K and Hopster, H (2005) Qualitative stakeholder analysis for the development of sustainable monitoring systems for farm animal welfare, *Journal of Agricultural and Environmental Ethics*, **18** (1), pp 27–56

Bryceson, K P and Ross, A (2020) Agrifood chains as complex systems and the role of informality in their sustainability in small scale societies, *Sustainability*, **12**, p 6535

Calker, K J V *et al* (2005) Identifying and ranking attributes that determine sustainability in Dutch dairy farming, *Agriculture and Human Values*, **22** (1), pp 53–63

Capper, J L (2011) The environmental impact of beef production in the United States: 1977 compared with 2007, *Journal of Animal Science*, **89** (12), pp 4249–61

Cederberg, C *et al* (2011) Including carbon emissions from deforestation in the carbon footprint of Brazilian beef, *Environmental Science Technology*, **45**, pp 1773–79

CCSBF (2016) [accessed 7 July 2021] Canadian Certified Sustainable Beef Framework, *CCSBF* [Online] www.crsbcertified.ca/about/ (archived at https://perma.cc/WQZ2-ZMJ3)

Cruz, J F, Mena, Y and Rodriguez-Estvez, V (2018) Methodologies for assessing sustainability in farming systems, in *Sustainability Assessment and Reporting*, ch 3, ed Soner Gokten and Pinar Okan Gokten, IntechOpen, doi:10.5772/intechopen.79220

Dainiene R and Dagliene, L (2015) A TBL Approach Based Theoretical Framework for Measuring Social Innovations Procedia – Social and Behavioral Sciences 213, 20th International Scientific Conference Economics and Management – 2015 (ICEM-2015)

Ding, G K C (2005) Developing a multicriteria approach for the measurement of sustainable performance, *Building Research & Information*, **33** (1), pp 3–16, doi:10.1080/0961321042000322618

Elkington, J (1994) Towards the sustainable corporation: win-win-win business strategies for sustainable development, *California Management Review*, **36**, pp 90–100

Elkington, J (1997) *Cannibals with Forks: The triple bottom line of 21st century business*, Capstone, Oxford

Elkington, J (2018) [accessed 7 July 2021] 25 years ago I coined the phrase triple bottom line. Here's why it's time to rethink it, *Harvard Business Review (Sustainability)*, [Online] https://hbr.org/2018/06/25-years-ago-i-coined-the-phrase-triple-bottom-line-heres-why-im-giving-up-on-it (archived at https://perma.cc/UFU3-GUKP)

European Union (EU) (2020) [accessed 7 July 2021] Social Sustainability – Concepts and Benchmarks, *European Union* [Online] www.europarl.europa.eu/supporting-analyses (archived at https://perma.cc/V84H-JR4D)

Frater, P and Franks, J (2013) Measuring agricultural sustainability at the farm-level: a pragmatic approach, *International Journal of Agricultural Management*, **2** (4), doi:10.5836/ijam/2013-04-04

Gamboa, G *et al* (2016) The complexity of food systems: defining relevant attributes and indicators for the evaluation of food supply chains in Spain, *Sustainability*, **8**, p 515

Gan, X *et al* (2017) When to use what: methods for weighting and aggregating sustainability indicators, *Ecological Indicators*, **81**, pp 491–502

Garriga, E and Mele, D (2004) Corporate social responsibility theories: mapping the territory, *Journal of Business Ethics*, **53**, pp 51–71

Gerber, P J *et al* (2013) Tackling Climate Change through Livestock—A Global Assessment of Emissions and Mitigation Opportunities, Food and Agriculture Organization of the United Nations (FAO), Rome, Italy

Gonsalves, R and Lopes, P (2014) Firm-specific determinants of agricultural financial reporting, *Procedia-Social and Behavioral Sciences*, **110**, pp 470–81

Grandview Research (2019) Market Analysis Report: Beef Market Size, Share & Trends Analysis Report By Cut (Brisket, Shank, Loin), By Slaughter Method (Kosher, Halal), By Region (North America, Europe, APAC, MEA, CSA), and Segment Forecasts, 2019 – 2025, Report ID: 978-1-68038-175-7, pp 117

Greenwood, P L, Gardner, G E and Ferguson, D M (2018) Current situation and future prospects for the Australian beef industry: a review, *Asian-Australasian Journal of Animal Sciences*, **31** (7), pp 992–1006, doi:10.5713/ajas.18.0090

GRSB (2017a) [accessed 7 July 2021] Global Sustainable Beef Framework, *GRSB [Online]* www. grsbeef.org/ (archived at https://perma.cc/M2NJ-RWAH)

GRSB (2017b) [accessed 7 July 2021] Principles and Criteria for Defining Global Sustainable Beef V1/10.17/100, *The Global Roundtable of Sustainable Beef, GRSB* [Online] https://grsbeef.org/resources/Documents/Principles%20and%20 Criteria/GRSB_Principles_F.pdf (archived at https://perma.cc/B4QF-8DVB)

Herrero, M *et al* (2013) Biomass use, production, feed efficiencies, and greenhouse gas emissions from global livestock systems, *Proceedings of the National Academy of Sciences of the United States of America*, **110** (52), pp 20888–93

Ingram, J (2011) A food systems approach to researching food security and its interactions with global environmental change, *Food Security*, **3**, pp 417–31

Lebacq, T, Baret, P V and Stilmant, D (2012) Sustainability indicators for livestock farming: a review, *Agronomy for Sustainable Development*, **33** (2), pp 311–27

Lélé, S M (1991) Sustainable development: a critical review, *World Development*, **19**, pp 607–21

Magee, L, James, P and Scerri, A (2012) Measuring social sustainability: a community-centred approach, *Applied Research in the Quality of Life*, **7** (3), pp 239–61

Maia de Souza, D *et al* (2017) A review of sustainability enhancements in the beef value chain: state-of-the-art and recommendations for future improvements, *Animals (Basel)*, **7** (3), pp 26

Marandure, T *et al* (2016) Indicator-based sustainability assessment of the small-holder beef cattle production system in South Africa, *Agroecology and Sustainable Food Systems*, **41** (1), pp 3–29, doi:10.1080/21683565.2016.1231152

McGuire, J, Sundgren, A and Schneeweis, T (1988) Corporate social responsibility and firm financial performance, *Academy of Management Journal*, **31** (4), pp 854–72

McKenzie, S (2004) [accessed 7 July 2021] Social sustainability: towards some definitions, Hawke Research Institute Working Paper Series PANDORA electronic collection, no 27, Hawke Research Institute, University of South Australia [Online] www.semanticscholar.org/paper/Social-sustainability%3A-towards-some-definitions-Mckenzie/7a7ec41a3d0c0fb4f9099db456b32166b25 275c9 (archived at https://perma.cc/E874-LDJ6)

Morelli, J (2011) Environmental sustainability: a definition for environmental professionals, *Journal of Environmental Sustainability*, **1** (1), Article 2

Muralikrishna, I M and Manickam, V (2017) Life cycle assessment, in *Environmental Management Science and Engineering for Industry*, Ch 5, pp 57–75, BSP Books Pvt Ltd, Elsevier, Amsterdam

Ogino, A *et al* (2016) Environmental impacts of extensive and intensive beef production systems in Thailand evaluated by life cycle assessment, *Journal of Cleaner Production*, **112**, pp 22–31

Oxford Dictionary (2020) Oxford University Press, Oxford

Rivera-Huerta, A *et al* (2019) Social sustainability assessment in livestock production: a social life cycle assessment approach, *Sustainability*, **11** (16), doi:10.3390/su11164419

Rotz, C A *et al* (2015) Cradle-to-farm gate environmental footprints of beef cattle production in Kansas, Oklahoma, and Texas, *Journal of Animal Science*, **93** (5), pp 2509–19

Rotz, C A *et al* (2019) Environmental footprints of beef cattle production in the United States, *Agricultural Systems*, **169**, pp 1–13

Savitz, A and Webber, K (2014) *The Triple Bottom Line: How today's best-run companies are achieving economic, social and environmental success – and how you can too*, 2nd edn, Jossey-Bass/Wiley, Hoboken, NJ

Scholten, M C T *et al* (2013) Livestock farming with care: towards sustainable production of animal-source food, *NJAS – Wageningen Journal of Life Sciences*, **66**, pp 3–5

Tai, S (2018) Food sustainability in the age of complex, global supply chains, *Arkansas Law Review*, **71** (2), pp 465–80

USBF (2019) [accessed 7 July 2021] US Sustainable Beef Framework, USBF [Online] www.beefsustainability.us/the-framework (archived at https://perma.cc/78DN-B3TS)

Wiedemann, S *et al* (2015) Environmental impacts and resource use of Australian beef and lamb exported to the USA determined using life cycle assessment, *Journal of Cleaner Production*, **94**, 67–75

Weidemann, S and Dunn, J (2021) Carbon Accounting Technical Manual, Project number V.SCS.0016, Meat & Livestock Australia, Sydney

Yapp, G *et al* (2001) [accessed 7 July 2021] Environmental Factors Affecting Australia's Livestock Industries: A Report for Meat & Livestock Australia, *Commonwealth Government of Australia* [Online] www.mla.com.au/globalassets/mla-corporate/generic/about-mla/enviro-issues-for-livestock-ind-_brs-repro-2001.pdf (archived at https://perma.cc/22ZK-TBXH)

Zabolotnyy, S and Wasilewski, M (2019) The concept of financial sustainability measurement: a case of food companies from Northern Europe, *Sustainability*, **11**, p 5139

Green practices in construction supply chains? 04

How a construction company manages and coordinates its green SCM practices

DR YIQING ZHAO, LINYI UNIVERSITY, CHINA

DR YING XIE, ANGLIA RUSKIN UNIVERSITY, CHELMSFORD, UK

Introduction

This chapter is presented as an investigative case study undertaken by the authors, evaluating the green supply chain management (SCM) practices of Company A in the Chinese construction industry. Organizations in the Chinese construction supply chain have struggled to improve their economic and environmental performance, although they have made some progress in the adoption of green SCM practices, for example:

- Within the Chinese context, the requirements of regulatory bodies, customers and internally driven environmental awareness have been increased and green SCM practices have emerged as systematic approaches for the construction industry in China.
- The adoption rates of green SCM practices shown in the investigation are high, indicating that green SCM is not a new concept in the Chinese construction industry. Companies have begun to change their focus from single-plant improvement to the entire supply chain.
- The introduction of an end-to-end supply chain analysis reflecting a more holistic approach to green SCM-wide practices, including internal environmental management, green procurement, green distribution and reverse logistics.

Therefore, this case study adopts a green practice in supply chain perspective and is based on the organizational knowledge available to us. First, the drivers and challenges of green SCM practices need to be explored.

Understanding the drivers and challenges of green SCM practices

Green SCM is considered a relatively advanced management practice to generate environmental benefits; it is also viewed as a new philosophy of environmental management which incorporates the entire SC (Narasimhan and Carter, 1998).The key elements needed for developing a green SCM approach (Nagel, 2000) include:

- attention to the production process;
- attention to the material content of components and products;
- awareness in the customer–supplier relationship;
- cost-effectiveness;
- concentration on environmentally sound technological innovation;
- the internal direct driver of green SCM; and
- a strategy-driven programme of green SCM.

It is recommended that the product and operational life cycle could be regarded as a more tactical set of organizational factors that necessarily impact both internal and external green SCM in organizations (Sarkis, 2003). The increasing pressure for the sustainability of the environment imposes an expectation on organizations, requiring them to implement a sustainability strategy to reduce or offset the environmental impacts of their services or products (Lewis and Gertsakis, 2001). Pressures generally arise from regulatory bodies, the market and competitors, incurred all over the world. The three types of driver can be further defined as:

- drivers from government agency or regulatory bodies (coercive);
- environmental concerns (normative); and
- pressures from competitors (mimetic).

However, organizations are not exposed to the same extent or to the same types of pressure for implementation of green SCM practices (Zhu and Sarkis, 2006). Large and medium-sized companies seem to encounter greater pressures on environmental protection than small ones, which are generally reactive to the national ecological strategy (Revell, 2007; Zhu *et al*, 2011). Small and medium-sized companies are generally reactive to the national ecological strategy, but large enterprises with stronger environmental commitment are better motivated to be proactive in environmental management (Roy and Therin, 2008). In addition, some industry sectors are more domestic focused whereas other industry sectors are more global in orientation and thus will have different pressures for adopting green SCM practices. For example, the construction sector is mainly domestically oriented, whereas the building material sector is more globally focused and thus will have differing domestic and international motivations and pressures for incorporating green SCM practices. With the international pressures for reducing greenhouse gas emissions, there may be differing and increased pressures on the building material sector which is traditionally a heavy emitter of greenhouse gases.

In China, the issues associated with green SCM have become more critical (Zhu, Sarkis and Geng, 2005). Although the country is developing its economy speedily, China still faces substantial environmental burdens (Rao, 2002). China has become increasingly industrialized and has been used as the point of end-of-life product disposal for developed countries and multinational organizations. Due to the increasing environmental burden on developed countries, end-of-life products are shipped to developing countries such as China where there are no tools or infrastructure available to deal with the products being disposed of (Puckett and Smith, 2002). The initial objective in this research seeks to determine whether companies in the Chinese construction industry are feeling these pressures/drivers for the adoption of green SCM practices.

SCM pressures/drivers of green practices in the Chinese construction industry

Chinese companies have experienced increasing environmental pressures from the government and customers while recognizing both the environmental and economic benefits of greening their SCs (Zhu and Sarkis, 2006; Zhu, Sarkis and Geng, 2005). As such, companies in China are beginning to proactively implement green SCM strategies to reduce negative impacts on the environment. Zhu and Sarkis (2006) support Chinese companies acquiring ISO 14000 certification to meet the expectations of foreign clients. Success in addressing environmental issues can not only provide new ways to add value to the business, but also provide new opportunities for competition (Hansmann and Claudia, 2001). In this research, pressures from regulations and the market are considered important drivers for the adoption of green SCM practices. Apart from pressures, one of the major drivers for implementing green SCM practices is the financial incentive. Christmann and Taylor (2001) claim that sales and exports to foreign customers are the major drivers for the environmental activities of organizations.

The pressures from corporate internal factors can also be considered as one of the drivers of environmental management practices. Approaches like environmental management systems and cleaner production have been implemented as green SCM practices to comply with regulatory requirements (Zhu, Sarkis and Lai, 2007). An environmental management system has been identified as an important source of competitive advantages, including:

- the quality advantage (Narasimhan and Schoenherr, 2012);
- business efficiency, regulatory compliance (Walker, 2008);
- cost reduction and differentiation (Maria, Lopez-Gamero and Molina-Azorin, 2009).

Zhu and Liu (2010) found that Chinese companies learned good environmental practices from leading competitors in developed countries and implemented them proactively in China. Zhu and Geng (2001, 2013) supported the notion that corporate internal factors motivate organizations to imitate the activities of their successful competitors, such as creating their environmental image, addressing environmental policies and missions, and accepting liability for the safe disposal of hazardous materials. In summary, pressures from regulation, the market and corporate internal factors motivate organizations to implement and promote environmental practices (Zhu *et al*, 2010). Institutional theory posits that environmental management activities are motivated by normative, coercive and mimetic pressures that come from regulations, the market and internal factors of organizations (Kilbourne, Beckmann and Thelen, 2002; Aerts, Cormier and Magnan, 2006; Ball and Craig, 2010). Organizations have improved environmental control to cope with the pressures and drivers on green SCM. In particular, green distribution and reverse logistics have important impacts on green SCM (Zhu, Sarkis and Geng, 2005). The operation of green distribution is most closely tied to the customers' requirements and characteristics. European and US companies have considered reverse logistics as an important aspect for green SCM (Zsidisin and Hendrick, 1998). Government involvement in green SC has shifted the emphasis from pollution control to the product life cycle (Lee, 2008). Government involvement ranges from direct financial and technical support to indirect infrastructure development and encouragement, with tax-cut incentives for environmental complexes (Holt *et al*, 2001). Adopting green SCM practices provides informal and formal mechanisms that reduce risk, promote trust and, in turn, increase profitability and innovation (Dodgson, 2000), while Alvaredz, Jimenez and Lorente (2001) argued that green SCM practices had a positive relationship with economic performance. Geffen and Rothenberg (2000) found that the relationship aided the development and adoption of innovative environmental technology. Results in Zhu and Cote (2004) showed that implementation of green SCM led to improvement in environmental performance. Hanna, Newman and Johnson (2000) found a strong relationship between the involvement of environmental management and meeting environmental goals. To help organizations achieve the environmental targets, a system of environmental management was confirmed as an information management tool and innovative environmental policy (Szwilski, 2000).

Green SCM practices in Company A

Company A,[1] established in the late 1990s, is one of the largest producers of construction materials in China. It has more than 3,500 employees, more than 500 product types and an annual turnover of 3 billion RMB. The company is certified by the ISO9001 international quality management system, ISO14000 environmental management, and by the local province.

Green SCM drivers/pressures faced by Company A

Laws, regulations and polices: Traditionally, construction material manufacturers produce heavy pollution in China; therefore, a number of laws and regulations were enacted. They require all construction material manufacturers to meet social and environmental standards, such as air emissions below specified standards, using clean energy and improving environmental performance. Company A is required to meet the following national environmental laws and regulations (to mention only some of them):

- Act of the People's Republic of China on Environmental Protection (1989);

- Act of the People's Republic of China on Environmental Impact Assessment (2003);
- Act of the People's Republic of China on the Prevention and Control of Atmospheric Pollution (2000);
- Act of the People's Republic of China on the Prevention and Control of Water Pollution (2008);
- Act of the People's Republic of China on the Prevention and Control of Pollution From Environmental Noise (1997);
- Act of the People's Republic of China on the Prevention and Control of Environmental Pollution by Solid Waste (2005);
- Cleaner Production Promotion Act of the People's Republic of China (2012);
- Act of the People's Republic of China on Water and Soil Conservation (2010);
- Regulation of the Administration of Construction Project Environmental Protection (1998);
- Notice of the State Council Approved the Issue of Acid Rain Control Zones and Sulphur Dioxide Pollution Control Zones (1998/5);
- Notice of the General Office of State Council, National Development and Reform Commission and Other Departments to Forward Notifications on Accelerating the Implementation of Cleaner Production (2003/100);
- Guiding Catalogue of Industrial Structure Adjustment (2011);
- Decision of the State Council on the Implementation of the Scientific Concept of Development to Strengthen Environmental Protection (2005/39);
- Notice on Regulating Consulting Fees Related to environmental impact issues (2002/125);
- Notice on Strengthening water conservation (2000/1015);
- Construction Project Environmental Impact Assessment Classification Catalogue (2008);
- Advices on the Implementation of Act of Clean Production Promotion of People's Republic of China (2003/60);
- Regulations on the Control over Safety of Dangerous Chemicals.

These environmental laws and regulations have imposed pressures on Company A to implement and improve its green SCM practices. The recent green agendas of the government have also forced Company A to eliminate backward production capacity, expanded from 5,000 t/a to 50,000 t/a, and part of the capacity is established as a reverse logistics system that considers environmental effects in the whole product life cycle and enables the company to actively engage in recycling end-of-life products from its customers. In addition to reducing waste and the impacts on the environment, the reverse logistics system offers a way for Company A to reuse raw materials retrieved from returned products and therefore save on costs.

As a supplier, Company A exports its products to the United States and Europe, which requires the company to meet international environmental regulations, such as F019 Final Rule released by the United States Environmental Protection Agency, and Regulation (EC) No.66/2010 of the European Parliament and of the Council. The environmental requirements from domestic and international regulatory bodies impose immense challenges on Company A, but they also force the company to build competency in the environmental dimension and consequently improve and maintain its environmentally sound image.

Pressures from the market faced by Company A

Company A has experienced motivational pressures and drivers from their domestic and foreign customers. Products exported to foreign markets need to fulfil various environmental requirements, including reduced environmental impacts during the whole product life cycle, reduced negative impacts on consumption of natural resources, and reduced impacts on climate, health and the environment.

To obtain factual and accurate information on the environmental impacts of the products and associated production processes, customers ask to visit the company's plants, observe its operations and evaluate employees' working environment. Furthermore, customers have major requirements for the design and development of products, including product functionalities, quality, reliability, durability and sources of raw materials. Company A invested in an environmentally friendly production line which reduces carbon emissions by 38 per cent[2] and pollution to zero, which led to an improved environmental image and a higher market share. Customers' expectations regarding the company's environmental image have driven Company A to initiate and implement green SCM practices.

Internal factors: corporate social responsibility in Company A

Corporate social responsibility (CSR) has also been integrated into Company A's business model. As part of its CSR strategy, the company is committed to building a sound green image and has taken liability for the responsible disposal of hazardous materials as required for ISO9001-2008 international quality management system certification and ISO14000-2004 environment system certification, which have paved the way for Company A to establish a sound green image. The general managers of Company A emphasized that the company has striven to improve its CSR performance. Company A develops source reduction strategies in the hierarchy of 3R (ie reduce, reuse, recycle) and makes continuous improvement in reducing noise, water, air and solid waste pollution from their premises (Chertow, 1998).

Internal environmental management applied in Company A

Senior managers in Company A put forward green SCM practices as a means of setting up the green image of the company and integrating CSR policy into its business model. Designing and producing environmentally friendly products is one of the key dimensions of green SCM practices for Company A to gain and maintain its competitiveness. Products produced by Company A are evaluated to be reliable and durable, to offer dynamic functions and to have low energy consumption and carbon emissions.

Since 2012, Company A has made the following investments:

- Invested about 8 million RMB to maintain and enhance its green image.
- Purchased equipment from Japan, Italy and Switzerland to eliminate noise, purify emissions and treat water and solid waste responsibly.
- Completed a project for water and solid waste treatment through interdepartmental cooperation.
- A system has been purchased to monitor, evaluate and manage the production process to meet domestic, Japanese, US and EU environmental standards.
- ISO9001 and ISO14001 facilitated Company A to meet the requirements of customers, minimize negative impacts on the environment and comply with regulatory and statutory environmental requirements. Such certifications also help Company A enter the global market and improve the quality of its products to meet international standards.

- Environmental issues are the main concerns for Company A during product design, development and manufacturing. To address these concerns, Company A has implemented cleaner production practices by closely cooperating with research institutes and Chinese universities, focusing on the eco-design of products, waste prevention and source reduction.

A green manufacturing process has also been developed by Company A, in order to achieve production efficiency, reduce environmental and occupational safety expenses, and lower raw material costs. Green manufacturing practices encompass the following:

- **3Rs**: Reduce, reuse and recycle materials such as aluminium, nickel, magnesium, silicon, hydrogen nitrate, sulphuric acid, coal and water.
- **Energy-efficient technology**:
  - Design product for using fewer resources.
  - Improve equipment uptime.
  - Increase product life span leading to higher productivity and efficiency.
  - Reduce energy consumption.
- **Hazardous substance control**:
  - Quality control and recheck before processing.
  - Rinse parts using reused water instead of chemicals.

Green procurement and distribution in Company A

Company A collects environmental information and has set up a database on the environmental situation of the materials and components related to suppliers. Company A believes that green purchase requires the selection of resources that minimize negative environmental impacts and that it is a solution for both economically conservative and environmentally concerned businesses. The supplier is assessed by Company A to ensure they meet various environmental requirements and can supply environmentally friendly materials on a permanent basis. Green purchase practices adopted by Company A include:

- **Green supplier selection**: Company A selects suppliers that meet environmental requirements and control hazardous resources responsibly.
- **ISO 14000**: Company A prioritizes suppliers that acquire ISO 14000 international environmental management certification or other environmental directives.

- **Environmental requirement**: Company A purchases materials or parts that meet environmental quality standards or pass the audit process following environment-related regulations.

Green distribution for Company A consists of green packaging and green logistics, both of which are outsourced to achieve just-in-time (JIT) production and require monitoring for economic and environmental performance. The findings in green distribution practices include:

- **Green packaging**:
  - Promote reuse and recycling of packaging.
  - Encourage and adopt returnable packaging methods.
  - Standardize packaging.
  - Downsize packaging.
- **Green transportation**:
  - Distribute products together rather than in smaller batches.
  - Optimize routing and minimize mileage to be travelled.

Company A's reverse logistics practices include waste collection, disposal and reprocessing. Findings include:

- **Waste collection**: Company A initially inspects, selects and sorts used parts, which are shipped to recycling plants.
- **Waste treatment**: Water waste and solid waste are treated by a final treatment/landfill company using secure solidification and stabilization systems.
- **Recycling plants**: Company A owns a recycling plant that collects used parts from customers or manufacturing plants and recycles metals.

The role of government involvement in Company A's green SCM practices

The government has involvement with Company A's green SCM practices as a facilitator, enabler and instructor. Government involvement facilitates maximizing the performance improvement resulting from the green SCM practices implemented, as evidenced by the reduced toxic releases to the environment and more effective use of renewable resources. The local government helps building materials manufacturers develop and implement a 'Design for Energy Saving' scheme, which aims to reduce energy consumption in the company. Company A has also benefited from technical assistance offered by government, such as workshops for energy conservation and minimizing wastes generated from production. Furthermore, 'end-of-life' is also considered by the government, focusing on eco-design. The government has encouraged and fostered collaborations between research institutions and Company A to investigate ways of maximizing the use of end-of-life products, including the potential for materials retrieval, energy recovery, high recyclability, re-manufacturability and reusability. Through the coordination and cooperation of the government, Company A has developed innovative products that can be reprocessed for raw materials and achieve resource efficiency. The innovative design also eliminates the production of hazardous materials.

The key components of Company A's green SCM practices are listed in Table 4.1.

Table 4.1 Key components of green SCM practices

Key competencies Company A	Descriptions
Internal environmental management	Its activities involve commitment from mid-level and senior-level management, inter-department cooperation, environmental compliance and auditing system, and improvement of manufacturing process.
Green procurement	Its activities involve cooperation with suppliers, environmental requirements and ISO14000 certification.
Green distribution and reverse logistics	Its activities involve environmentally friendly transportation, excess inventory and materials, used material and scrap, and technology utilization.
Government involvement	Its activities involve government coordination, infrastructure, assistance from government and knowledge popularization.

Conclusion

The practices of Chinese green distribution involve green packaging and green transportation that increase space utilization and lower materials usage and the amount of handling required. However, Chinese companies lack cooperation with customers and/or suppliers during the green distribution process. Therefore, companies would benefit from cooperating with customers and/or suppliers during the distribution process to increase energy efficiency and reduce carbon emissions.

The Chinese government's involvement facilitates maximizing the performance improvement resulting from green SCM practices, organizes workshops and offers guidelines and a framework for implementing green SCM practices, and suggest measures to be taken, provides leadership by increasing awareness of environmental protection, offers financial incentives and helps companies to develop and implement energy-saving schemes that aim to reduce energy consumption in the company. Chinese companies benefited from the technical assistance offered by government, such as workshops for energy conservation and minimizing wastes generated from production. The government encourages and fosters collaborations between research institutions and companies to maximize the use of end-of-life products, including the potential for materials retrieval, energy recovery, high recyclability, remanufacturability and reusability.

We base our conclusions on an end-to-end operational analysis supporting the holistic development of green SCM practices and strategy:

- The Chinese government has issued an array of regulations and standards; however, it lacks enforceable environmental laws and regulations to provide guidelines and directives for the industry. Therefore, the Chinese government should introduce such laws and regulations and also enhance public awareness of carbon emissions.
- Company A needs to check second-tier suppliers' environmental assessments, which will allow clear opportunities to introduce and develop emerging green practices for Company A.
- The current distribution models employed by Company A entail lack of cooperation with customers and/or suppliers for green packaging and transportation and with major multiple retailers and their logistics subcontractors, which needs to be developed and restructured.

- Further, the research considered an 'end to end' environmental analysis which evaluates opportunities for SC-wide practices to be developed.

In conclusion, although Company A has introduced and applies many green practices comparable with international partners, the zeal to approach the same goal supply chain wide to include partners of Company A needs further development and perhaps more subsidies.

The major findings of this study and the consequent discussions of Chinese green SCM can be summarized as follows:

- Green SCM pressures/drivers have driven green SCM practice adoption in Chinese enterprises to gain 'benefits' ranging from straightforward cost reduction to facilitating the development of cooperative relationships with suppliers, and even encouraging a life-cycle, holistic approach in managerial decision making.
- Green SCM practice has a positive influence on reducing energy consumption, which is one of the indicators for improved environmental performance.
- Adoption and implementation of green SCM practices in the Chinese construction industry may take longer, as the environmental and economic benefits are not perceived to be significant.
- Chinese companies are facing several challenges to implement green SCM practices that will also affect the construction industry.

Learning outcomes

- Regulations and internal factors are considered as important green SCM drivers and pressures. Medium and large Chinese companies face higher regulatory pressures than small firms.
- Case studies confirm that green SCM is not a new concept in the Chinese construction industry. Companies have begun to change their focus from improvement in one supply chain entity to the entire supply chain.
- Chinese construction companies seem to be more mature in their adoption of green procurement practices than companies in the building material sector.

Questions

1 Green SCM practices bring challenges as well as opportunities to introduce and develop green practices. Discuss Company A's green SCM practices in line with this statement.

2 As a result of this case study, list the factors which you would now include in developing green SCM practices to support a construction supply chain.

3 Referring to the discussion in the chapter on the importance of governance and international collaboration, discuss the implications for Company A.

Endnotes

1 The names and numbers have been altered to safeguard the anonymity of the company.

2 Numbers have been altered to protect the anonymity of the case company.

References

Aerts, W, Cormier, D and Magnan, M (2006) Intra-industry imitation in corporate environmental reporting: an international perspective, *Journal of Accounting and Public Policy*, **25** (3) pp 299–331

Alvaredz, G M J, Jimenez, J B and Lorente, J C (2001) An analysis of environmental management, organizational context and performance of Spanish hotels, *Omega*, **29** (6), pp 457–71

Ball, A and Craig, R (2010) Using neo-institutionalism to advance social and environmental accounting, *Critical Perspectives on Accounting*, **21** (4), pp 283–93

Chertow, M R (1998) Waste, industrial ecology, and sustainability, *Social Research*, **65** (1), pp 31–53

Christmann, P and Taylor, G (2001) Globalization and the environment: determinants of firm self-regulation in China, *Journal of International Business Studies*, **32** (3), pp 439–58

Dodgson, M (2000) *Management of Technology*, Routledge, Abingdon

Geffen, C and Rothenberg, S (2000) Sustainable development across firm boundaries: the critical role of suppliers in environmental innovation, *International Journal of Operations and Production Management*, **20** (2) pp 166–86

Hanna, M D, Newman, W R and Johnson, P (2000) Linking operational and environmental improvement through employee involvement, *International Journal of Operations and Production Management*, **20** (2) pp 148–65

Hansmann, K W and Claudia, K (2001) Environmental management policies, in *Green Manufacturing and Operations: From design to delivery and back*, ed J Sarkis, pp 192–204, Greenleaf Publishing, Sheffield

Holt, D, Anthony, S and Viney, H (2001) Supporting environmental improvements in SMEs in the UK, *Greener Management International*, **35**, pp 29–49

Kilbourne, W E, Beckmann, S C and Thelen, E (2002) The role of the dominant social paradigm in environmental attitudes: a multinational examination, *Journal of Business Research*, **55** (3), pp 193–204

Lee, S (2008) Drivers for the participation of small and medium-sized suppliers in green supply chain initiatives, *Supply Chain Management*, **13** (3), pp 185–98

Lewis, H and Gertsakis, J (2001) *Design Environment: A global guide to designing greener goods*, Greenleaf Publishing, Sheffield

Maria, D, Lopez-Gamero, J F and Molina-Azorin, E C (2009) The relationship between environmental variables and firm performance: competitive advantage and firm resources as mediator variables, *Journal of Environmental Management*, **90**, pp 3110–21

Nagel, M H (2000) Environmental supply-chain management versus green procurement in the scope of a business and leadership perspective, *IEEE Proceedings of the 2000 IEEE International Symposium*, **8/10**, pp 219–24

Narasimhan, R and Schoenherr, T (2012) The effects of integrated supply chain management practices and environmental management practices on relative competitive quality advantage, *International Journal of Production Research*, **50** (4), pp 1185–201

Narasimhan, R and Carter, J R (1998) *Environmental Supply Chain Management*, Research monograph, Centre for Advanced Purchasing Studies, Tempe, AZ

Puckett, J and Smith, T (2002) Exporting harm: the high-tech trashing of Asia, The Basel Action Network, Seattle: Silicon Valley Toxics Coalition

Rao, P (2002) Greening the supply chain: a new initiative in South East Asia, *International Journal of Operations and Production Management*, **21** (6), pp 632–55

Revell, A (2007) The ecological modernisation of SME in the UK's construction industry, *Geoforum*, **38**, pp 114–26

Roy, M J and Therin, F (2008) Knowledge acquisition and environmental commitment in SMEs, *Corporate Social Responsibility and Environmental Management*, **15**, pp 249–59

Sarkis, J (2003) A strategic decision making framework for green supply chain management, *Journal of Cleaner Production*, **11** (4) pp 397–409

Szwilski, T B (2000) Using environmental management systems to systematically improve operational performance and environmental protection, *International Journal of Surface Mining, Reclamation and Environment*, **14** (3), pp 183–91

Walker, D (2008) Sustainability: environmental management, transparency and competitive advantage, *Journal of Retail and Leisure Property*, **7**, pp 119–30

Zhu, Q and Cote, R P (2004) Integrating green supply chain management into an embryonic eco-industrial development: a case study of the Guitang Group, *Journal of Cleaner Production*, **12**, pp 1025–35

Zhu, Q and Geng, Y (2001) Integrating environmental issues into supplier selection and management: a study of large and medium-sized state-owned enterprises in China, *Greener Management International*, **35**, pp 27–40

Zhu, Q and Geng, Y (2013) Drivers and barriers of extended supply chain practices for energy saving and emission reduction among Chinese manufacturers, *Journal of Cleaner Production*, **40**, pp 6–12

Zhu, Q and Liu, Q (2010) Eco-design planning in a Chinese telecommunication network company: benchmarking its parent company, *Benchmarking*, **17** (3), pp 363–77

Zhu, Q and Sarkis, J (2006) An inter-sectorial comparison of green supply chain management in China: drivers and practices, *Journal of Cleaner Production*, **14**, pp 472–86

Zhu, Q, Sarkis, J and Geng, Y (2005) Green supply chain management in China: pressures, practices and performance, *International Journal of Operations and Product Management*, **25** (5), pp 449–68

Zhu, Q H, Sarkis, J and Lai, K H (2007) Green supply chain management: pressures, practices and performance within the Chinese automobile industry, *Journal of Cleaner Production*, **15**, pp 1041–52

Zhu, Q *et al* (2010) Green supply chain management in leading manufactures: case studies in Japanese large companies, *Management Research Review*, **33** (4), pp 380–92

Zhu, Q *et al* (2011) Evaluating green supply chain management among Chinese manufacturers from the ecological modernization perspective, *Transportation Research Part E: Logistics and Transportation Review*, **47**, 808–21

Zsidisin, G A and Hendrick, T E (1998) Purchasing's involvement in environmental issues: a multi-country perspective, *Industrial Management and Data Systems*, **7**, pp 313–20

05 Mechanized zones in food regional distribution centres

A sustainability case study

DR TONY CRAGG, ECOLE SUPÉRIEURE DE LOGISTIQUE INDUSTRIELLE, REDON, FRANCE

DR TOM MCNAMARA, RENNES SCHOOL OF BUSINESS, FRANCE

Introduction

This case study involves the project of a leading supermarket brand to install mechanized zones to speed up the sorting and pallet preparation in both fresh and ambient product regional distribution centres (RDCs) across France. For reasons of confidentiality, the brand name of the supermarket will not be used in this case study but will be referred to as 'Company Flow'. RDCs are the interface between suppliers/producers and retail outlets and therefore represent an important node in the supply chain. Their role is to receive, check, store, pick and then finally despatch approximately 10,000 stock keeping units (SKUs) or product references to around 50 supermarkets in the same region. They act as consolidation centres that facilitate the distribution of goods to supermarkets and customers.

In France, the warehousing sector employs an estimated 700,000 people in what have been described as 'package factories' (Gaborieau, 2016). In recent years, RDCs have been growing in number and size, facilities have been reorganized, new sites opened and projects for automated systems are either under way or already installed. As evidence, one study in the United States found that 7 in 10 decision makers planned to accelerate warehouse technology investment by 2020 (Zebra, 2016).

Clearly, digitalization (Attaran, 2020) and the enhanced speed of information flows have placed the spotlight on the relative slowness of physical flows connected with the order fulfilment process. Mechanization zones can be seen as one strategic response to this imbalance in the pace of physical and information flows. In RDCs, time becomes the 'overarching measure of performance' and a vital source of competitive advantage (Stalk, 1988). The means to reduce logistic process time needs to be found and put in place, while respecting time constraints, such as delivery windows. The theory of swift, even flow (Schmenner and Swink, 1998) underpins this thinking and states that the productivity of any process rises as the speed of materials flowing through the system increases.

Along with Amazon and other online retailers, one of the main 'winners' of the Covid pandemic from a business perspective has been the supermarket brands. In France, at the beginning of February 2021, Didier Duhaupand, president of one of the leading supermarkets, Intermarché, described it as 'an exceptional year, marked by a pathbreaking acceleration' (Le Monde, 2021). Research by one consultancy, Kantar Worldpanel, showed that in 2020, sales in the sector had increased by 7.7 per cent, a rise that has never been seen before (Prudhomme, 2021). Traditionally, stable sales volumes and intense competition between the major players have marked the supermarket sector. The pandemic and sales growth have placed pressure on logistics to perform, as supermarkets remain open to meet the essential needs of the population under lockdowns and curfews. Even before the pandemic, supermarket brands realized that warehouse productivity or speeding goods through the various nodes of the supply chain could lead to a competitive advantage.

Logistics strategy

It is important to note that supermarket brands do not adopt the same logistics strategy. Since 2014, Intermarché, for example, has been engaged in a programme to reduce the number of RDCs from 42 to 22 with major investments in process automation and anticipated job losses (LSA, 2019). The company's strategy is to group together the maximum number of logistic operations in a smaller number of sites of around 70,000 sq metres, simultaneously handling frozen, fresh and dry goods. The creation of these mixed sites aims to 'massify' the flow of goods and thereby achieve economies of scale. These large sites are also designed to respond to the demands that the different possible distribution channels place on existing logistic networks (Wollenburg *et al*, 2018), in particular since the pandemic has increased the trend towards online grocery sales. For example, in 2020 Intermarché benefited from a growth in online sales of 80 per cent between 18 May and 14 June, compared with the previous year (Fournier, 2020).

Not all brands develop mixed sites. ULOG, the Logistics branch of the French retailer Super U, for example, keeps frozen, fresh and dry goods not only in separate warehouses, but also in distinct geographical locations. Other firms, such as Carrefour, often outsource logistics activities such as the handling of fresh and frozen goods to specialist subcontractors. Equally, transport between RDCs and stores is subcontracted or not, depending on company policy.

The national brands continue to engage in a price war in a highly competitive market with no wholly dominant player. The market leader is Leclerc with 23.3 per cent of market share, with several other brands close behind (Fournier, 2020). Increasingly, supermarkets in France are putting in place supply chain strategies, focusing on the upstream, to improve storage, order preparation and transport performance. This approach confirms academic research, which shows that logistics can provide a way for a firm to achieve the necessary level of performance on the competitive dimensions of cost, quality and time (Stock *et al*, 1999). A firm can obtain a competitive advantage through efficient logistics.

Mechanized zones

For the efficient functioning of supermarket RDCs, handling approximately 70,000 packages daily, the key activity is order preparation, which accounts for up to 55 per cent of operating costs (De Koster *et al*, 2007). Optimizing and accelerating the process of order retrieval, pallet preparation and delivery to the appropriate loading bay has become a major management objective. In this context of continuous process improvement, a series of technologies exists to increase the efficiency of order-picking performance (Richards, 2017). Some of them involve speeding up the work of each picker, using headsets or terminals, while others involve significant investments in mechanized and automated systems, with the intervention of workers being limited to a stationary role at the beginning or end of the area.

This case study concerns the latter: the major long-term project of a leading supermarket brand to install mechanized zones to speed up the sorting and pallet preparation in both fresh and ambient product RDCs across France. The case study is based on numerous visits to warehouse sites belonging to Company Flow and other firms, personal observations and interviews with managers in connection with professional responsibilities as teachers and researchers.

The mechanization and automation of a warehouse affect the whole logistics ecosystem and the success of any project has to be gauged in the long term rather than seen as a short-term panacea. The initial challenge is to receive authorization from shareholders for the investment of several tens or hundreds of millions of euros. Rigorous methods of project management are required to convince and reassure financiers, lawyers and insurers and to fight against internal resistance to a major organizational change. Once the mechanized zone is in place, it comprises huge logistic machineries, with metallic moving parts, sorters, robotic arms, and conveyor belts, often with humans excluded from the zone for their own safety (Strategies Logistique, 2019). For Company Flow there are two main reasons for the programme to install mechanized zones in both fresh and dry product RDCs:

- **The human factor:** One of the main drivers behind automation is recruitment difficulties in the sector. Physically demanding labour leads to a lack of attractiveness for warehouse work. In June 2019, the quarterly barometer report 'Data Emploi et Territoires' (The Addeco Group, 2019) revealed that companies were looking to recruit 430,000 workers in the transport and logistics sector, in particular warehousemen and order pickers. Company Flow also anticipated possible stricter regulatory standards for the maximum weight of goods carried per picker per day. Therefore, at the outset the plan was to mechanize the handling of the heaviest packages with the highest levels of demand.
- **Productivity improvement:** Productivity gains took much longer to achieve than originally planned and return on investment (ROI) even longer. It took six years to reach the initial objectives for the total number of packages handled by the mechanized zone per year. Today, in fresh

> product RDCs a zone handles approximately 50% of a site's references. The experience of Company Flow in mechanization of logistics processes confirms Christensen's (2013) thesis that improving a product takes time and many iterations. As leaders on the market, Company Flow has been subject to the innovator's dilemma, and other firms, later adopters, have been able to learn from their experience and reduce the transition period required for the new technology.

In the mechanized zone for fresh products, installed at Company Flow, the operators are placed at the entrance and exit of the machine. At the entrance, they inject the supplier pallets and place the packages one by one on the belts. The barcode reader identifies each package by checking the necessary information, such as reference, expiry date, weight, and then assigns these packages to the stores in line with the orders. At the exit of the sorting belt, ramps are used to evacuate the packages; facing these ramps are floor spaces with pallets. Each location corresponds to a store, so the packages destined for exit from this location are the packages ordered by the store linked to this location. The operators posted at these ramps are responsible for stacking the pallets by assembling the packages as they are evacuated. Once fully stacked, the pallets are then taken to the loading bays to await outbound transport.

One important impact of mechanization is on the standard and quality of supplier packaging. Each different supplier package has to be tested on the conveyor belt to check that it will not be damaged by the movement along it, as part of the gradual load build-up. If the packaging is substandard, procurement managers request suppliers to use more and stronger packaging, so that packages can survive the knocks and bumps in the mechanized zone. Since increased packaging requires both more cardboard as a raw material and generates more end waste, there is a risk that mechanization runs counter to environmental sustainability criteria.

The transition period

There are several reasons for the length of time it took for Company Flow to begin to make gains from mechanization. The first and perhaps most important is that employees resisted the change. Workplace committees refused to accept mechanized zones for fear of job losses and changes to working conditions, resulting in lengthy negotiations and a significant involvement of the human resources department. Second, a long period of adaptation was required to discover how to use the machine and combine it with traditional manual order picking with a view to improved warehouse performance.

For Company Flow, bringing online a new mechanized zone involves two key stages, which impact productivity:

1. A 'downtime' for the installation period of between six months and a year, when the subcontractor responsible for the design and construction of the zone is on site. This installation period requires the non-use of several thousand square metres of physical space in the warehouse.
2. There is a 'trial period' when the different products that can be loaded into the zone are tested and gradually increased. This trial period means the use of that space at sub-optimal efficiency. Hence, there is a requirement for existing capacity (traditional human order preparation methods) to compensate for this loss and speed up. The longer the mechanized zone is not operational, the greater the risk that orders from supermarkets will not be fulfilled.

The role of humans

Traditional human order picking serves the mechanized zone and not vice versa, because the former is more flexible than the latter. If difficulties arise in the mechanized zone, such as a maintenance problem, then traditional picking must pick up the slack. Furthermore, the need to synchronize (Hirsch-Kreinsen, 2016) flows, for example, from the two zones to arrive at loading bays is recurrent. Loading of outbound trucks at RDCs takes place at specific time windows or slots, and some of the pallets to be loaded into each truck will come from the mechanized zone and others from traditional human picking. Therefore, a need exists to coordinate these flows. Minimizing the risk of desynchronization becomes essential and part of the process of learning to work with the machine. Another example in fresh RDCs of the impact of the mechanized zone on processes concerns the rapid pace of packages along the conveyor belt. This means that they pass the barcode reader much faster than in the case of a hand-held reader. The barcodes on the product, previously acceptable, now have to be perfect, requiring work with upstream suppliers to ensure compliance and illustrating the point that speeding up one node in a supply chain has implications for other nodes.

Muilerman *et al* (2005, p. 10), in a study of firms in the food sector, found that it was certainty rather than process acceleration that was the priority for firms: 'The main focus in time-based logistics strategies is on reducing uncertainties, rather than on accelerating logistics processes in absolute terms, as was shown by the dominance of the factor "on-time reliability" over the attribute "transit time".' In modern food RDCs, however, the challenge is that in order to achieve 'on-time reliability', firms need to build resilience (Ali *et al*, 2017) and remain agile (Christopher. 2000) with sufficient human and machine capacity in place. If it isn't, then existing resources need to be accelerated to their maximum potential. Given that the capacity of a mechanized zone is limited, the flexible human factor needs to adapt, either by recruiting extra temporary staff or by speeding up existing staff or both.

Traditional order preparation

In fresh product RDCs, the traditional mode is a floor-based zone-picking system, where suppliers' pallets, loaded with packages, are laid out across a large surface and order pickers on electric vehicles complete each supermarket's orders by circulating between these pallets and picking the goods. Here, the objective, therefore, is to empty the picking space within a few hours. To speed up workers, one firm has put in place software not only to monitor each picker's performance but also to predict how that performance will evolve over the shift. Such predictions allow management to inform poor-performing workers of their pick rate and for the workload to be redistributed, if necessary. Indicators are available for past, present and future performance against time.

The principal disadvantage of the floor-based picking system is the risk of accidents, as pickers rush to the next picking location, cross paths with others on electric vehicles and lift packages from a low position. As a result, these workers face an elevated risk of back and other musculoskeletal injuries – one of the factors leading senior management to invest in mechanization in the first place. However, an advantage of the traditional picking method is that communication between workers and physical movement are possible. In the mechanized zones, operatives remain stationary at their individual workstations either unloading cartons onto the conveyor belt from a raised pallet or, at the other end of the zone, loading them onto a pallet. Communication between workers separated by several metres is more difficult and movement is mainly limited to the upper body. However, another advantage of the mechanized zone is improving quality indicators by minimizing preparation error and breakages.

The Covid pandemic

In fresh food RDCs, goods are picked when orders from supermarkets are received, and supplies are procured in line with forecasts based on the previous year's sales at particular times – so June's sales of beer will determine procurement levels and varieties for the following June. The pandemic completely disrupted forecasts for orders and for staffing requirements, rendering agility essential. For example, at the onset of the first lockdown in March 2020, demand for staple dry foods, such as pasta, suddenly rose unexpectedly, and unrelated to forecast demand levels. In the week that started on 9 March, pasta sales in supermarkets tripled compared to normal. The following week, the increase was again exceptionally high, before suddenly normalizing in mid-March (Leclerc, 2020). We have seen that the pandemic led to increased sales volumes for supermarkets. Since supply chain management is about finding a balance between resources and demand, to cope with sudden increases, extra capacity was required.

Logistics managers plan for the future and then work backwards (retro planning), so that a delivery window at a supermarket will determine transport, loading, picking and unloading times – a process of thinking downstream to plan upstream or laying out the future to control the present. Time constraints are so carefully choreographed that a minor disruption can have impacts throughout the chain. This led Rossiter (2014) to describe the ambitions of logistics as 'operational fantasies', because the unpredicted and unpredictable, such as the pandemic, keep breaking in.

Evaluating the sustainability of a mechanized zone

Academic literature exists on evaluating sustainability in supply chains (Cucchiella *et al*, 2012) and specifically in warehouses (Torabizadeh *et al*, 2020) in terms of the three triple bottom line criteria – economic, social and environmental. In the economic dimension, total cost, net revenue, return on investment and productivity gains are taken as indicators (Seuring and Müller, 2008; Seuring, 2013). For warehouses, utilization of storage capacity, order fulfilment and picking performance will need to be taken into consideration.

In the environmental dimension, researchers have focused on life-cycle assessments (LCAs), energy demand and CO_2-emissions, natural resources, such as water or energy, as well as waste generation. In warehousing, indicators would include the ratio of recyclable material used to total material used, systems of energy generation, the reduction of energy consumption, attempts to mitigate the environmental impact of products and services, and the percentage of products sold with recycled packaging materials. In the case of major new warehousing projects, consideration would need to be given to local environmental impacts, including noise, light pollution and traffic levels.

In a study of the literature on the social dimension, Yawar and Seuring (2015) developed seven constructs: the working conditions of the employees, child labour, human rights, health and safety, the development of minority groups, the inclusion of disabled/marginalized people and finally gender equality. In warehousing, indicators might include an analysis of employees by age, gender and ethnicity, staff turnover and opportunities for job development, the use of temporary as opposed to permanent staff, travel distances for workers to and from the site, a breakdown of the type and rate of accidents and injuries, occupational diseases and the number and type of complaints registered. In order to evaluate the sustainability of Company Flow's mechanized zone project in the social dimension, these indicators (and others) would need to be applied. For example, researchers could compare workers' physical health problems under the traditional picking system with those experienced by workers in the mechanized zones, to see if there is an improvement and whether different types of problem arise or not.

Conclusion

In food warehousing, the shorter the product sell-by date, the greater the urgency to reduce the warehouse transit time. In the case of dairy products, for example, the aim is to receive, sort and then despatch within a matter of hours. The internal organization of the warehouse needs to be such that the time between the unloading of the supplier's truck and the loading of the outgoing truck to the supermarket is as short as possible. The ambition is to maximize the time a product is available to customers before the sell-by date by minimizing the logistic transit time. The reduction in the transit time through mechanization can be seen as a continuation of the logic of industrialization, whose greatest effect, according to Beniger (1986), has been to speed up a society's material processing system. So, warehouses for perishable foods are no longer places for storing and holding goods, but for moving goods through at speed.

In the food retailing sector, leading brands compete for market share and imitate (Højer *et al*, 2018) rivals' logistic processes in bids to increase productivity, while faced with recruitment difficulties. The mechanization process shows that there is a long process to reassure and prepare workers for the new technological solutions (Klumpp and Zijm, 2019), progressively increase the references that the zone can handle and ensure maximum capacity utilization by using human resources flexibly.

For RDCs, the pandemic has served to enhance the need for two simultaneous strategies – an offensive strategy of agility and, secondly, a defensive strategy of risk minimization. With agility, firms seek to remain sufficiently flexible by having the capacity in place to respond to rapid evolutions in supply and demand. Given the unreliability of forecasts based on last year's data, agility becomes more important. With risk minimization, firms seek to build secure and resilient supply chains that can withstand the impacts on performance of the full range of risk events (Manuj and Mentzer, 2008), such as mechanical breakdowns, failure of IT systems, security breaches, labour and recruitment difficulties and panic buying. In these circumstances, warehouse managers must ensure that they balance flexibility and extra capacity with the need to reduce risk exposure in volatile times.

Learning outcomes

- This case has highlighted the importance of RDCs in terms of providing reliable distribution networks and high levels of customer service.
- The case provides examples of various logistics strategies that firms can use in order to gain a competitive advantage.
- The case provides a detailed explanation, as well as an informed critical analysis, of the steps needed to introduce a mechanized and automated warehouse system into a firm's supply chain.
- The case highlights the social and environmental concerns associated with the introduction of a mechanized and automated warehouse system.

Questions

1 What are the main challenges for a warehouse in setting up a mechanized zone?

2 To evaluate the sustainability of a mechanized zone, what criteria given in the case study do you think are the most important? Please justify your selection and add any further criteria.

3 Through internet research, find examples of other warehouse mechanization projects and learn about whether they are sustainable or not.

References

Ali, I, Nagalingam, S and Gurd, B (2017) Building resilience in SMEs of perishable product supply chains: enablers, barriers and risks. *Production Planning & Control*, **28** (15), pp 1236–50

Attaran, M (2020) Digital technology enablers and their implications for supply chain management, *Supply Chain Forum*, **21** (3), pp 158–72

Beniger, J (1986) *The Control Revolution: Technological and economic origins of the information society*, Harvard University Press, Boston, MA

Christensen, C M (2013) *The Innovator's Dilemma: When new technologies cause great firms to fail*, Harvard Business Review Press, Boston, MA

Christopher, M (2000) The agile supply chain: competing in volatile markets, *Industrial Marketing Management*, **29** (1), pp 37–44

Cucchiella, F *et al* (2012) Evaluating ecological sustainable performance measures for supply chain management, *Supply Chain Management*, **17**, pp 78–92

De Koster, R, Le-Duc, T and Roodbergen, K J (2007) Design and control of warehouse order picking: a literature review, *European Journal of Operational Research*, **182** (2), pp 481–501

Fournier, L (2020) [accessed 7 July 2021] Leclerc et Intermarché grands gagnants de la période post-confinement, *Capital*, 1 July [Online] www.capital.fr/entreprises-marches/leclerc-et-intermarche-grands-gagnants-de-la-periode-post-confinement-1374169 (archived at https://perma.cc/W5SB-NUQP)

Gaborieau, D (2016) [accessed 7 July 2021] *Des usines à colis: trajectoire ouvrière des entrepôts de la grande distribution* (Doctoral dissertation, Paris 1), Theses [Online] www.theses.fr/s91353 (archived at https://perma.cc/BV77-YN36)

Hirsch-Kreinsen, H (2016) Digitization of industrial work: development paths and prospects, *Journal for Labour Market Research*, **49** (1), pp 1–14

Højer, L *et al* (2018) Escalations: theorizing sudden accelerating change, *Anthropological Theory*, **18** (1), pp 36–58

Klumpp, M and Zijm, H (2019) Logistics innovation and social sustainability: how to prevent an artificial divide in human–computer interaction, *Journal of Business Logistics*, **40** (3), pp 265–78

Le Monde (2021) Les grands gagnants de « l'économie du confinement», *Le Monde*, 6 February

Leclerc, M (2020) [accessed 7 July 2021] Une croissance extraordinaire mais en trompe-l'oeil pour les féculents, *LSA*, 27 May [Online] www.lsa-conso.fr/une-croissance-extraordinaire-mais-en-trompe-l-oeil-pour-les-feculents,349909 (archived at https://perma.cc/5M2Y-8G7R)

LSA (2019) [accessed 9 July 2021] L'amont au service des points de vente, LSA, 26 June [Online] www.lsa-conso.fr/l-amont-au-service-des-points-de-vente,322826 (archived at https://perma.cc/PM85-ZJE7)

Manuj, I and Mentzer, J T (2008) Global supply chain risk management strategies, *International Journal of Physical Distribution & Logistics Management,* **38** (3), pp 192–223

Muilerman, G J, Van Der Hoorn, T and Van Der Heijden, R (2005) Determining the impacts of time-based logistics strategies in the Dutch food industry, *International Journal of Logistics: Research and Applications*, **8** (3), pp 237–47

Prudhomme, C (2021) [accessed 7 July 2021] In 2020, the French had fun … in supermarkets, *Archyde*, 28 January [Online] www.archyde.com/in-2020-the-french-had-fun-in-supermarkets/ (archived at https://perma.cc/5FTV-ZDNJ)

Richards, G (2017) *Warehouse Management: A complete guide to improving efficiency and minimizing costs in the modern warehouse*, Kogan Page, London

Rossiter, N (2014) Logistical worlds, *Cultural Studies Review*, **20** (1), pp 53–76

Schmenner, R W and Swink, M L (1998) On theory in operations management, *Journal of Operations Management*, **17** (1), pp 97–113

Seuring, S (2013) A review of modeling approaches for sustainable supply chain management, *Decision Support Systems*, **54** (4), pp 1513–20

Seuring, S and Müller, M (2008) From a literature review to a conceptual framework for sustainable supply chain management, *Journal of Cleaner Production*, **16** (15), pp 1699–710

Stalk, G (1988) Time – the next source of competitive advantage, *Harvard Business Review*, July–August, pp 41–51

Stock, G N, Greis, N P and Kasarda, J D (1999) Logistics, strategy and structure: a conceptual framework, *International Journal of Operations & Production Management*, **29** (4), pp 224–39

Strategies Logistique (2019 [accessed 7 July 2021] Mécanisation et automatisation de l'entrepôt, un projet au long cours, no 176, Strategies Logistique [Online] www.strategieslogistique.com (archived at https://perma.cc/YPN4-5772)

The Adecco Group (2019) [accessed 7 July 2021] Plus de 3,5 millions de recrutements prévus en France en 2019, The Adecco Group [Online] www.groupe-adecco.fr/wp-content/uploads/2019/06/03062019_CP-Barome%CC%80tre-Emploi-The-Adecco-Group_National_VDEF.pdf (archived at https://perma.cc/V9U5-RX3S)

Torabizadeh, M *et al* (2020) Identifying sustainable warehouse management system indicators and proposing new weighting method, *Journal of Cleaner Production*, **248**, pp 119–90

Wollenburg, J *et al* (2018) From bricks-and-mortar to bricks-and-clicks, *International Journal of Physical Distribution & Logistics Management*, **48** (4), pp 415–38

Yawar, S A and Seuring, S (2015) Management of social issues in supply chains: a literature review exploring social issues, actions and performance outcomes, *Journal of Business Ethics*, **141** (3), pp 621–43

Zebra (2016) [accessed 7 July 2021] Zebra Technologies Study Finds 7 in 10 Decision Makers to Accelerate Warehouse Technology Investment by 2020, 26 April, Zebra [Online] www.zebra.com/us/en/about-zebra/newsroom/press-releases/2016/study-finds-increased-warehouse-tech-investment-by-2020.html (archived at https://perma.cc/2P6D-TUM4)

Elevating business processes in sustainable supply chain management

06

The case of a chocolate supply chain network

DR KATE MCLOUGHLIN, MANAGEMENT, MANCHESTER METROPOLITAN UNIVERSITY, MANCHESTER, UK

DR DAVID LASCELLES, MANCHESTER METROPOLITAN UNIVERSITY, MANCHESTER, UK

PROFESSOR SAI S NUDURUPATI, INSTITUTE OF MANAGEMENT, GANDHI INSTITUTE OF TECHNOLOGY AND MANAGEMENT, VISAKHAPATNAM, INDIA

Introduction

This chapter develops the case of a chocolate supply chain network as multiple stakeholders therein seek to multilaterally align and coordinate their activities to achieve the common goal of sustainability. This case aims to describe the inter-organizational business processes that integrate economic, environmental and social dimensions. Operational and logistical processes are omitted as this research model focuses on business processes.

Sustainable supply chain management

Sustainable supply chain management refers to establishing a coordinated supply chain which integrates environmental, social and economic aspects aligning with its supply-chain-wide business systems:

> in order to effectively and successfully manage the flow of materials, information, and capital associated with the supply, the production and the distribution of products and services in order to fulfil the requirements of interested subjects and the improvement in the profitability, the competitiveness, and the vulnerability of the organization in short and long-term prospect. (Ahi and Searcy, 2013)

Sustainability tenets dictate changes to the traditional elements of supply chain management (SCM) and its inter-organizational processes. This is due to the fact that sustainability fundamentally encompasses a broader paradigm, namely, that of sustaining life, beyond the economic remit of business. It is important to understand how the tenets of sustainability are fundamentally altering the SCM paradigm so that a new model of sustainable supply chain management (SSCM) is emerging. With the importance of the sustainability agenda in SCM, the conceptual understanding of SSCM is being extended to an emergent set of principles on how to manage supply chain sustainably. Some of the issues which have been highlighted within this context are:

- accounting for and reconciling sustainability dimensions (Seuring and Müller, 2008; Morali and Searcy, 2013; Carter and Rogers, 2008);
- taking a fully integrated, holistic approach to vertical (Pagell and Wu, 2009) and horizontal alignment of supply chains (Carter and Rogers, 2008; Seuring and Müller, 2008);
- considering multiple stakeholders in supply-chain decision making (Seuring and Müller, 2008; Vachon and Klassen, 2008; Pagell and Wu, 2009);
- greater collaboration with supply chain partners resulting in a change of mindset from competitive to collaborative advantages (Vachon and Klassen, 2008; Gold *et al*, 2010; Gunasekaran *et al*, 2015);

- extending the boundaries of responsibility and the necessity for collaborative activities across supply chain networks (Vachon and Klassen, 2008; Vurro *et al*, 2009; Miemczyk *et al*, 2012).

These changes in business practices are essential because the scale of issues requires an understanding of common goals and collective action, hence changing the orientation and strategic management of the supply chain. As such, managing supply-chain-wide relationships through a systemic, holistic understanding of network nodes and how they relate to each other is necessary (Shook *et al*, 2009). As part of this discourse, academics are developing various theoretical rationale to explain SSCM concepts, processes and practices (Burgess *et al*, 2006; Shook *et al*, 2009). Yet several issues arise. SCM strategies are being reappraised to integrate sustainability due to the need for a holistic, systemic approach (Bocken *et al*, 2014). This requires a shift in mindset from shareholder (Friedman, 1970) to stakeholder value (Freeman, 2010). This is due to increased interdependencies beyond the economic rationale of contract that results in varying socio-economic interrelationships (McLoughlin and Meehan, 2021). This broadening of boundaries of responsibility extends the necessity to develop partnerships with multiple stakeholders, many of whom have an organizational mandate beyond the economic rationale, such as civil organizations. Subsequently, an emerging tenet of business sustainability is the shifting focus from a linear to a system view of the network of relationships and the relationship-based processes and practices that manage these (Evans *et al*, 2017). As such, there is a change in focus on the sets of activities required to manage relationships in a different way that facilitates the integration of sustainability. Ahi and Searcy (2013) recommend that supply chains are managed sustainably by integrating the three dimensions of economic, environmental and social sustainability into key inter-organizational business systems and stakeholder network interrelationships. McLoughlin and Meehan (2021) explain that this is achieved by understanding that SSCM practices are shaped by different logics from SCM.

What are 'sustainable' business processes?

Business processes are formalized sets of repetitive activities or task flows across internal business functions and between supply chain partners (Croxton *et al*, 2001; Ahi and Searcy, 2013). In the context of SSCM, the business processes that enable process integration are strategic planning, design, governance, integration, collaboration, pre-competitive collaboration, stakeholder management, and performance monitoring and evaluation (Figure 6.1) (McLoughlin *et al*, 2021). Setting the sustainable business processes is important as it refers to how a business can translate, create, deliver and retain value in environmental, economic and social areas in a sustainable way.

Process management

It is well established that SSCM necessitates the consideration of multiple stakeholders, partnerships and collaborators (Seuring and Müller, 2008; Vachon and Klassen, 2008). Sarkis also raises the issue of the diversity of perceptions and preferences, alongside how strategic decision making will affect network stakeholders and, therefore, 'considering critical factors and their interdependencies is necessary for accomplishing this goal' (2003: 405). As such, managing business processes requires a phased approach of alignment, implementation and maintenance.

Storey *et al* (2006) contend that the tenets of management are alignment and integration. However, this 'process' view is limited as it does not consider the necessity of collaboration which is a core tenet of SSCM. As Lambert explains, 'SCM is the integration of key business processes across the supply chain and the processes can be linked successfully only if the relationships with the other members of the supply chain are managed properly' (2008: 235). Furthermore, Kleindorfer, Singhal and van Wassenhove (2005), Vachon and Klassen (2006) and Beske and Seuring (2014) stress the importance of SSCM maintenance. Therefore, McLoughlin *et al* (2021) explain that the phases of management are alignment, implementation and maintenance.

The case study – a global chocolate supply chain network

The food and beverage (F&B) sector was selected as the research context. There is ample evidence in the literature and expert sources (French, 2008) that this sector provides valuable insights into how to manage sustainable supply chains. How society has evolved has been dependent on food supply.

This is exemplified by the interrelationship between food supply and the three pillars of sustainability, as seven billion people need food. This is set to grow to nine billion by 2050 (IPCC, 2015). The £1.5 trillion F&B sector provides a rich arena to explore sustainable supply chains. The global confectionery market was worth an estimated £1.5 billion retail value in 2016, of which chocolate confectionery was worth £79 billion. The world consumes over three million tonnes of chocolate annually. Between 2014 and 2019, this is expected to grow by 7.2 per cent (Statista, 2016). Chocolate production is adapting to meet changing macroeconomic and consumer trends. Consumers' appetite for high-quality, sustainable and ethically supplied products is growing (van der Vorst *et al*, 2009; Alvarez *et al*, 2010). Thirty-three thousand 'responsible' products were introduced to the top 'sustainability friendly' markets of France, the UK, the United States and Germany from 2009 to 2010 (Agriculture and Agri-Food Canada, 2011). However, within this growth market there are serious challenges:

- This sector captures the zeitgeist of sustainability issues such as planetary boundaries, macroeconomics, geopolitics and human rights.
- The sector is expected to produce 4.5 million tonnes by 2020 to meet this demand yet production is declining. Over 70% of production comes from developing world countries where sustainability issues come into relief as risks and impacts are heightened (Barometer Consortium, 2016).
- Macroeconomic and geopolitical issues such as decrease in distributed income and migration to cities has resulted in growing demand and declining production. Environmentally the quality and quantity of stock are decreasing due to ageing plants, unsustainable farming practices and climate change.
- The chocolate industry is one of the earlier cohorts impacting upon and being impacted by sustainability issues, alongside examples such as bananas, coffee and tea.
- The sector's impetus for action was the Harkin–Engel Protocol on child labour in 2001 (Slave Free Chocolate, 2013). Since then, there have been multiple partnerships and multi-stakeholder collaborations convened to tackle the issues that require collective action.

The inherent tensions between the global economic system and sustainability threaten the well-being of supply chain stakeholders. Companies are having to understand the trade-offs between different stakeholders that have implications for demand, market commodities and price of commodities.

Figure 6.1 The chocolate supply chain and sustainability impact (McLoughlin and Meehan, 2021)

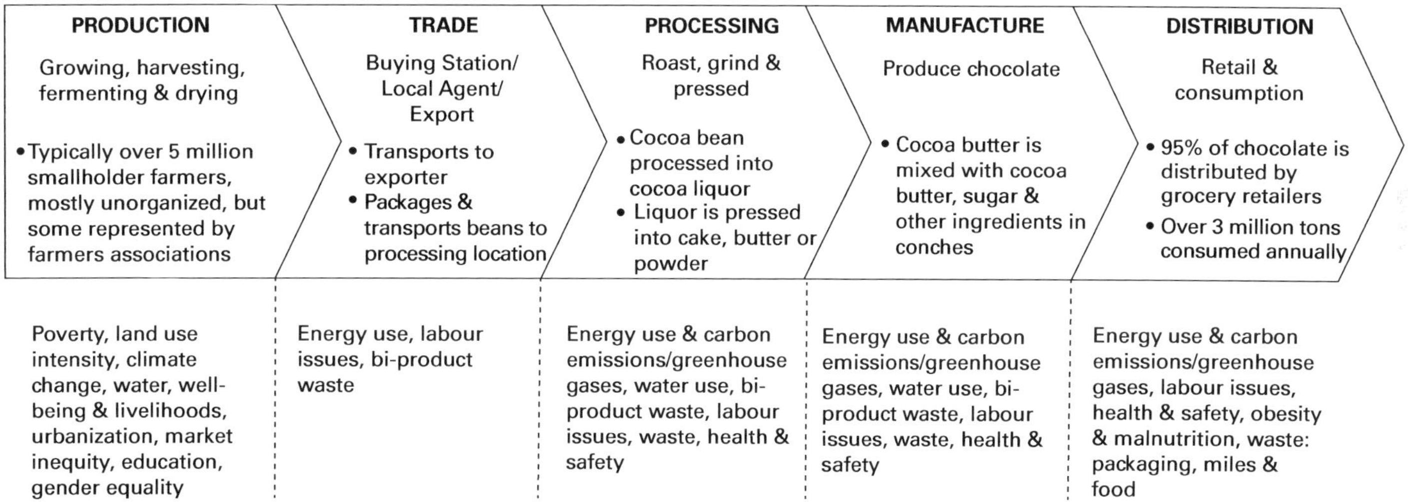

Sustainable sourcing and market supply have become vital components of core business strategy and operations. This can be seen by the 60 per cent increase in sustainability reports between 2001 and 2013 as 92 per cent of the world's largest 250 companies and over 90 per cent of 45,000 publicly traded companies globally reported on sustainability performance (United Nations Environment Programme *et al*, 2014). Since the first reports were submitted to the Global Reporting Initiative (GRI) in 1991, seven of the 'Top 10' Food & Beverage companies[1] identified by Oxfam as having the largest revenues globally have assessed their supply chain policies and practices along either GRI or non-GRI guidelines. Therefore, the industry has over 25 years' experience in sustainability reporting on policy and practices in tackling some of the world's largest and most critical issues and the challenges of putting those plans into practice.

The global sustainable chocolate supply chain network (ending in the UK retail sector) was selected as a critical case as it met the contextual and case study conditions. This is a growth market that is beset with sustainability challenges and opportunities end-to-end, from supply to manufacturing, market and waste trends (Figure 6.1). The network presents an array of stakeholders with varying principles regarding sustainability and propositions as to how they capture its value across the supply chain. It is also a relatively small network – in comparison to soy and palm oil for example – and within the resources of the researcher to study.

Overview of the network

The chocolate SC network consists of multiple stakeholders, including commercial and non-commercial organizations (Table 6.1). The network was mapped by identifying the connections among organizations who are collaborating to manage sustainability. Secondary data were used to identify actors across multiple online sources. For example, UTZ (2017) listed over 1,800 registered cocoa supply chain actors that interacted with their organization. This started with access to a manufacturing MNC from which their stakeholders and partners were identified. Next, a stakeholder analysis of the main cocoa and chocolate companies was carried out. Their partnerships were mapped into 351 relationships, listing two primary categories – commercial and non-commercial partners – and their respective subcategories, and constitute a range of private and civil stakeholders engaged in sustainability issues across the five stages of the supply chain illustrated in

Table 6.1 Categories of organizations mapped in supply chain network

Primary category	Subcategory	Quantity of nodes
Commercial	Farming association	1
	Processor/Traders	5
	Brand manufacturers	7
	Retailers	7
	Packaging company	1
Non-commercial	Trade associations	10
	NGO	15
	Certifiers	6

Figure 6.1. Contact was made through existing network relationships used to gain introductions or cold-calling by the researcher. Data were collected through 33 interviews and 265 publicly available documents. Sensitizing concepts were used from the literature to thematically analyse data using NVivo software. Thematic analysis is defined as 'a method of identifying, analysing and reporting patterns (themes) within data' (Braun and Clarke, 2006:79). Axil codes were generated from the sensitizing concepts identified in the literature to identify processes. Pattern matching of outcomes in causal relationship variables signalled the emergent theme (Miles and Huberman, 1994). This process was satisfied once saturation occurred (Neuman, 2014).

Defining the issue

After approximately 20 years of practice within the chocolate sector, organizations have aligned their activities to collaborate and work collectively using a set of repetitive tasks that this project seeks to formalize, such as a range of non-profit initiatives, including the World Cocoa Foundation's Cocoa Action convener and strategy holder or WRAP's working groups to share knowledge. In practice, diverse stakeholder organizations seek to align partners' goals with their own, put plans into practice and extend activities both within their own supply chains and across the sector, all indicative of an organized set of management processes. This study examined an end-to-end supply chain network of multiple stakeholders. These actors (1) capture the diversity of organizational types, from commercial to non-commercial, ranging across the private and civil sectors (Alter, 2007) and (2) align and coordinate their activities and find a common goal in order to address sustainability issues.

To carry out such an effort, according to authors McLoughlin *et al* (2021) there are eight integral business processes that are critical to SSCM which were stated as (1) strategic planning, (2) design, (3) governance, (4) integration, (5) collaboration, (6) pre-competitive collaboration, (7) stakeholder management and (8) performance monitoring and evaluation. McLoughlin *et al* (2021) put forward the proposition that 'The set of eight business processes are a set of logically organized tasks that collectively stimulate communities of sustainable practice to emerge in which knowledge is constructed and shared beyond organizational boundaries within complex, heterogeneous environments'.

Identifying the set of key eight business processes in chocolate SSCM

In-depth explanations of how each of these key business processes is critical in the integration of sustainability across the supply chain are imperative to understand and evaluate their role within the chocolate supply chain and its operational strategy (McLoughlin *et al*, 2021). These key processes are explained within the context of sustainability specifically, which is elaborated below in detail.

(1) Strategic planning

Strategic planning refers here to the object or aim or an action and on which its effects can be examined on task performance. It is a key process as it (a) identifies sustainable and ethical aims within and across the supply chain (SC) and aligns them with corporate strategy, and (b) entails also the subprocesses of impact mapping and analysis, goal setting and making the business case.

Within the case study of the chocolate supply chain network this related to mapping the supply chain and identifying where sustainability impacts are critical. This allows partners to agree a common vision, align goals and subsequently implement activities. Planning also provides the framework for maintenance and continuous improvement for the organization and others to learn from. As one manufacturing respondent explained:

> Often it's about identifying the agenda. So, we don't necessarily work directly with other colleagues on deforestation but by defining the agenda and agreeing on the priorities, it means that we pursue [these] through our own engagement with our own suppliers. We might be working to an increasingly harmonized agenda. Therefore, we clearly manage all our own relationships with our direct suppliers ourselves but by being signed-up to a global agenda on deforestation it means that increasingly complex questions are being asked.

(2) Design

Design within the context refers to the organization of materials, information and resources through product and business processes and systems including three main features:

1. redesigning product sustainability through product coordination and SC design;
2. reconceptualizing the SC business processes for enhanced sustainability performance; and
3. reengineering business processes analytically and radically to change activities across the SC.

Within the case of the chocolate supply chain network this related to the configuration of global supply networks being redesigned and contracts changing to become more resilient to risk while seeking opportunities and innovating. Supply chain networks being re-conceptualized and business processes being re-engineered are naturally closely aligned with the strategic planning, governance and performance processes. This means increased sustainability value being created, as multiple stakeholders are adapting innovatively to integrate sustainability efficiently and effectively. For example, within-case three manufacturers analysed and radically changed activities within business functions and across the supply chain to embed sustainability more firmly, with one company investing $3.5 billion.

(3) Governance

Governance in this context is defined as frameworks and structured to establish standards, align institutions with supply chain members within and outside, and provide an umbrella for strategic management. Corporate responsibility has extended the governance of an organization beyond its direct realm of influence and control, across boundaries into the supply chain network. This involves executive, legislative and policy responsibilities at a strategic level from which management receive their mandate and directive to implement operationally.

Within the case of the chocolate supply chain network this related to the executive providing power, leadership, mandate and legitimacy to drive change and influence others. Another crucial component of governance is policy and standards, as they provide guidelines for operations and supply chain relationships. Experience has taught those engaged in sustainability programmes that 'they can't just throw money at it ... it's going to be about policies' (manufacturing respondent). One of the functions of governance is due diligence and compliance with legislation and regulation by the board. There is recognition sector-wide that effecting sustainability impact requires shared responsibility. This extends the onus of responsibility from responsible businesses to government to create an enabling environment. Together with local governments and key stakeholders, organizations collaborate pre-competitively to align their goals and activities.

(4) Integration

Integration here refers to the structural coordination of intra- and inter-organizational processes. As such, effective integration requires knowledge and skills exchange, resource coordination and an alignment (reduction in goal discrepancy) of capabilities and priorities through both the product and process.

Within the case of the chocolate supply chain network this related to linking strategy, design, governance and performance. This was heavily substantiated by respondents who verified the arc of integration theory (Frohlich and Westbrook, 2001). They believe that for sustainability to be successfully managed in the supply chain, it needs to be integrated in terms of both depth and breadth. A trade association respondent explained, 'now the time is right for this more, this big, larger scale and more integrated approach which brings resilience and sustainability together'.

(5) Collaboration

Collaboration here is defined as the processes by which partners cooperate and work jointly. Due to the scale of sustainability issues, they require collective action, thus it builds collaborative advantage across the network and that advantage is characterized by time and resources and as boundary-spanning.

Within the case of the chocolate supply chain network this related to managing varying relationships across a multi-stakeholder network; sustainability can be conceptualized differently and strategic priorities can vary among partners, and they can have different approaches to collaboration and goal alignment. Respondents said that more is achieved by the supply chain partners working together rather than acting alone. Supply chain partners collaborate to gain the differentiation and competitive advantage of the supply chain for customers and in the market. Therefore, agreement on how that is best achieved sustainably is essential to have all partners working towards a shared vision. As a manufacturing respondent described it, 'So, it's all working together and trying to get to a point where we can deliver on this community action plan. That's one of the key priorities.'

(6) Pre-competitive collaboration

This refers to the structural coordination of business, public and civil arenas entailing the experience and the scale of issues that have been taught to practitioners underlying the necessity for collective action and shared responsibility.

Within the case of the chocolate supply chain network this related to collaborations based on anti-trust laws and non-profit organization. Network determinants play a highly influential role in this process as it has enabled a galvanized sector in terms of alignment, coordination and collective action. The most common arena is through trade association initiatives whereby the boundary of activity is any activity that contravenes competition law and is considered anti-trust by regulators. Another important aspect is that it provides a corporate veil whereby the trade association can represent the collective without negatively impacting on any one individual. While all companies choose their level of participation (if at all), findings indicate a spectrum of levels of commitment to the phases of management that is pre-determined by organizational orientation.

(7) Stakeholder management

Stakeholder management here refers to all entities that have a stake in the supply chain but that the company is not in collaboration with, including commercial and non-commercial actors and organizations, the planet and its ecosystems. Increased sustainability orientation requires a greater consideration of stakeholders.

Within the case of the chocolate supply chain network this related to the importance of identifying, analysing and engaging with stakeholders. They provide a good indicator as to where the big sustainability challenges are; however, because the scale is so broad and complex, the challenge is in working out which areas to focus on. This means that planning and governance are critical in identifying goals as all stakeholders across the SC network cannot be satisfied. Respondents said that they find this a challenge, as is finding the balance in managing their expectations and supporting key stakeholders. For example, a retail respondent explained that:

> The challenge we have sometimes is that they [employees] care so much that we can't actually do the things they want us to! So, I guess we're quite the other end in terms of managing our stakeholders to maybe someone who just cares about the share price.

While a manufacturing respondent explained: 'So, just finding the right stakeholders is not so easy.' Ultimately, this depended on how the company identified and analysed stakeholders and the type of relationship they wanted to manage. Essentially, it was about enhanced communication to manage reputation and expectations, alignment, coordination, consultation and to provide guidance and support. There is a sense of long-term commitment and increased accountability and responsibility. Also, that these relationships need to be managed so that they are not disruptive but rather constructive to the supply chain.

(8) Performance monitoring and evaluation

This refers to the process of assessing and improving the implementation of strategic goals. It provides important information about the business case for integrating sustainability and improving efficiency, effectiveness and innovation while meeting strategic goals.

Within the case of the chocolate supply chain network this enables efficiency, effectiveness and innovation while meeting strategic goals. Respondents described how monitoring and evaluation subprocesses are important for numerous reasons. Having the correct procedures and measures enables verification, self-assessment, consequence management and accountability. Activities are designed to comply with certification and regulations, providing the information for accreditation, auditing, compliance, reporting and transparency. The system also provides information for internal company reports, such as annual and sustainability reports, and external reporting systems. These activities and mechanisms are strategically designed to address complex challenges that take time to solve and required a phased approach. For example, a trader reports: 'Tackling poverty is a long-term solution to child labour, but in the short term we need to put in place solid monitoring and remediation systems, in order to identify and forever eliminate child labour' (Barry Callebaut, 2016: 12).

The process is dependent on other key processes, namely, identified key goals and metrics in the strategic planning process and collaboration with multiple stakeholders to educate, enforce standards and achieve scale. The system developed procedures such as key performance indicators to prevent, monitor and remediate partners' compliance.

Aligning real-world issues with the SSCM process models

Guiding principles that outline how the SSCM process model is managed have been set up by McLoughlin *et al* (2021) as indicated in Figure 6.2, with the model illustrating;

- How to create value through the alignment of principles and priorities, deliver value through the implementation of key business processes, and capture value through the maintenance activities such as continuous improvement, resilience and scaling-up approaches.
- Utilizing as a mechanism for interpreting real-world issues into a management model.

Regarding the management of the process model, there is a strategic significance in linking and managing of relationships across the supply chain network. The management of the link and the quantity and combinations of these components are performative (Lambert and Cooper, 2000; Frohlich and Westbrook, 2001). The greater the number of links the greater the efficiency of flows, coordination and collectivism (Rowley, 1997).

Figure 6.2 The development of business and management processes in response to real-world issues in SSCM

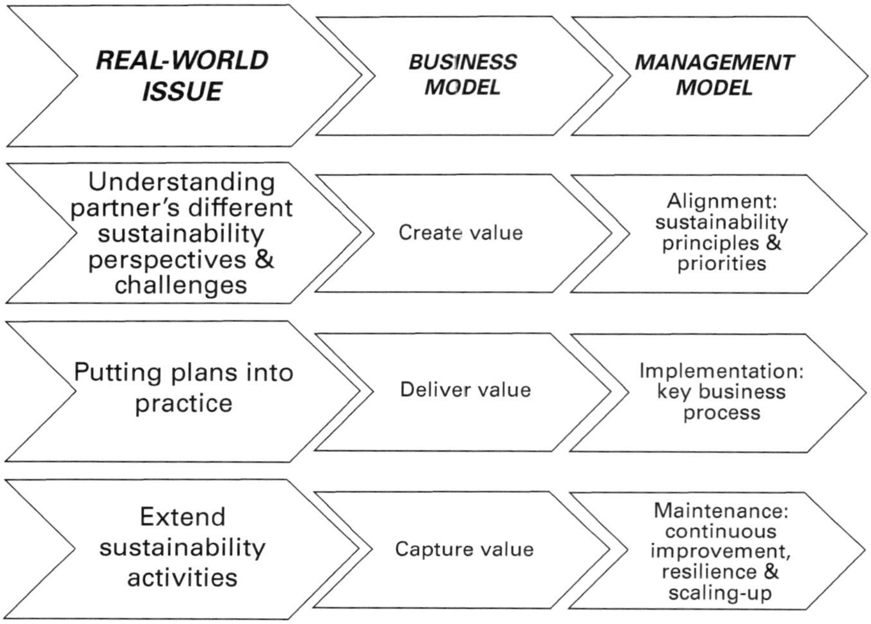

Storey *et al* (2006) contend that the tenets of management are relational alignment and structural integration. As Lambert explains, 'SCM is the integration of key business processes across the supply chain and the processes can be linked successfully only if the relationships with the other members of the supply chain are managed properly' (2008: 235). Furthermore, Kleindorfer *et al* (2005), Vachon and Klassen (2006) and Beske and Seuring (2014) stress the importance of SSCM maintenance through utilization of the management phases which include alignment, implementation and maintenance, denoting a maturity model.

Within the case of the chocolate supply chain network, the extended model illustrates how practitioners create value through the alignment of principles and priorities, deliver value through the implementation of key business processes, and capture value through the maintenance activities such as continuous improvement, resilience and scaling-up approaches. This process gives continuity from the business model to the management model in response to real-world issues.

Managing the impact of a spectrum of sustainability principles in multi-stakeholder networks

Consistent with the findings in the literature, respondents discussed how companies create value in different ways. All business models in this study captured some aspect of responsibility. However, depending on the institutional logics, an organization captures sustainability value in its business model based on varying social and economic logics, attitudes to stakeholders, and inter-organizational activities (McLoughlin and Meehan, 2021). As such, different types of business models exist, ranging from classical economy to alternative economic theories. Parallels can be drawn between the stages of value creation and the organizational orientation towards sustainability, with increasing sustainability orientation and paradigmatic transformation leading to new business model creation. As the chocolate sector continues to develop sustainability by managing the impact of a spectrum of sustainability principles in multi-stakeholder networks, it faces three key issues:

1. understanding sustainability across the supply chain;
2. putting plans into practice; and
3. scaling-up sustainability.

These issues are insightful to the theoretical development of this research project as they illustrate the 'real life' manifestation of how organizations are managing sustainable supply chains. Furthermore, these issues meet the requirements of the SSCM process model – (a) alignment, (b) implementation and (c) maintenance respectively.

(a) Alignment of the strategic orientation in the supply chain

Organizational orientation is a company's predisposition towards goals and activities as a result of its structure, culture and strategy. In this instance, it refers to an orientation towards sustainability. What Banerjee (2001) refers to as internal environmental orientation, Gold *et al* (2013) explain that orientation towards sustainability manifests in the behaviours, norms and mores both at an individual and at a corporate level. The level of integration determines the sustainability of the organization and its holistic management across supply chains (Ahi and Searcy, 2013). This in turn influences sustainable supply chain orientation (Pagell and Wu, 2009; Kleindorfer *et al*, 2009). A manufacturing respondent explained alignment within a linear supply chain:

> We take a standard, if you like the standard definition of sustainability as being economically, socially and environmentally sustainable in the long run. We take a pragmatic perspective on it. We look to see where are the biggest impacts and therefore the biggest opportunities to make a difference. And we seek to integrate as closely as possible within our business model. So, it's quite broad-based ... By defining the agenda and agreeing on the priorities, it means that we pursue [these] through our own engagement with our own suppliers – we might be working to an increasingly harmonized agenda ... The idea is that we work together as a partnership. So, we all feel some ownership, and we're all there for different reasons. Ultimately, we're there because we want the cocoa to make chocolate. Barry Callebaut is there because they want to buy cocoa and sell cocoa. The farmers are there because they want to get a better income. So, there's slightly different reasons why you're there but I think at the end of it we all want the same thing.

At the heart of this discourse is how organizational orientation is a causal mechanism that shapes practice (Wu and Pagell, 2011; Beske *et al*, 2014). This is a dynamic process which captures the mindset and strategic values of a company in its movement towards sustainability across the supply chain (Pagell and Wu, 2009).

(b) Implementation: Developing a strategic response

To address these, each organization has developed a strategic response bespoke to its business model, value proposition and organizational culture. As a manufacturing respondent explained, within the case of the chocolate supply chain network, 'We work with thousands of suppliers, consultants and business partners around the world. We are taking steps to align what they do for us with our own values and goals.' Concepts are kept broad and simple, with emphasis on the dimensions and economic model consistent across the supply chain. For example, a retailer explained the alignment activities of a retail group as a pre-competitive level:

> So, what we've done is we've said that what we have to do is we have to have accountability or custodianship by the key actors. We have to be able to evaluate how well they are delivering against our policy requirements. So, what

we've done is, as a retail group, we're all pretty consistent in our policies in the top line; there may be subtle differences in the detail but top line we're all looking at the same thing.

(c) Maintenance in the supply chain

Within the case of the chocolate supply chain network, respondents explained the challenges in putting plans into practice as the complexity (21 sources) and siloed thinking (14 sources) from which challenges regarding the scale of issues, divergent attitudes and varying levels of commitment internally in business functions and across interconnected businesses become evident. This requires members to trust, be patient, flexible and provide transparency across their supply chains to disclose risks. For example, a trade association respondent explained how a retail member wanted to take a landscape approach, rather than a commodity one, to organize collective activities. This is illustrative of a company with more experience and sophistication in the approach they take that not all association members collaborating pre-competitively would have. Therefore, the respondent explained how it is very complicated to get agreement among members as, generally, the business case is built around commodities, which determines the level of commitment, investment and activity. Another retailer explained this as:

> How do we create solutions that give us lowest inconvenience, lowest cost, easiest communication and implementation, and how do we need to develop? The best bet for our sector will be, in effect, an 'off the shelf' solution for our suppliers and as standardized as possible, as simple as possible.

To overcome these challenges and share commitment, businesses are exploring ways to deliver value at various levels. Respondents explained that the degree to which plans are put into effect depends on the capacities of individual members to integrate and collaborate. At a network level, due to the scale of these issues, the solution requires shared responsibility and collective action. This extends collaborative ties, not only with one's supply chain partners but also with potential partners – commercial and non-commercial, competitive and non-competitive. Partnership requires a shared vision. Within the case of the chocolate supply chain network, this related to creating buy-in and enabling shared responsibility and collective action, as explained by a manufacturing respondent who is a leader in trade associations: 'What we're seeking to do is find a way of getting to that point where everybody in the sector is approaching issues in similar ways.'

Research indicates that companies have different sustainability principles and priorities due to bespoke strategies unique to that organization type. A focus on network theory emerged due to the premise that 'managing inter-organizational relationships is central to success' (Shook *et al*, 2009: 4) given the need for a systemic, holistic view, a wider view of stakeholders being taken into consideration and increased interrelationships resulting in interdependencies. Rowley (1997) explains that stakeholder influences, and how a company responds to these, require an understanding of the interconnected networks of relationships. The network view accommodates an understanding of multiple, interdependent stakeholders' influences and how a company manages these. Within the case of the chocolate supply chain network, this related to how organizations use a variety of relational processes: collaboration, pre-competitive collaboration and stakeholder management. This addresses the breadth of socio-economic impacts that extend beyond the economic rationale of commercial relations and contract (McLoughlin and Meehan, 2021). For example, a manufacturing respondent explained:

> The other area that I would highlight is that for the socio-economic stuff it's a lot harder because it's harder to form a view of where the biggest impacts are. Because socio-economic impacts [are] often not well researched within supply chains and so we are increasingly focusing on how to build the view, in a systematic way, of where key socio-economic impacts within supply chains [are] so that we can then seek to address them. And again, all those complexities about being difficult and time-consuming, and use of indirect influence come to play, very much so within social issues in the supply chain.

Understanding how to manage a supply chain sustainably requires this wider view of how direct and indirect stakeholders are embedded (Miemczyk *et al*, 2012). Stakeholders become more embedded through the degree to which they become interconnected through integrative and collaborative processes and the links that facilitate these. Diverse stakeholders collaborate on issues of concern even though their requirements do not necessarily align (Ferrell *et al*, 2010). Therefore, concurrent with Ferrell *et al*'s (2010) conclusions, stakeholder orientation requires a more expansive perspective than supply chain orientation (SCO) allows in SSCM.

Conclusion

The purpose of this study was to describe key business processes in SSCM. This was achieved by analysing a chocolate supply chain network that captured the diversity of stakeholders who had to find common ground to work together. This created a comprehensive understanding of the model and its structure through phases of management, as greater orientation towards sustainability is achieved within multilateral partnerships. The function of processes has changed from being process to impact driven. Their relationships, through the process model, are actualized in response to real-world events; therefore their character is heterogeneous depending on their context and the mechanisms that generate them.

Learning outcomes

- This case has highlighted how the concepts of sustainability and SCM merge, resulting in business processes being reappraised to facilitate a sustainable value proposition.
- The case provides an example of how standard business processes are elevated to critical SSCM using thick description of the processes and their subprocesses, in response to the emergent set of principles in SSCM.
- The case helps to appreciate how the processes themselves are not unique to SSCM but, through phases of management, they perform as a maturity model in service of sustainability goals.
- The case highlights how organizational orientation towards sustainability fundamentally alters a supply chain.
- The centrality of sustainability in the value proposition determines the extent to which an organization engages in the phases of management.

Questions

1. How does an organization map its supply chain network in order to identify sustainability impacts?
2. How does an organization strategically select and plan its supply chain sustainability strategy?

3 Based on the eight business processes, how can an organization manage relationships effectively?

4 How does an organization create value in the supply chain that extends beyond that of an economic nature?

5 How does an organization communicate this value to its stakeholders?

Endnote

1 Associated British Foods, Coca-Cola, Danone, General Mills, Kellogg's, Mars, Mondeléz, Nestlé, PepsiCo and Unilever

References

Agriculture and Agri-Food Canada (2011) *Global Trends: Sustainable food and beverages*, Ottawa, Canada

Ahi, P and Searcy, C (2013) A comparative literature analysis of definitions for green and sustainable supply chain management, *Journal of Cleaner Production*, **52**, pp 329–41

Alter, K (2007) *Social Enterprise Typology*, Virtue Ventures LLC, Wilmington, DE

Alvarez, G, Pilbeam, C and Wilding, R (2010) Nestlé Nespresso AAA sustainable quality program: an investigation into the governance dynamics in a multi-stakeholder supply chain network, *Supply Chain Management*, **15** (2), pp 165–82

Banerjee, S B (2001) Managerial perceptions of corporate environmentalism: interpretations from industry and strategic implications for organizations, *Journal of Management Studies*, **38** (4), pp 489–513

Barometer Consortium (2016) *Cocoa Barometer 2015*, Netherlands

Barry Callebaut (2016) [accessed 9 July 2021] "Forever Chocolate": Barry Callebaut Targets 100% Sustainable Chocolate by 2025, *Barry Callebaut*, Zurich [Online] = www.barry-callebaut.com/news/2016/11/"forever-chocolate"-barry-callebaut-targets-100-sustainable-chocolate-2025 (archived at https://perma.cc/66N2-TCJH)

Beske, P and Seuring, S (2014) Putting sustainability into supply chain management, *Supply Chain Management*, **19** (3), pp 322–31

Beske, P, Land, A and Seuring, S (2014) Sustainable supply chain management practices and dynamic capabilities in the food industry: a critical analysis of the literature, *International Journal of Production Economics*, **152**, June, pp 131–43

Bocken, N M P *et al* (2014) A literature and practice review to develop sustainable business model archetypes, *Journal of Cleaner Production*, **65**, pp 42–56

Braun, V and Clarke, C (2006) Using thematic analysis in psychology, *Qualitative Research in Psychology*, **3** (2), pp 77–101

Burgess, K, Singh, P J and Koroglu, R (2006) Supply chain management: a structured literature review and implications for future research, *International Journal of Operations & Production Management*, **26** (7), pp 703–29

Carter, C R and Rogers, D S (2008) A framework of sustainable supply chain management: moving toward new theory, *International Journal of Physical Distribution & Logistics Management*, **38** (5–6), pp 360–87

Croxton, K L *et al* (2001) The supply chain management processes, *The International Journal of Logistics Management*, **12** (2) pp 13–36

Evans, S *et al* (2017) Business model innovation for sustainability: towards a unified perspective for creation of sustainable business models, *Business Strategy and the Environment*, **26** (5) pp 597–608

Ferrell, O C *et al* (2010) From market orientation to stakeholder orientation, *Journal of Public Policy & Marketing*, **29** (1) pp 93–96

Freeman, R E (2010) *Strategic Management: A stakeholder approach*, Cambridge University Press, Cambridge

French, L (2008) *Sustainability Reporting in the Food Processing Sector: A survey conducted by the Global Reporting Initiative*, Amsterdam

Friedman, M (1970) A Friedman doctrine – the social responsibility of business is to increase its profits, *The New York Times*, 13 September

Frohlich, M T and Westbrook, R (2001) Arcs of integration: an international study of supply chain strategies, *Journal of Operations Management*, **19** (2), February, pp 185–200

Gold, S, Seuring, S and Beske, P (2010) Sustainable supply chain management and inter-organizational resources: a literature review, *Corporate Social Responsibility and Environmental Management*, **17**, pp 230–45

Gold, S, Hahn, R and Seuring, S (2013) Sustainable supply chain management in 'Base of the Pyramid' food projects: a path to triple bottom line approaches for multinationals? *International Business Review*, **22** (5), October, pp 784–99

Gunasekaran, A, Subramanian, N and Rahman, S (2015) Green supply chain collaboration and incentives: current trends and future directions, *Transportation Research: Part E*, **74**, pp 1–10

IPCC (2015) Climate Change 2014 Synthesis Report Summary for Policymakers, Geneva, Switzerland

Kleindorfer, P R, Singhal, K and Van Wassenhove, L N (2005) Sustainable operations management, *Production & Operations Management*, **14** (4), Winter, pp 482–92

Kleindorfer, P R, Singhal, K and Wassenhove, L N (2009) Sustainable operations management, *Production and Operations Management*, **14** (4), pp 482–92

Lambert, D M (2008) *Supply Chain Management: Processes, partnerships, performance*, 3rd edn, Supply Chain Management Institute, Sarasota, FL

Lambert, D M and Cooper, M C (2000) Issues in supply chain management, *Industrial Marketing Management*, **29** (1), pp 65–83

McLoughlin, K *et al* (2021) Sustainability in supply chains: reappraising business process management, *Production Planning & Control*, pp 1–68, doi:10.1080/09537287.2021.1884764

McLoughlin, K and Meehan, J (2021) The institutional logic of the sustainable organisation: the case of a chocolate supply network, *International Journal of Operations & Production Management*, doi:10.1108/IJOPM-11-2020-0773 (archived at https://perma.cc/8S7Y-KYJ7)

Miemczyk, J, Johnsen, T E and Macquet, M (2012) Sustainable purchasing and supply management: a structured literature review of definitions and measures at the dyad, chain and network levels, *Supply Chain Management*, **17** (5), pp 478–96

Miles, M and Huberman, A (1994) *Qualitative Data Analysis: An expanded sourcebook*, 2nd edn, SAGE, London

Morali, O and Searcy, C (2013) A review of sustainable supply chain management practices in Canada, *Journal of Business Ethics*, **117**, pp 635–58

Neuman, W L (2014) *Social Research Methods: Qualitative and quantitative approaches*, 7th edn, Pearson, Harlow

Pagell, M and Wu, Z (2009) Building a more complete theory of sustainable supply chain management using case studies of 10 exemplars, *Journal of Supply Chain Management*, **45**, pp 37–56

Rowley, T J (1997) Moving beyond dyadic ties: a network theory of stakeholder influences, *Academy of Management Review*, **22** (4), October, pp 887–910

Sarkis, J (2003) A strategic decision framework for green supply chain management, *Journal of Cleaner Production*, **11** (4), pp 397–409

Seuring, S and Müller, M (2008) From a literature review to a conceptual framework for sustainable supply chain management, *Journal of Cleaner Production*, **16** (15), pp 1699–710

Shook, C L *et al* (2009) Towards a 'theoretical toolbox' for strategic sourcing, *Supply Chain Management*, **14** (1), pp 3–10

Slave Free Chocolate (2013) [accessed 7 July 2021] The Harkin–Engel Protocol [Online] = www.slavefreechocolate.org/harkin-engel-protocol/ (archived at https://perma.cc/R6WM-5NP8)

Statista (2016) [accessed 7 July 2021] Retail Consumption of Chocolate Confectionery Worldwide From 2012/13 to 2018/19 (in 1,000 metric tons), *Statista* [Online] = www.statista.com/statistics/238849/global-chocolate-consumption/ (archived at https://perma.cc/SB5F-CF7V)

Storey, J *et al* (2006) Supply chain management: theory, practice and future challenges, *International Journal of Operations & Production Management*, **26** (7) pp 754–74

United Nations Environment Programme, The Global Reporting Initiative, KPMG and The Centre for Corporate Governance in Africa (2014) *Carrots and Sticks: Sustainable reporting practices worldwide – today's best practice, tomorrow's trends*, 4th edn, South Africa

UTZ (2017) UTZ Registered Cocoa Supply Chain Actors, Amsterdam

Vachon, S and Klassen, R D (2006) Extending green practices across the supply chain: the impact of upstream and downstream integration, *International Journal of Operations & Production Management*, **26** (7) pp 795–821

Vachon, S and Klassen, R D (2008) Environmental management and manufacturing performance: the role of collaboration in the supply chain, *International Journal of Production Economics*, **111** (2), February, pp 299–315

van der Vorst, J, Tromp, S O and van der Zee, D J (2009) Simulation modelling for food supply chain redesign; integrated decision making on product quality, sustainability and logistics, *International Journal of Production Research*, **47** (23), pp 6611–31

Vurro, C, Russo, A and Perrini, F (2009) Shaping sustainable value chains: network determinants of supply chain governance models, *Journal of Business Ethics*, **90**, pp 607–21

Wu, Z and Pagell, M (2011) Balancing priorities: decision-making in sustainable supply chain management, *Journal of Operations Management*, **29** (6), pp 577–90

Exploring the inefficiency of medicine delivery processes in pharmaceutical supply chain (PSC) waste 07

The case of the UK and Greece

DR MARINA PAPALEXI, MANCHESTER METROPOLITAN UNIVERSITY, MANCHESTER, UK

Introduction

This case study discusses the inefficiency observed in the delivery process of pharmaceuticals employed within two diverse geographical areas: the UK and Greece. It highlights the perceived waste in this complex delivery process and provides potential solutions through using innovative approaches. In summary:

- The UK and Greek healthcare systems have been structured in a different manner:
  - The healthcare system in the UK focuses more on developing the primary healthcare settings; there are multiple prescribers and different prescribing processes.

   - The healthcare system in Greece concentrates more on secondary healthcare provision; there is only one prescriber (the physicians).
- Both healthcare systems have to deal with a number of issues, such as high level of complexity, wastage, eg cost, expired products, and communication issues.

After analysing both pharmaceutical delivery processes, the adoption of innovative approaches, such as lean and reverse logistics, as potential solutions is discussed.

The pharmaceutical sector

The pharmaceutical sector operates globally, manufacturing and distributing products to millions of people every day; therefore, it generates a considerable income and affects nearly everyone in the developed world (Mustaffa and Potter, 2009). As mentioned in Statista (Mikulic, 2019), worldwide drug expenditure was approximately \$1.2 trillion in 2018, with an expected growth to \$1.52 trillion by 2023. However, the pharmaceutical sector is characterized as a complex enterprise because it has to deal with conflicting objectives and numerous intractable constraints (Rossetti *et al*, 2011). In particular, it aims to meet customer demand effectively.

In this context the case study investigates the delivery process of pharmaceuticals employed within two diverse geographical areas: the UK and Greece. It analyses their inherently complex process and classifies the perceived waste, which is associated to process inefficiency. Furthermore, it recommends innovative approaches that can overcome issues, especially the fact that pharmacies have to deal with and optimize the medicine delivery process. Finally, the case study provides further theoretical insight into the highly complex pharmaceutical delivery process that can guide pharmacies and healthcare organizations to develop more efficient, effective and sustainable supply chain strategies, expanding our understanding of the pharmaceutical supply chain (PSC) downstream domain beyond the context of a single country setting.

The UK and Greece pharmaceutical supply chain

For a better understanding of the environment in which the medicine delivery process takes place, reference to some general data related to both

Table 7.1 Key facts for the UK and Greece (adapted from OECD Health Statistics, 2020)

	United Kingdom	Greece
Population	66.4 million	10.72 million
Gross domestic product (GDP)	$2.829 trillion	$209.853 billion
Healthcare expenditure		
Health expenditure as a % GDP	10.3%	7.8%
Public expenditure on health as a % GDP	8.0%	4.6%
Out-of-pocket payments for health care as a % GDP	2.3%	3.2%
Pharmaceutical expenditure (% health expenditure)	12.3%	26.2%

countries is necessary, as presented in Table 7.1. The UK's population was 66.4 million and its gross domestic product (GDP), or the value of all final goods and services produced within the nation, was $2.829 trillion, according to measurements carried out in 2019 (World Bank, 2020a). Based on the same measurements, Greece's population totalled 10.72 million people and its GDP was $209.853 billion in 2019 (World Bank, 2020b).

Focusing on the healthcare sector, in the UK total expenditure on healthcare as a percentage of GDP was 10.3 per cent in 2019; on the other hand, the share of GDP allocated to health spending in Greece was 7.8 per cent in 2019 (OECD Health Statistics, 2020). From Table 7.1, it can also be seen that public sources in the UK accounted for 8.0 per cent as a percentage of GDP and 2.3 per cent covered private expenditure in 2019 (OECD Health Statistics, 2020). Regarding Greece, public expenditure accounted for 4.6 per cent as a percentage of GDP and 3.2 per cent was related to private expenditure in 2019 (OECD Health Statistics, 2020). Regarding pharmaceutical expenditure, the UK spent 12.3 per cent and Greece 26.2 per cent of overall health spending in 2019 (OECD Health Statistics, 2020).

Based on the statistics presented, one could conclude that there are differences between these two countries in terms of their healthcare spending and existing healthcare structure.

Pharmaceutical delivery process

PSCs play an imperative role in the distribution and delivery of medicine and manage the inherent risks, which may 'disrupt the supply of medicine in many ways such as their quantity and quality and their delivery to the right place and customers and at the right time' (Jaberidosst, 2013: 1). The literature reveals that the supply chain associated with pharmaceutical products is vital in providing adequate supplies of medicine due to its impact upon people's health and well-being (Mustaffa and Potter, 2009). For a better understanding of the PSC, the description focuses only on the distribution of finished products where there are a number of different channels:

- The dominant intermediary is the wholesaler; approximately 80 per cent of pharmaceutical items flow through this channel.
- Pharmacies receive a number of products directly from the manufacturer's distribution centre.
- In some cases, group purchasing organizations may have responsibility for supplying pharmacies with the required products.

This case will focus on hospital pharmacies as well as community pharmacies. Figure 7.1 illustrates the process map of the medicine delivery process in hospital pharmacies in both countries. It presents the suppliers: wholesalers and pharmaceutical companies, the hospital pharmacy and the three different sorts of supply route. It describes not only the forward but also the reverse components of the defined pharmaceutical logistics process.

Figure 7.1 The process map of drug delivery in hospital pharmacies (adapted from Papalexi *et al*, 2017)

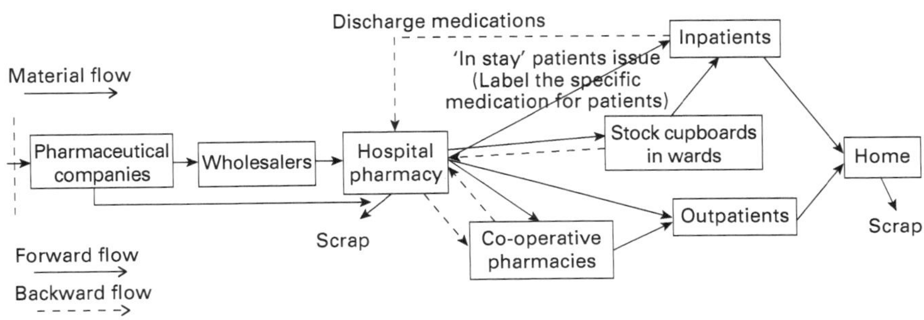

The arrows in Figure 7.1 show the forward logistics process and the dashed arrows the way that items can be reused or destroyed. Data related to the actual time spent on delivering the products and returning them into the system were not available; such data are difficult to estimate because the PSCs include different supply routes, and a number of stakeholders have diverse roles and have to deal with the diversity in demand. There is difficulty in predicting the exact demand for medicines, partially due to the lack of standard nomenclature and partially to the fact that medicines are stored in several areas of a healthcare organization (Mustaffa and Potter, 2009). The unavailability of those data, therefore, is due to the highly complex delivery system and the lack of standardized processes.

Figure 7.2 presents the process map of the medicine delivery process in community pharmacies in both countries:

- Community pharmacies order approximately 90% of the required products through wholesalers and the rest directly from pharmaceutical companies.
- In addition, they are able to collect spare medication; they cannot reuse it, but they can collect and destroy it. Therefore, similarly to Figure 7.1, the arrows show the forward logistics process and the dashed arrows describe how medicines can be destroyed.
- There were also difficulties in estimating the actual time required to deliver and return medication back to the system due to the perceived complexity of the delivery system.

Figure 7.2 Medicine delivery in community pharmacies (adapted from Papalexi *et al*, 2017)

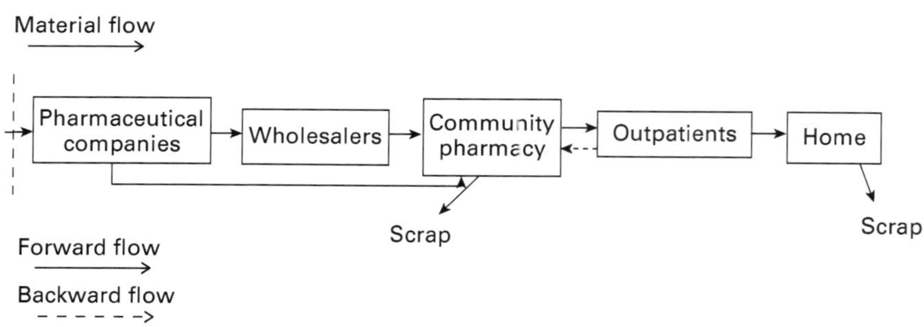

Table 7.2 Operational process waste identified within the PSC (adapted from Papalexi *et al*, 2016)

Type of waste	Type of waste within the PSC
Duplication	• Lack of communication and of knowledge and information sharing • Low level of transparency during the delivery process • Lack of team-working spirit • Duplication during the prescribing and dispensing processes • Re-labelling and discharging returned medication • Separation of the medicines that can be reused from those that have to be destroyed
Waiting	• Providing the required information • Receiving medication
Defect/Error	• Unclear prescription • Un-labelled medicines • Inappropriate packaging of medication
Inappropriate processing	• Lack of communication and of knowledge and information sharing • Low level of transparency during the delivery process • Lack of team-working spirit • Wards do not manage their stock properly • Discharged medication has been issued to the wards when patients have already left – approximately £36,000 per annum of stock is re-used • Complying with the national guidance and regulations
Unnecessary inventory	• Different storage policies • Safety stock • Complying with the national guidance and regulations • Staff and patients culture, following a 'just in case' not 'just in time' approach • Periodic lack of adequate storage capacity
Unnecessary transportation	• Unnecessary delivery of medicines
Unnecessary motion	• Lack of communication and of knowledge and information sharing • Clinical staff or patients ask for required medication

To provide a more parsimonious analysis, Table 7.2 shows the amount of operational process waste occurring within pharmacies. The classification of the PSC operational process waste is based on the list of the types of waste created by Taiichi Ohno in the Toyota Production System (Ohno, 1988). These include: overproduction, waiting, transportation, inappropriate processing, unnecessary inventory, unnecessary motion and the cost of defects.

Healthcare organizations could use this classification as guidance to identify the waste occurring within their systems, recognizing the causes that generated them; as a result, this action would enable them to undertake the required improvement, achieving delivery process perfection (Jones *et al*, 1997). In particular, the inherent types of waste included:

- duplication of service caused mainly due to the lack of a team-working environment;
- waiting to receive the required information and products;
- waste generated due to a number of defects;
- inappropriate processing, generated by the lack of transparency in the system;
- unnecessary inventory caused through application of push logistic systems;
- unnecessary transportation and motion that exist due to the weak communication system.

Key differences between the Greek and UK PSCs

There are key region-dependent issues observed in the healthcare system structure implemented in these two diverse contexts, which specifically affect the pharmaceuticals delivery process. Powell Davies *et al* (2008) explained that the healthcare system in the UK focuses more on developing the primary healthcare settings in order to minimize UK National Health System (NHS) expenditure and improve patients' experience. Conversely, the healthcare system in Greece concentrates more on secondary healthcare provision because there is not enough capacity to offer developed primary healthcare services, as highlighted by Papanikolaou and Zygiaris (2012). These different structures in both country settings cause some specific issues during the medicine delivery process. Table 7.3 presents the emerging issues associated with the different healthcare systems that influence the PSC's effectiveness.

Table 7.3 Key issues associated with Greek and UK PSCs (adapted from Papalexi *et al*, 2020)

<table>
<tr><th colspan="2">The issues associated within the pharmaceutical supply chain</th></tr>
<tr><th>The UK context</th><th>The Greek context</th></tr>
<tr><td>Strong primary healthcare structure</td><td>Weak primary healthcare structure</td></tr>
<tr><td>Existence of multiple prescribers</td><td>Existence of only one prescriber – physicians</td></tr>
<tr><td>Differences in prescribing process
• Differences in prescribing practices between nurse practitioners and physicians</td><td>More 'privatized' healthcare system
• Non-existence of family physicians serving as gatekeepers to more specialized care</td></tr>
<tr><td colspan="2">Increasing complexity of the PSC</td></tr>
<tr><td colspan="2">Increasing spending on pharmaceuticals</td></tr>
<tr><td colspan="2">Increasing level of wastage</td></tr>
<tr><td colspan="2">Difficulties in the healthcare providers' communication system</td></tr>
</table>

Although the UK and Greek healthcare systems have been structured in a different manner, based on the available resources and capacity, the issues emerging are similar (Table 7.3). One could conclude that system-related issues stem not from the system itself but from how it is managed. This view is also supported by:

- Sirmon *et al* (2011) and Brandon-Jones *et al* (2014) who suggested that orchestrating resources and capabilities across the supply chain could be very challenging, but at the same time it creates opportunities to develop an effective system and be competitive.
- Macinko *et al* (2003) explained that well-established primary care is associated with better population health, lower socio-economic inequality and higher rates of satisfied patients.
- Although developing primary care provision can lead to less expensive healthcare services through better control of the overall healthcare costs (Ansari *et al*, 2003), maintaining a strong primary care structure requires great investment (Rosano *et al*, 2011).

- Kringos *et al* (2013) highlighted that sustaining a high-performing primary care system is costly because developments have to be promoted, such as: decentralization of services delivery, an educational system for primary care professionals and protection of patients' rights.

Overcoming inefficiencies in the PSC

One of the core issues related to the PSC is associated with the complexity of the delivery process. This complexity is mainly derived from the particular characteristics of the products managed within this supply chain:

- **High value of product**: Cherrett *et al* (2012) explained that pharmaceuticals are considered to be highly expensive and sensitive products; their inappropriate use can convert them into dangerous or useless products due to their short expiration dates.
- **Stockout and stock expiration**: The existence of expired and unwanted medication increases the potential threat to human health and the ecological environment, as suggested by Papalexi *et al* (2017) and Wang *et al* (2015). In addition, those products are perceived as waste, which means that they need to be disposed of. This action increases the cost within the PSC; medical waste was estimated to be $13.3 billion in 2020 (Markets and Markets Research, 2018). Papalexi *et al* (2020) and Xie and Breen (2014) highlighted the importance of managing both the forward and reverse components of the delivery process in order to reduce the waste associated with pharmaceuticals and prevent their negative effect on society. However, the literature indicates that the management of those products could be very challenging due to their variety and variation (Tran *et al*, 2014).
- **Variety of demand and product range**: In addition, Mustaffa and Potter (2009) reported that the main root of the medicine delivery process's inefficiency is related to the existing difficulties in predicting exact demand. They explained this further, stating that those difficulties are derived from the lack of standard nomenclature and the fact that those products are stored in several areas within healthcare organizations. Pharmacies, therefore, need to develop and improve not only the forward but also the reverse components of the logistics process in order to synchronize the products' characteristics with the organization's environment and as a result satisfy their customers' needs (Cardoso *et al*, 2013; Fawcett *et al*, 2014).

Within this context there are several considerations to improve PSC efficiency:

- **Focus on reverse supply chain management (RSCM)**: The aim of RSCM is to manage the activities required effectively in order to retrieve useless products from the market and subsequently dispose of them or recover their value (Prahinski and Kocabasoglu, 2006; Defee *et al*, 2009). In particular, RSCM supports organizational sustainability focusing on three primary components: economic, social, and environmental (Robins, 2006). By implementing RSCM within the PSC, healthcare organizations would be able to reduce healthcare spending on pharmaceuticals and increase the quality of healthcare services. The data collected from reverse logistics could actively inform the supply and replenishment of medicines. Breen and Xie (2009) highlighted that these data could also be used to inform and assess the efficiency of the prescribing and dispensing process.
- **Inclusion of information-sharing practices across PSC**: One output of this data analysis could be the effective prediction of market demand and the associated cost. The success rate of this initiative requires effective communication and knowledge and information sharing between the PSC stakeholders (Figure 7.3). Figure 7.3 also shows that the suggested innovative programmes need to be supported by integrated IT systems that can facilitate the delivery process through enhancing the communication between the PSC partners.

These improvements can be undertaken through orchestrating the organization's resources and capabilities (Drucker, 2014) without significantly disrupting the way that healthcare personnel tend to operate. On the contrary, those initiatives can improve communication, synchronization and transparency throughout the PSC; enhance knowledge and information sharing, which will positively affect the prescribing and dispensing processes; minimize the perceived waste and as a result lead to continuous improvements and subsequently to a competitive advantage. Breen (2006) reported that enhancing communication can positively influence the management of returns. Erol *et al* (2010) found that the main reason for adopting RSCM within the PSC is mostly due to legislative liabilities. Álvarez-Gil *et al* (2007) stated that pressures from external stakeholders, such as the government, affect organizations' decisions to apply return policies. Breen and Xie (2015: 89) explained that 'in the case of recycling engagement, performance can be influenced by organizational policies and procedures informed by strategy, but also by the personal principles and convictions held by staff.'

- **Develop a lean strategy**: There is a need for integrating RSCM practices within an overarching operational strategy in order for them to be communicated effectively across the PSC, influencing staff and customers' culture. This could be achieved by providing the required knowledge and information related to those practices, highlighting their importance. Chen *et al* (2012) stated that knowledge and education raise consciousness of recycling.
  - According to Cheng *et al* (2015) and Govindan *et al* (2015), the adoption of lean approaches can overcome the issues of lack of communication and limited knowledge and information sharing within organizations. Brandão de Souza (2009) and Martínez-Jurado and Moyano-Fuentes (2014), among others, defined lean as an improvement philosophy aiming to reduce the perceived waste existing in a system, while improving the quality of products and services. There are a number of lean tools and techniques that can be adapted to fit in with organizations' needs and environment, such as value stream mapping (VSM), just-in-time (JIT), Kanban, Benchmarking and PDSA cycles (Baczewski, 2005; Bamford and Greatbanks, 2005).

Figure 7.3 The integrated information systems in PSC (adapted from Papalexi, 2017)

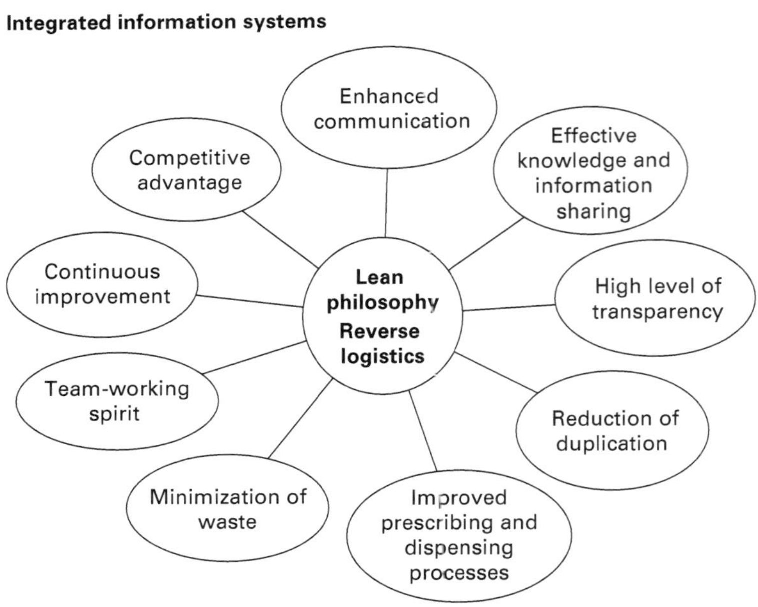

Figure 7.4 The conceptual framework of the discussion (adapted from Papalexi, 2017)

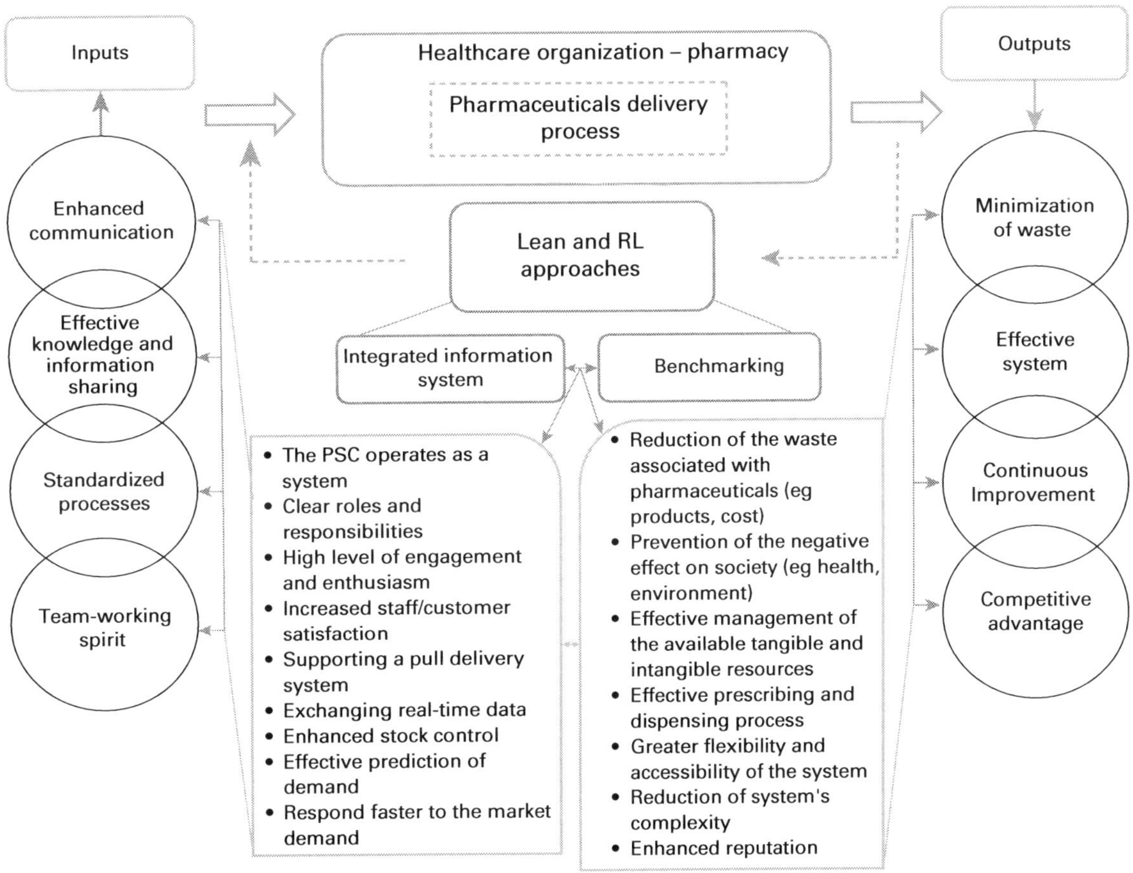

In particular, the combination of lean and reverse logistics (RL) approaches can benefit pharmacies in both contexts because, on the one hand, they seek to deal with the identified issues, and on the other, they do not require great investments. Pharmacies in both countries have the capacity and capabilities required, such as staff and equipment, to adopt and fit these approaches to their own needs. The only challenge that they have to face refers to the integration of the new practices across the PSC. They need to involve these approaches into their organizational strategy and communicate their mission and vision to their supply chain partners. Benchmarking can help them to take this forward, as it provides best practices for implementing innovative programmes, highlighting the associated benefits.

From an operations management perspective, the pharmaceutical delivery process can be represented by an input, transformation and output operation. Figure 7.4 presents the transformation process for improving the pharmaceutical delivery process and subsequently the quality of healthcare services. This figure describes how pharmacies can overcome the issues associated with delivery process inefficiency, presents the areas that can be improved through implementing lean and RL practices, and highlights the benefits that can be achieved. In particular, if the recommended innovative programmes are implemented throughout the pharmaceutical delivery process, the emphasis will be placed on improving the communication system, exchanging knowledge and relevant information, promoting standardized processes and operating under a teamworking umbrella.

The outputs of adopting this innovative approach will be the minimization of any type of perceived waste in the delivery system, a continuous improvement philosophy, a high level of service quality and, as a result, healthcare organizations will be able to compete with and sustain an advantage over their competitors. As Figure 7.4 shows, lean and RL approaches need to be supported by integrated information systems (IS), which facilitate communication between the PSC stakeholders, enabling them to exchange real-time data and respond faster to market demand. In addition, benchmarking is a useful tool for healthcare organizations, as they can use it to assess different supply chains and adopt the best practices that fit within their environment. It is believed that the adoption of this framework supports the optimization of the medicine delivery process in both contexts.

Learning outcomes

- This case explores the downstream domain of the PSC and highlights its complexity and perceived inefficiency.
- The case analyses the medicines delivery system employed within two diverse geographical areas and presents the differences between them.
- The case recommends that the adoption of innovative approaches can deal with the systems' inefficiency.
- The case highlights the importance of managing the forward and reverse logistics for creating a successful supply chain.

Questions

1. What are the issues observed within the PSC?
2. What are the key region-dependent issues observed within the UK and Greek healthcare systems?
3. Why can innovative approaches such as lean and reverse logistics potentially provide a solution? Is there any other solution that you can think of?

References

Álvarez-Gil, M *et al* (2007) Reverse logistics, stakeholders' influence, organizational slack, and managers' posture, *Journal Of Business Research*, **60** (5), pp 463–73

Ansari, Z *et al* (2003) The Victorian ambulatory care sensitive conditions study: rural and urban perspectives, *Soz Praventivmed*, **48** (1), pp 33–43

Baczewski, R A (2005) Four methods for improving performance: a comparison, *Healthcare Financial Management*, **59** (7), pp 101–03

Bamford, D and Greatbanks, R (2005) The use of quality management tools and techniques: a study of application in everyday situations, *International Journal of Quality & Reliability Management*, **2** (4), pp 376–92

Brandão de Souza, L (2009) Trends and approaches in lean healthcare, *Leadership in Health Services*, **22** (2), pp 121–39

Brandon-Jones, E *et al* (2014) A contingent resource-based perspective of supply chain resilience and robustness, *Journal of Supply Chain Management*, **50** (3), pp 55–73

Breen, L and Xie, Y (2009) Examining the role of the customer in facilitating reverse logistics system in NHS community pharmacy in the UK, *Proceedings of the Logistics Research Network annual conference*, Cardiff, pp 588–91

Breen, L (2006) Give me back my empties or else! A preliminary analysis of customer compliance in reverse logistics practices (UK), *Management Research News*, **29** (9), pp 532–51

Breen, L and Xie, Y (2015) Waste not, want not. What are the drivers of sustainable medicines recycling in National Health Service hospital pharmacies (UK)? *International Journal of Project Management*, **8** (1/2), p 82

Cardoso, S, Barbosa-Póvoa, A and Relvas, S (2013) Design and planning of supply chains with integration of reverse logistics activities under demand uncertainty, *European Journal of Operational Research*, **226** (3), pp 436–51

Chen, X *et al* (2012) [accessed 7 July 2021] Perceived Exposure to Environmental Harm Influences Environmental Behaviour in Urban China, *Royal Swedish Academy of Sciences* [Online] http://csis.msu.edu/sites/csis.msu.edu/files/ www.springerlink. com_content_q5t161n15q882p38_fulltext.pdf

Cheng, S *et al* (2015) Improving access to health services – challenges in Lean application, *International Journal Of Public Sector Management*, **28** (2), pp 121–35

Cherrett, T J *et al* (2012) Reverse logistics for the management of waste, in *Green Logistics: Improving the environmental sustainability of logistics*, ed A McKinnon *et al*, pp 242–62, Kogan Page, London

Defee, C *et al* (2009) The role of followers in supply chains, *Journal of Business Logistics*, **30** (2), pp 65–84

Drucker, P (2014) *Innovation and Entrepreneurship*, Routledge, New York

Erol, I *et al* (2010) Exploring reverse supply chain management practices in Turkey, *Supply Chain Management*, **15** (1), pp 43–54

Fawcett, S E, Ellram, L M and Ogden, J A (2014) *Supply Chain Management: From vision to implementation*, Pearson, Harlow

Govindan, K, Azevedo, S G and Carvalho, H (2015) Lean, green and resilient practices influence on supply chain performance: interpretive structural modelling approach, *International Journal of Environment Science and Technology*, **12**, pp 15–34

Jaberidoost, M *et al* (2013) [accessed 12 July 2021] Pharmaceutical supply chain risks: a systematic review, *DARU Journal of Pharmaceutical Sciences*, **21** (69) [Online] https://doi.org/10.1186/2008-2231-21-69 (archived at https://perma.cc/DG2T-6Y4D)

Jones, D T, Hines, P and Rich, N (1997) Lean logistics, *International Journal of Physical Distribution & Logistics*, **27** (3/4), pp 153–73

Kringos, D *et al* (2013) Europe's strong primary care systems are linked to better population health but also to higher health spending, *Health Affairs*, **32** (4), pp 686–94

Macinko, J, Starfield, B and Shi, L (2003) The contribution of primary care systems to health outcomes within Organization for Economic Cooperation and Development (OECD) countries, 1970–1998, *Health Services Research Journal*, **38** (3), pp 831–65

Martínez-Jurado, P and Moyano-Fuentes, J (2014) Lean management, supply chain management and sustainability: a literature review, *Journal of Cleaner Production*, **85**, pp 134–50

Markets and Markets Research (2018) [accessed 7 July 2021] Medical Waste Management Market, *Markets and Markets Research* [Online] www.marketsandmarkets.com/Market-Reports/medical-waste-management-market-1256.html (archived at https://perma.cc/L8CY-9YQA)

Mikulic, M (2019) [accessed 7 July 2021] Global Spending on Medicines from 2010, 2018 and a forecast for 2023 (in billion US dollars), *Statista* [Online] www.statista.com/statistics /280572/ medicine-spending-worldwide (archived at https://perma.cc/9LRB-LQSS)

Mustaffa, N H and Potter, A (2009) Healthcare supply chain management in Malaysia: a case study, *Supply Chain Management*, 14 (3), pp 234–43

OECD (2020) [accessed 7 July 2021] Health Statistics, *OECD* [Online] https://data.oecd.org/healthres/health-spending.htm#indicator-chart (archived at https://perma.cc/SH66-MLKA)

Ohno, T (1988) *The Toyota Production System: Beyond large-scale production*, Productivity Press, Portland, OR

Papalexi, M (2017) An Investigation into the Aspects of Innovation Within the Downstream Domain of the Pharmaceutical Supply Chain, PhD thesis, University of Huddersfield

Papalexi, M, Bamford, D and Breen, L (2020) Key sources of operational inefficiency in the PSC, *Supply Chain Management*, 25 (6), pp 617–35

Papalexi, M, Bamford, D and Dehe, B (2017) A case study of Kanban implementation within the pharmaceutical supply chain, *International Journal of Logistics Research and Applications*, **19** (4), pp 239–55

Papanikolaou, V and Zygiaris, S (2012) Service quality perceptions in primary health care centres in Greece, *Health Expectations*, **17** (2), pp 197–207

Powell Davies, G *et al* (2008) Coordinating primary health care: an analysis of the outcomes of a systematic review, *Medical Journal of Australia*, **188** (8), pp S65–S68

Prahinski, C and Kocabasoglu, C (2006) Empirical research opportunities in reverse supply chains, *Omega*, **34** (6), pp 519–32

Robins, F (2006) The challenge of TBL: a responsibility to whom? *Business and Society Review*, **111**, pp 1–14

Rosano, A *et al* (2011) Hospitalization for ambulatory care sensitive conditions and the role of primary care, *Italian Journal of Public Health*, **8** (1), pp 77–88

Rossetti, C, Handfield, R and Dooley, K (2011) Forces, trends, and decisions in pharmaceutical supply chain management, *International Journal of Physical Distribution & Logistics Management*, **41** (6), pp 601–22

Sirmon, D G *et al* (2011) Resource orchestration to create competitive advantage: breadth, depth, and life cycle effects, *Journal of Management*, **37** (5), pp 1390–412

Tran, N *et al* (2014) Suitability of artificial sweeteners as indicators of raw wastewater contamination in surface water and groundwater, *Water Research*, **48**, pp 443–56

Wang, Z *et al* (2015) Comprehensive evaluation of pharmaceuticals and personal care products (PPCPs) in typical highly urbanized regions across China, *Environmental Pollution*, **204**, pp 223–32

World Bank (2020a) [accessed 7 July 2021] World Development Indicators database – GB, *World Bank* [Online] https://data.worldbank.org/country/GB (archived at https://perma.cc/E39R-XPQ4)

World Bank (2020b) [accessed 7 July 2021] World Development Indicators database – Greece, *World Bank* [Online] https://data.worldbank.org/country/greece (archived at https://perma.cc/9BR9-SHJ2)

Xie, Y and Breen, L (2014) Who cares wins? A comparative analysis of household waste medicines and batteries reverse logistics systems, *Supply Chain Management*, **19** (4), pp 455–74

Packaging design and sustainability

08

The case of the paper packaging supply chain

DR NICOLETA S TIPI, OPEN UNIVERSITY, UK

DR ELIAS D GEORGAKOUDIS, MULTI-PACK S.A., GREECE

Introduction

This chapter introduces the role of packaging in the supply chain, describes its functions and focuses the discussion on paper packaging and its role in sustainability, packaging being a very important and integral element/part of any supply chain. Traditionally, the main function of packaging was to protect the product, but over the years this has developed further, with innovative venues for sustainability. In the following case study, a typical paper packaging supply chain is introduced and various options discussed from the point of view of sustainability.

Packaging design and sustainability

Packaging refers to products made of any material for the use of containment, protection, handling, delivery and presentation of goods, from the raw materials to processed goods, from the producer to the user or consumer, with the primary function being to protect the product until it is ready for use (Prendergast, 1995; Prendergast and Pitt, 1996). Therefore, packaging is a very important and integral element/part of any supply chain. Traditionally, packaging's main function was to protect and store the product. Over the years this notion has further developed, and we now can see the function of packaging developing from protecting, containing and handling the product to playing a key role in transporting it, with varied implications for the transportation function. Packaging also provides relevant information about the product; it incorporates several roles, ranging from a marketing and display role to a supporting and promoting innovation role and can carry out a key role in sustainability. Here, we can also mention the role of packaging in promotion, since an effectively designed package may attract the consumer and increase sales. Furthermore, there is a major packaging role in marketing, which has developed in recent years with the use of modern technologies such as RFID tags. Such uses include interaction between two (tagged) packages or an increase in safety, which adds further uses for this kind of packaging. García-Arca *et al* (2017) indicate that packaging should be designed not only to differentiate the product but also to bring simplification to the logistics activities in the supply chain and have a positive role in sustainability by reducing the negative impact on the environment and society.

Looking at the packaging function, packaging becomes waste as soon as the product reaches its destination. Eurostat (2018) indicates that:

- In 2018 the waste generated per inhabitant was estimated to be an average of 174 kg in the 27 European Union (EU) Member States, compared to a total of 156.7 kg reported in 2015 (Monnot *et al*, 2019).
- There were variations in the amount of waste generated by European countries. For example, 227.5 kg of waste was generated per inhabitant in Germany, whereas it was 67.8 kg in Croatia.
- In the UK, 178.08 kg of waste were recorded, with a total of 110.55 kg being recycled.
- The waste generated by packaging material was 40.9% for paper and cardboard, 19% for plastic, followed by 18.7% for glass, 16.1% for wood and 5% for metal (see Figure 8.1).

Europe is promoting 'closing the loop' of the product life cycle with a target of recycling 65 per cent of municipal waste and 75 per cent of packaging waste by 2030 (European Commission, 2015). Hence, the context of packaging waste and what makes it count as waste rests on the characteristics of its constituents.

Figure 8.1 Packaging waste generated by packaging material in the EU-27, 2008–2018 (Eurostat, 2018)

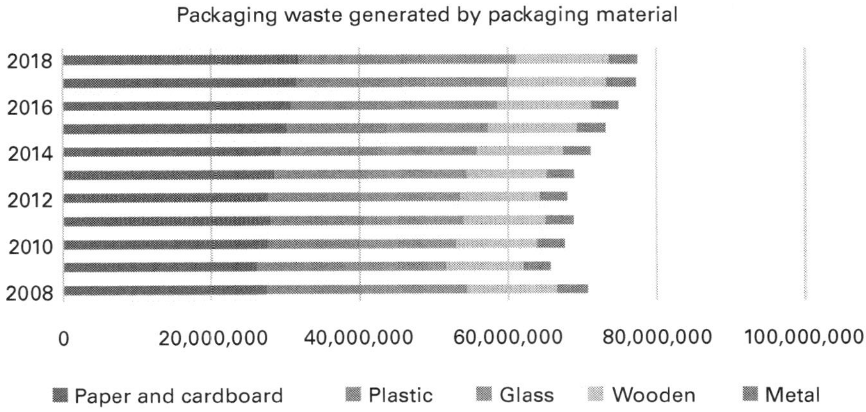

Packaging characteristics

With such a high percentage of waste generated by paper and cardboard packaging (see Figure 8.1 showing waste presented in tonnes per packaging material), it is relevant to further understand the role of packaging and the implications this has on the environment and on the supply chain. Therefore, below we explore packaging characteristics with a focus on sustainable development and supply chains. Some typical questions that come to mind when discussing packaging are:

- *Which packaging material is best for a particular product?* When answering this question, product and packaging designers are looking at product characteristics and life cycle, the characteristics and needs of the market where the product is going to be sold, the required durability, the storage conditions, the distance to be travelled, the modes of transport to be used, the final destination of the product, and so on.
- *What is the overall weight gained by a product when packaging is added?* Transport organizations and packaging manufacturers are concerned with this aspect when additional weight is being added to the overall transportation of products (Georgakoudis *et al*, 2018). Products carrying unnecessary weight will incur additional transportation costs as well as having an effect on CO_2 emissions.

- *At which point in the product design is packaging design input best incorporated?* Incorporating packaging design considerations earlier in product design decisions has the advantage of using optimum packaging design considerations that can have a primary role of product protection and at the same time contribute to the recovery and recycle function of the packaging used. In addition, well-designed and efficient packaging may further lower the capacity of the carried load and result in reduced CO_2 emissions per unit.
- *What role does packaging play in distributing products globally?* Packaging design decisions not only affect packaging manufacturers and their customers, but also transportation companies, shipping companies and warehouse operators situated far from the packaging manufacturers and product manufacturers as well as the final consumers.

With the complex function packaging plays in the supply chain, many other questions can be considered, some of which are detailed in the following sections of this chapter.

Types of packaging materials

As mentioned, there are five main types of packaging material (Figure 8.1) that are commonly used: paper and cardboard, plastic, glass, wood and metal. These are also used in combination, such as paper with plastic, or the main packaging material being plastic with a paper label, or metal with paper label, or plastic with metal cap, or wood with paper and so on. A mixed type of packaging is not as easy to categorize for recycling purposes; however, a number of materials have been recently developed that consider recycled plastic, and there are packaging materials that incorporate textiles. In general, there are three levels of packaging and they all play a key role in the packaging supply chain (see Figure 8.3).

Primary packaging

Primary packaging is the first layer used to pack the product, or in other words, the packaging which comes in direct contact with the product itself. The purpose of the primary packaging is to contain and protect the product. In cases where product details are directly printed on the primary packaging, we see packaging being used as a communication tool, having the role of providing information such as nutritional information, content details, expiry date and weight, and can also be used for advertising and display. Sometimes, the primary packaging can be considered as the packaging that a consumer sees in a shop. However, this is not always the case, especially when the product is sensitive or has an irregular shape and needs a secondary packaging in order to be placed on the shelf. We see examples of each type of material being used as primary packaging, such as paper to pack food products (eg sugar), paper to protect a book or magazine, paper envelopes which are also a form of primary packaging and many other examples. Glass, for example, is the primary packaging for beer, wine, jam, perfume and so on. Plastic is used in many examples as primary packaging, for cereals, water, milk, household chemicals, medicine (see Figure 8.2) and a large number of other products in daily use. Metal is frequently used for products such as drinks, and for other products such as aerosols, paint, glue and many others. Wood has also been introduced in primary packaging for food-type products, industrial goods or more sophisticated products of high value. In general, primary packaging is handled at the manufacturing point, at the retail point in the supply chain and by the final consumer.

Figure 8.2 Primary and secondary packaging

Secondary packaging

Secondary packaging is the packaging used outside the primary packaging (see Figure 8.2). For example cereals can be first packed in a plastic bag followed by a cardboard box as a secondary packaging; or medication is first packed in a combination of plastic and metal material followed by a cardboard box as secondary packaging; or a set of shampoo bottles are packed first in plastic bottles which are then packed in a cardboard box as secondary packaging; or beer cans are the primary packaging and the cover box that keeps them together is the secondary packaging. Secondary packaging is also used to group a set of products together to form a stock keeping unit (SKU) and is used to handle small shipments. With the example given for medicine, the secondary packaging can collate a number of smaller sets of products into a single bigger pack to enable the customer to better handle and store these products. The secondary packaging can also be the corrugated cardboard box that contains a number of smaller primary packaging containers. As in the case of primary packaging, secondary packaging can also be used to carry information about the product it contains, it can be specifically designed to meet a particular marketing function, it can use particular colours and designs to attract attention, or it can be designed in such a way as to minimize the space it occupies on a retail shelf. The secondary packaging provides additional protection to a product by helping to prevent damage to the primary packaging and therefore to the main product. Secondary packaging can also prevent situations such as pilferage, which is very common, especially in long supply chains. In the supply chain, secondary packaging appears at most points from manufacturing to distribution, warehouse, transport and retail, and in some cases the final consumer comes into contact with the primary as well as secondary packaging.

Tertiary packaging

Tertiary packaging is the packaging that collects a number of secondary packaged items such as SKUs and prepares them for transportation (see Figure 8.3). When products are grouped in this format, they need to be handled, for example, on the journey from a manufacturing facility to a warehouse, or from a warehouse to a retail centre, using various modes of transport. Typically, consumers of primary products do not come in contact with tertiary packaging; however, industrial customers at warehouses, distribution centres and retailer points as well as transport companies do handle tertiary packaging. As final consumers do not come in contact with tertiary packaging, there is no need for marketing considerations in the design of

Figure 8.3 Different stages of packaging before a product reaches the final consumer

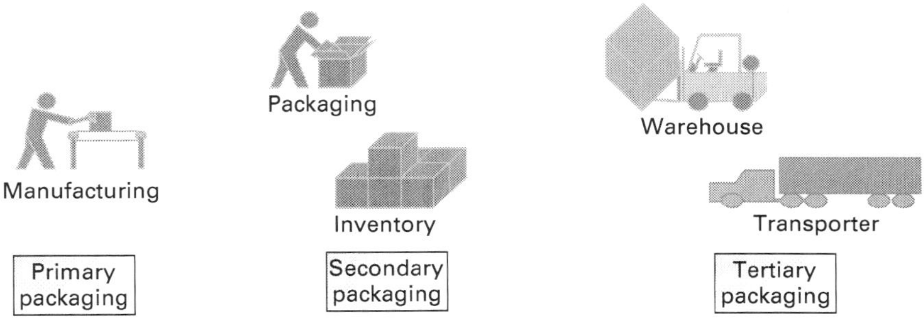

this packaging. Tertiary packaging can be anything from a large box containing a number of smaller secondary packaged items to a full pallet formed of stakes of corrugated boxes, secured with a streaked plastic wrap. Their primary objective is to protect the shipment when it is in transit, and to allow for easy movement of inventory and storage when products in this format are being transported as well as stored in a warehouse.

Figure 8.4 Damaged secondary packaging

It is important to note that damage to secondary packaging (see Figure 8.4) will have a negative effect on the primary packaging, but it can have a negative impact on the tertiary packaging as well.

Other terminology

Other terminology used to refer to packaging (as presented in Gustafsson *et al*, 2006) is *consumer and sales packaging* which are seen in Gustafsson *et al* (2006) as primary packaging. There is a reference here to *transport packaging* that mainly refers to the type of packaging designed for transportation handling. Like transportation packaging, we see references to *industrial packaging*, *bulk packaging*, *container and distribution packaging*. Reference to *display packaging* and *retail packaging* is made here that make a reference to tertiary packaging. It is also relevant to note the reference made in Gustafsson *et al* (2006) to *used packaging*, *waste packaging* and *returnable packaging*. Each of these packaging types and aspects is particularly important to protect the product, therefore it is relevant to consider packaging decisions from the start of product development and how this product will be transported and handled in the supply chain. Returning and reusing the packaging material should also be given consideration when designing a product. Some of these elements are further discussed later in this chapter.

Packaging function

As previously introduced, one of the primary roles of packaging is 'to protect' the product from contamination, damage, spillage, breakages, weather conditions such as high or low temperature and humidity, or when products need to be refrigerated. Packaging has the function 'to contain' the product. Packaging is used for products in liquid, gas or dry form to contain them, such as beverages, detergent, facial creams, aerosols and spray paints, to list just a few. This function is also seen when more than one product is grouped together to be sold as a unit, for example vegetables, eggs, or bulk products such as rice and sugar; although the product can be handled by the consumer as an individual product, they are grouped for displaying, handling and selling the set as a single unit (see Figure 8.5).

Figure 8.5 Food primary packaging containers

The role of packaging

The packaging may serve different roles and have different purposes (see Figure 8.6), such as:

- Marketing purposes: Packaging is used for marketing purposes, to promote a product and improve the attractiveness of the product. A customer will recognize a product based on the packaging, logo and colour used to identify it. A very attractive design may result in increased sales while poorly designed packaging may not be appealing to the final consumer. For marketing purposes, for a well-known global brand, we often see changes in packaging to meet local needs, such as changes in the language used to describe the product, in some cases the colour used, storage conditions and other things.
- Differentiation purposes: Packaging is used to differentiate a product. A product, for example a soft drink, may carry the same brand as others, with many similar characteristics (weight, shape, some of the main ingredients, place of manufacturing), but it could be of a different flavour (for example, lemon flavour versus orange flavour), and this is represented in packaging. Another example is the different colours used in the cap of some products such as aerosol paint, which correspond to the colour of the paint included in order to facilitate the consumer's selection.
- Transport facilitation purposes: Packaging has the role of facilitating transportation and can be designed for easy handling. A smart packaging design will give consideration to the shape of the packaging used so that it is easy to carry, easy to store, has the correct durability to protect the product it carries and is easy to handle in transportation.

Figure 8.6 The main roles of packaging

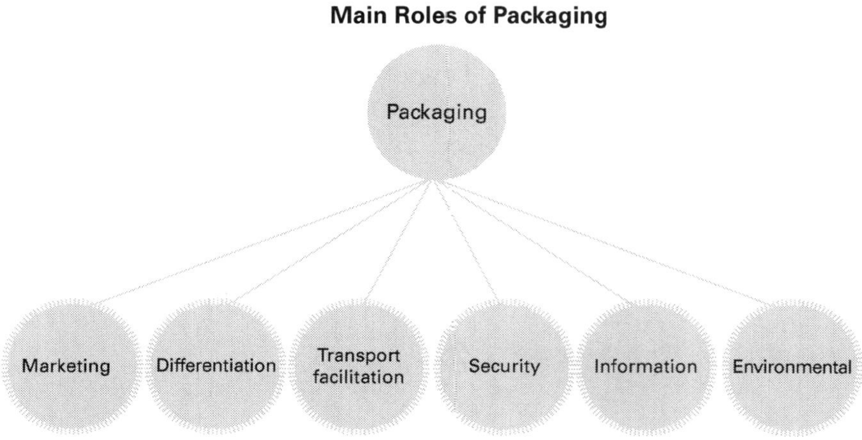

- Security purposes: Security is also attributed to packaging as a key characteristic. An intact box indicates that there was no interference with the product inside the package.
- Information purposes: Packaging has the function to provide information about specific characteristics of the product: ingredients, place of origin, expiry date of the products it contains, net and gross weight and so on. This way, packaging is used to connect and communicate with customers.
- Environmental purposes: Packaging has an environmental role. The way the packaging is designed and the types of material used to form the packaging give an indication of how these could be reused, recycled and, if the packaging ends up in landfill, how long it will take for the packaging to decompose.

Packaging in the supply chain

Looking at the supply chain functions and their characteristics, it can be observed that packaging has a key role in the majority of the functions in the supply chain. Packaging is present in the supply function, from transporting raw materials to their customers, from customers, industrial customers making informed decisions when purchasing products, raw material for production. As previously exemplified, packaging is key in facilitating the transportation function.

In product design and manufacturing, packaging is embedded in the process of manufacturing from product level to SKU and managing inventory.

Products are identified by the barcode that is printed on the product packaging. This is directly connected to the enterprise resource planning (ERP) system and information technology (IT) supply chain system until the product reaches the final consumer. Packaging is present in the distribution of the product as well as in the warehouse(s), where the product waits until it is delivered to the retailer and its final destination. Considering the reverse supply chain, packaging has a similar key function in containing and protecting the returned product(s), in facilitating transportation based on the selected function of return, recycle, or packaging being reused to transport a new set of products. However, we have to mention that in reverse supply chains some major packaging operations, such as the protection of the product, its promotion or the safety of the contained product, have disappeared after the package has reached its destination or after it has been opened.

Packaging and sustainability

As observed in the previous sections, packaging is present in most aspects of the supply chain. Looking at the typical paper packaging supply chain system, it is evident from observing the supply chain from a packaging point of view, that other aspects can be emphasized. In the example shown in Figure 8.7 there is the assumption that the starting point is from a raw material supplier of recycled paper packaging, but this chain can be further extended to indicate the manufacture of paper.

Figure 8.7 An example of a paper packaging supply chain

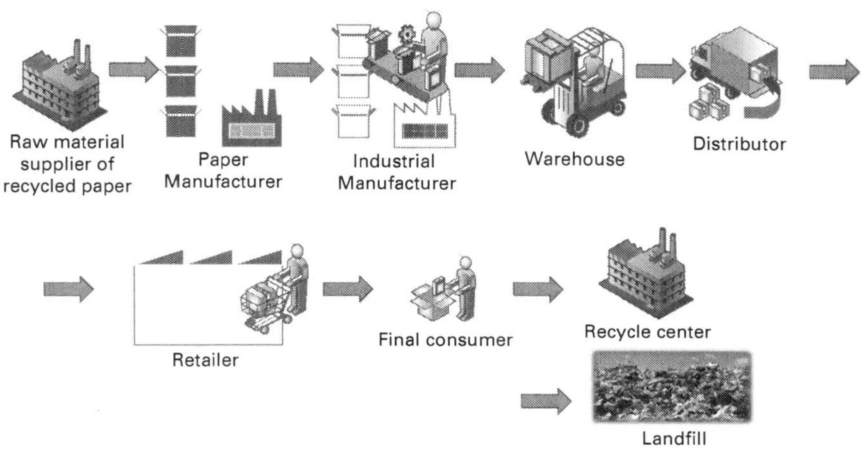

Packaging improvements that could be incorporated to reach sustainability could come from several stages in the packaging supply chain. The recycled paper processor could consider collection points from a larger number of suppliers. The paper manufacturer could incorporate order decisions to meet the requirements of the entire chain and take into consideration product characteristics when designing the packaging. Industrial manufacturers are making use of packaging for most of their products. Some opportunities for optimizing the use of packaging by the industrial manufacturer are: to incorporate packaging design decisions earlier in the product design process; eliminate unnecessary packaging, based on the product it carries, working to reduce the bullwhip effect and operate only with the volume of packaging required; return or repurpose unused packaging, and many others. Packaging is present at warehouses, distribution centres and retail sites. Packaging reduction, recycle or reuse opportunities are present at these points in the supply chain as well. Opportunities for reuse, recycle or upcycle of packaging material are present at the end-consumer point. The main scope is to minimize the volume of packaging material sent to the landfill (see Figure 8.7).

Other opportunities for sustainability that can be considered are linked to the selection of packaging material. Packaging selection is one of the key approaches in ensuring a reduction in packaging waste and therefore a reduction in resource depletion (Almeida *et al*, 2017). In the case of the paper packaging supply chain, in the majority of cases, packaging can be manufactured from recycled paper material. Here we should underline that, from an environmental point of view, the use of recycled paper is not always the most important issue since the selection of paper that could be further recyclable is important too. For example, coated paper may not be recyclable, especially when it has a plastic coating or, in some cases, it may include materials that need more energy or water in order to be able to be recycled.

Sustainability issues can be observed in the issue of *overpackaging* as discussed in Georgakoudis and Tipi (2020), where solutions on how to rethink the design of packaging products to consider using less material, while maintaining all the other packaging functions, offer a solution on how overpackaging can be avoided. Escursell *et al* (2021) summarize their review research and indicate that policies to avoid overpackaging should be further considered by organizations and their supply chains.

Conclusion

A general case of a paper packaging supply chain has been discussed here, with some of the challenges that are associated with product design, supply chain design and sustainability. Packaging is present in the majority of supply chains, where paper packaging appears at various stages. As the most commonly used packaging material, paper can be transformed into numerous shapes and gives solutions to multiple problems. It is therefore relevant to consider at what level of supply chain design and product design packaging can be incorporated in the design decisions.

At every stage in the supply chain there is an opportunity for optimization (Tipi, 2021) that will have a direct effect on packaging. In fact, this is one of the biggest challenges for the designers: the chance to adjust the packaging in order to be efficient throughout the supply chain. The paper packaging introduced in the supply chain by the packaging manufacturer will most probably be returned in a new chain, in a different location, based on the types of product and their destination to the final customer. While environmental protection becomes more and more of a global issue and as there is a dramatic growth in laws to protect the environment, imported products are causing environmental effects in local supply chains. A well-designed packaging focusing not only on its primary aims mentioned above, but also, for example, on the use of materials that can be easily recycled, is becoming more and more important and is easily identifiable by consumers. It should be underlined that a successful product is one that is being sold, and while consumers are becoming highly educated and strongly conscious of the environment, the product that meets their expectations will be the winner in the field.

Learning outcomes

- Provide an understanding of the current situation linked to packaging, with specific reference to paper packaging.
- Bring the key characteristics of sustainability into the discussion linked to packaging in the supply chain.
- Discuss the potential for sustainability from the point of view of paper packaging.

Questions

1. Primary and secondary packaging design has the potential to influence sales for a particular product or set of products. By selecting a product from the food industry, evaluate its packaging needs from a supply chain perspective. What considerations should be given to packaging to make this more sustainable?
2. Packaging is present along different points in the supply chain as well as in the reverse supply chain. As a paper packaging manufacturer, what packaging design aspects would you consider essential? Explain your answer.
3. Supply chain organizations are keen to maintain their sustainability goals. Which do you think are the most important goals from a packaging point of view and why? Explain your answer.

References

Almeida, C M V B *et al* (2017) Material selection for environmental responsibility: the case of soft drinks packaging in Brazil, *Journal of Cleaner Production*, **142**, pp 173–79.

Escursell, S, Llorach-Massana, P and Roncero, M B (2021) Sustainability in e-commerce packaging: a review, *Journal of Cleaner Production*, **280**, doi:10.1016/j.jclepro.2020.124314 (archived at https://perma.cc/Y5RW-BC2J)

European Commission (2015) [accessed 7 July 2021] Closing the Loop: Commission Adopts Ambitious New Circular Economy Package to Boost Competitiveness, Create Jobs and Generate Sustainable Growth, *European Commission* [Online] https://ec.europa.eu/commission/presscorner/detail/en/IP_15_6203 (archived at https://perma.cc/3769-ZKCY), Accessed 3rd April 2021

Eurostat (2018) [accessed 7 July 2021] Packaging waste statistics – Statistics Explained (europa.eu), *Eurostat* [Online] https://ec.europa.eu/eurostat/statistics-explained/index.php?title=Packaging_waste_statistics (archived at https://perma.cc/T3AF-5GRR)

García-Arca, J, Garrido, A and Prado-Prado, J (2017) Sustainable packaging logistics: the link between sustainability and competitiveness in supply chains, *Sustainability* (Basel, Switzerland), **9** (7), p 1098

Georgakoudis, E and Tipi, N (2020) An investigation into the issue of overpackaging – examining the case of paper packaging, *The International Journal of Sustainable Engineering*, **13** (1), pp 1–10, doi:10.1080/19397038.2020.1780337

Georgakoudis, E, Tipi, N S and Bamford, C (2018) European packaging regulations and the environment – a case of a Greek packaging supply chain system, *International Journal of Sustainable Engineering*, **11** (5), pp 307–20, doi:10.1080/19397038.2018.1445789

Gustafsson, K *et al* (2006) *Retailing Logistics and Fresh Food Packaging: Managing change in the supply chain*, Kogan Page, London

Monnot, E *et al* (2019) 'Thinking outside the packaging box': should brands consider store shelf context when eliminating overpackaging? *Journal of Business Ethics*, **154** (2), pp 355–70, doi:10.1007/s10551-017-3439-0

Prendergast, G (1995) The logistical implications of the EC directive on packaging and packaging waste, *Logistics Information Management*, **8** (3), pp 10–17

Prendergast, G and Pitt, L (1996) Packaging, marketing, logistics and the environment: are there tradeoffs? *International Journal of Physical Distribution & Logistics Management*, **26** (6), pp 60–72

Tipi, N (2021) *Supply Chain Analytics and Modelling: Quantitative tools and applications*, Kogan Page, London

Factors affecting sustainability adoption in small and medium-sized manufacturing enterprises (SMMEs) in Vietnam 09

HUY Q PHAN, BRISTOL BUSINESS SCHOOL, UNIVERSITY OF THE WEST OF ENGLAND, UK

PROF MOHAMMED SAAD, BRISTOL BUSINESS SCHOOL, UNIVERSITY OF THE WEST OF ENGLAND, UK

PROF VIKAS KUMAR, BRISTOL BUSINESS SCHOOL, UNIVERSITY OF THE WEST OF ENGLAND, UK

Introduction

This chapter is presented as an investigative study undertaken by the authors, including 58 Vietnamese small and medium-sized manufacturing enterprises

(SMMEs) and their sustainable SCM practices. Several factors may influence the level of sustainability engagement among SMMEs due to various external and internal moderating effects, such as:

- Sustainability has gained substantial attention in recent years. However, despite its growing popularity in developing countries such as Vietnam, sustainability has not yet been widely explored.
- In Vietnam, SMEs account for 97% of the country's total companies (Tran and Jeppesen, 2016) and play a vital role in the economy by creating jobs and helping reduce poverty. Specifically, Vietnamese SMEs have created over half a million new jobs, account for over 51% of the labour force and contribute 40% of the GDP (Phan *et al*, 2015). Therefore, it is necessary to understand the circumstances under which SMEs, particularly in the manufacturing sector in developing countries, address sustainability practices (Hasan, 2016; Jamali, Lund-Thomsen and Khara, 2017).
- The adoption rates of green SCM practices shown are impacted by the tax system, employee resistance and firm size, while customer pressure significantly impacts the level of social sustainability engagement.

Therefore, this chapter introduces the SMMEs investigation of 58 Vietnamese SMEs based on the triple bottom line (TBL) performance measures, including economic, social and environmental factors.

Background

Over the past decade, sustainability has become increasingly significant in business research and practice (Hassini, Surti and Searcy, 2012). The main objective of sustainable development is to '[meet] the present's needs without compromising the ability of future generations to meet their own needs' (World Commission on Economic Development, 1987: 43). Though the concept of sustainability applies to all types of businesses, regardless of size or sector, it has been predominantly discussed and implemented in the context of larger corporations (Searcy, 2012; Johnson and Schaltegger, 2016). Moreover, the concept has mostly been discussed in developed countries such as the United States, the UK, Europe and Japan (Hassini, Surti and Searcy, 2012; McMurray *et al*, 2014). Although SMEs play a vital role in the growth and development of a country and make up the most significant component of the business community (Mabhungu and Van Der Poll, 2017), limited attention has been paid to their sustainability practices. There is still a significant gap in the literature in the specific context of small and medium-sized manufacturing enterprises (SMMEs) in developing countries (Hasan, 2016; Jamali, Lund-Thomsen and Khara, 2017). A specific investigation of sustainability practices in SMMEs in developing countries is vital for the following two reasons:

1 Developing countries account for 80% of the world's population and are expected to play a central role in ensuring sustainable development in the 21st century (Organisation for Economic Co-operation and Development, 2019), with sustainability receiving little attention (Barkemeyer, 2011; Anisul Huq, Stevenson and Zorzini, 2014).
2 Large corporations are currently adopting sustainability strategies in their manufacturing operations due to pressure from consumers, regulators and the community. Thus, these companies have extended these practices to their suppliers to achieve higher sustainability performance within their supply chains (Lee and Klassen, 2008). Eighty per cent of these suppliers are SMMEs (Singh, Olugu and Musa, 2016) that are increasingly under pressure to enhance their sustainability performance to contribute to sustainability in the supply chain (Revell and Blackburn, 2007; Bourlakis *et al*, 2014; Hsu, Chang and Luo, 2017).

Understanding the TBL and its impact on SMMEs

The term sustainability is frequently used in connection with the TBL in business research (Marrewijk and Werre, 2002; Montiel, 2008; Amini and Bienstock, 2014). The concept suggests that corporations should not only focus on the economic value they add but also consider the social and environmental value that they deliver or compromise (Elkington, 2001; Assaf, Josiassen and Cvelbar, 2012; Gimenez, Sierra and Rodon, 2012). Accordingly, firms adopting the TBL approach may capture a whole set of values, issues and processes to maximize the positive impact of their sustainability-related practices (Elkington, 1997). Furthermore, firms should address all three pillars of TBL in an integrated manner to ensure sustainable development (Slaper and Hall, 2011; Khurana, Haleem and Mannan, 2019), because tackling any one of the dimensions in isolation may result in unintended consequences in the other dimensions (Rachuri *et al*, 2009). From a holistic perspective, the TBL approach is a unified sustainability concept of business activity performance (Elkington, 2001; Slaper and Hall, 2011).

Stakeholders are increasingly evaluating a business's performance from the TBL perspective (Azapagic, 2003; Searcy, 2012). Therefore, firms have been advised to accept stakeholder pressure by adopting TBL sustainability measures to demonstrate higher accountability in environmental and social issues in addition to economic activities (Roxas and Chadee, 2012; Høgevold *et al*, 2015; Elkington, 1997; Cordano *et al*, 2010; Shevchenko *et al*, 2016; Wiengarten *et al*, 2017). As such, stakeholder pressure is considered a primary factor in forcing firms to fulfil their responsibilities and commitments towards environmental, social and economic impacts that result from their operations (Markley and Davis, 2007; De Giovanni, 2012; Govindan *et al*, 2013). Notwithstanding, it is still assumed that stakeholders are commonly associated with large corporations, whereas SMEs are favoured by shareholders (Jenkins, 2006; Russo and Perrini, 2010). However, this perspective has been challenged by corporate sustainability studies, which have demonstrated that firms of all sizes have stakeholder interests as a priority (Azmat, 2010). In line with this reasoning, it is important to understand and respond to stakeholders' requirements, and firms have to demonstrate corporate sustainability progress (Harding, 2006; Jamali and Mirshak, 2007). However, stakeholders are diverse and varied and may have different expectations (Polonsky, 1995) and conflicting interests (Adams and Frost, 2008; Dobers and Halme, 2009). For example, some stakeholders (decision makers and non-specialists) may demand simple, structured information. In contrast, others (such as NGOs and industries) may need an intermediate level of detail, and academics and policymakers may prefer technical information (Hák, Janoušková and Moldan, 2016). Ideally, sustainability information should reach the target stakeholders.

Compared to larger counterparts, SMEs frequently have a smaller number of stakeholders (Preuss and Perschke, 2010). By their very nature, SMEs have close relationships with key players (Perrini and Tencati, 2006) and are highly dependent on them for survival (Fuller and Lewis, 2002). Nejati *et al* (2014) emphasize that stakeholders' roles in fostering SMEs' sustainability engagement should not be underestimated. Bansal (2005) argues that valuing relations with stakeholders is vital in a firm's strategy to move towards sustainability. More specifically, empirical studies provide ample evidence showing a relationship between stakeholders and SMEs' sustainability performance. For example, a survey by Nejati *et al* (2014) found that employees and customers are primary stakeholders who significantly influence the environmental performance of SMEs. Further, Massa *et al* (2015) identified managers as key stakeholders in determining the process of developing sustainability reports in

SMEs. The research reviewed here suggests that the approach to identifying SMEs' stakeholders must be simple (Garengo *et al*, 2005). Therefore, only crucial stakeholders should be taken into consideration when investigating SMMEs' sustainability practices.

SME sustainability practices and proposition development

SMEs are not scaled-down versions of larger corporations, due to their characteristics (Jenkins, 2006; Masurel, 2007; Darcy *et al*, 2014); these characteristics vary in different geographical regions (Ghazilla *et al*, 2015). Moreover, it is argued that these characteristics may enable or inhibit SMEs' engagement in sustainability practices; hence, for this reason, the following key enablers and inhibitors that impact sustainability practices in SMMEs, specifically in Vietnam, have been identified:

1 **Taxation system and its implications**: Many published studies describe the role of the institutional environment in emerging and developing countries, which is commonly weaker compared to that in developed nations (Dobers and Halme, 2009; Rettab *et al*, 2009; Hilson, 2012; Abdalla and Siti-Nabiha, 2015; Dissanayake *et al*, 2016). From a macro perspective, institutional voids are frequently recognized as barriers hindering sustainability initiatives for businesses (Silvestre, 2015). For example, Silvestre (2015) analysed institutional voids and sustainability trajectories in Brazil and concluded that the complexities of bureaucracy, corruption and intricate tax systems were problems that hindered economic development. SMEs' issues in other emerging economies are similar to those facing SMEs in Vietnam, particularly private enterprise laws. Taxation systems are overly complex and difficult to understand (Benzin *et al*, 2005; Nguyen *et al*, 2015). Based on these arguments, we formulate the first proposition:

   P1. Firms with owners and managers who believe that intricate tax systems affect their businesses are more likely to have a relatively lower level of SPE.

2 **Regulation and its enforcement implications**: Further, empirical evidence reveals that low enforcement of regulations in emerging economies hinders firms from engaging in sustainability practices. Cui *et al* (2015) found from a sample of 630 Chinese private firms that many firms that damage the environment have rarely been fined. Further, Anisul Huq *et al* (2014) noted a dilemma in the Bangladeshi ready-made garments industry. Although the

International Labour Organization convention allows only an eight-hour work shift and local laws limit overtime to two hours per day, these standards are not always adhered to locally. Although Vietnam has enacted some rules and regulations related to social and environmental aspects, in reality, most of them are routinely flouted, as they are weakly enforced by the pervasively corrupt authorities (Nguyen *et al*, 2015; Tran and Jeppesen, 2016). Based on this evidence, we explore the following proposition:

> *P2*. Firms with owners and managers who believe that there is a low level of regulation enforcement are more likely to have a relatively lower level of SPE.

3 **External market pressures and their implications**: External pressures are prominent factors driving firms to engage in sustainability practices. In a recent study, Jamali, Lund-Thomsen and Khara (2017) showed concern about the pressure of international buyers on manufacturing SMEs in developing countries. These buyers demand that firms lower their prices year after year, placing seasonal orders and asking for ever-shorter lead-times and flexibility in production, while labour wages and the prices of raw materials are on the rise (Jamali, Lund-Thomsen and Khara, 2017). This viewpoint was reinforced by Hasan's (2016) qualitative research which studied Bangladeshi SMMEs and found that customers were more concerned with cheaper prices and earning more profit than the value of sustainability activities of supply firms. However, what is not yet clear is the actual relationship between customer pressure and the level of sustainability practice engagement (SPE) in Vietnamese SMMEs. Based on these arguments, we formulate the following proposition:

> *P3*. Firms with owners and managers who believe that a cheaper product price, rather than sustainability issues, affects the buying decisions of customers are more likely to have a relatively lower level of SPE.

4 **Sustainability engagement benefits for SMEs**: There are indications in the literature that many SME owners and managers are aware that engagement in sustainability activities could provide cost reduction and waste and discharge reduction (Gadenne, Kennedy and McKeiver, 2009), enhancements of corporate image and reputation (Masurel, 2007), customer satisfaction (Garengo *et al*, 2005) and a better relationship with the local community (Tsalis *et al*, 2013). Other benefits and drivers include staff satisfaction and retention, partnership strengthening, the potential attraction of customers, resource efficiency (Revell and

Blackburn, 2007) and improvements in working conditions (Zorpas, 2010). Therefore, we formulate the following proposition:

> *P4.* Firms with owners and managers who believe that there are benefits associated with sustainability activities are more likely to have a relatively higher level of SPE.

5 **Sustainability financial implications for SMEs**: The adoption of sustainability practices requires financial resources (Jenkins, 2006; Palmer, Russell and McIntosh, 2012; Chen *et al*, 2014; Leonidou *et al*, 2017). However, SMEs may not have the financial resources to support such endeavours (Pedersen, 2009; Roxas and Chadee, 2012). SMEs tend to refrain from setting a separate sustainability budget to support sustainability activities beyond their core business operations (Jenkins, 2006; Palmer *et al*, 2012). Previous empirical studies support this argument. For example, Kallmuenzer *et al* (2017) studied Australian SMEs and found that most SME owners and managers were reluctant to adopt sustainability practices because they require additional human resources, resulting in higher costs. Lee (2009) conducted two case studies of South Korean SMEs and found that executives feared that early investment in green management would only become an extra cost burden without any financial rewards later. These results reinforced the following proposition:

> *P5.* Firms with owners and managers who believe that they do not have the financial resources to address sustainability issues are more likely to have a relatively lower level of SPE.

6 **Sustainability time consumption and its implications for SMEs**: Extant literature reveals that although SMEs may be willing to become more sustainable entrepreneurs, they find it difficult to devote the necessary time and effort (Roxas and Chadee, 2012; Singh, Olugu and Musa, 2016). Engagement in sustainability practices requires SMEs to invest substantial time in the writing, layout and printing of sustainability reports (Crals and Vereeck, 2005). According to Lepoutre and Heene (2006), many SMEs are deficient in the knowledge essential to implement sustainability initiatives, and they frequently do not have enough time to gather such knowledge. Hence, we formulate the following proposition:

> *P6.* Firms with owners and managers who believe that they do not have the time to address sustainability issues are more likely to have a relatively lower level of SPE.

7 **Sustainability knowledge and its implications for SMEs**: Engagement in sustainability practices requires prior knowledge (Ahi and Searcy, 2013; Høgevold *et al*, 2015), where SMEs may have limited knowledge to undertake sustainability initiatives. In a study of 3,626 Italian firms, Russo and Tencati (2009) noted that lack of sustainability knowledge was a barrier hindering SMEs' engagement in sustainability practices compared to their larger counterparts. The issues discussed are extremely relevant, interesting and challenging in the context of SMEs from developing countries, where SME owners' and managers' educational levels are frequently lower compared to those in developed countries (Nichter and Goldmark, 2009). Based on this argument, the following proposition was formulated:

> *P7*. Firms with owners and managers who believe that they do not have enough knowledge to address sustainability initiatives are more likely to have a relatively lower level of SPE.

8 **Sustainability support from external parties and its implications for SMEs**: SMEs could overcome the lack of sustainability knowledge by seeking support from external parties such as government, non-profit organizations (NGOs) and advocacy organizations (Hoogendoorn *et al* 2015). In Vietnam, Nguyen *et al* (2015) contended that firms had received little attention from external parties to develop sustainability. Indeed, government policies and external support are not limited to financial support because the implementation of sustainable practices is not solely dependent on monetary assistance (Roxas and Chadee, 2012). Hence, the following proposition has been devised:

> *P8*. Firms with owners and managers who believe that they need more support from external parties are more likely to have a relatively lower level of SPE.

9 **Sustainability top management engagement and its implications for SMEs**: The level of engagement in sustainability practices is primarily dependent on the vision of the owners and managers to protect, maintain and grow the business (Aragón-Correa *et al*, 2008; Lee, Herold and Yu, 2016). Accordingly, if owners and managers prioritize sustainability issues, their firms are likely to do the same (Spence and Schmidpeter, 2003; Jenkins, 2006). Many authors (eg Kerr, 2006; Zhu *et al*, 2008) stressed that top management support and leadership play a vital role in a firm's level of sustainability practice. Therefore, we formulate the following proposition:

> *P9*. Firms with owners and managers who believe that top management support is necessary to address sustainability issues are more likely to have a relatively higher level of SPE.

10 **Employee resistance and reward systems and their implications for SMEs**: Employee resistance and scepticism are normally viewed as barriers hindering firms from pursuing sustainability (Nejati *et al*, 2014; Wiesner, Chadee and Best, 2018; Caldera *et al*, 2019; Orji, 2019). Empirical evidence reveals that resistance at the firm and individual employee level can vary across firms, and frequently depends on a firm's organizational culture and values (Sroufe *et al*, 2010; Shevchenko, Lévesque and Pagell, 2016). Lucas, Cunningham and Lamberton (2009) studied a sample of 195 Australian SMEs and found that despite firms' socially and environmentally responsible actions, they had a relatively low commitment to sustainability practices. Mabhungu and Van Der Poll (2017) suggested that owners and managers should establish incentives and communicate them effectively to encourage staff to achieve sustainability targets. What remains unclear is how such issues affect the level of SPE in Vietnamese SMMEs. Thus, we explore the following propositions:

> *P10.* Firms with owners and managers who believe that there is employee resistance to addressing sustainability issues are more likely to have a relatively lower level of SPE.

> *P11.* Firms with owners and managers who believe that they should offer rewards and recognition for addressing sustainability issues are more likely to have a relatively higher level of SPE.

11 **Sustainability education and training implications for SMEs**: Education, training and increasing organizational learning capabilities may increase employees' abilities to recognize and acquire new knowledge (Caloghirou, Kastelli and Tsakanikas, 2004; Bond *et al*, 2010; Tilleman, 2012; Johnson, 2017). Employees equipped with the necessary skills and expertise are more likely to know how to undertake sustainability initiatives (Rao *et al*, 2006; Horisch, Johnson and Schaltegger, 2015; Jones and Corral de Zubielqui, 2015; Lee, Herold and Yu, 2016). Thus, we formulate the following proposition:

> *P12.* Firms with owners and managers who believe that providing education and training is necessary to address sustainability issues are more likely to have a relatively higher level of SPE.

12 **Sustainability and SME ownership characteristics implications**: SME owners' and managers' characteristics, such as age, gender and education level influence the level of SPE (Petts, Herd and O'Heocha, 1998; Schaper, 2002; Gadenne, Kennedy and McKeiver, 2009). For

example, Schaper (2002) surveyed 154 retail SMEs in Western Australia and found a negative correlation between age and a positive attitude towards sustainability. Specifically, this finding revealed that younger owners and managers tended to be more concerned about the environment and the community. This finding was reinforced by Jahanshahi and Brem (2017) who surveyed 40 top management teams in Iranian SMEs and found that younger managers tended to generate novel ideas in sustainability innovation. However, little is known about how the characteristics of SMME owner/managers in developing countries influence the adoption of sustainability practices (Hasan, 2016; Jamali, Lund-Thomsen and Khara, 2017). We still expected that the characteristics of owners and managers with larger firms would be more positively associated with the SPE. Therefore, we formulate the following propositions:

P13. Firms with younger owners and managers are more likely to have a relatively higher level of SPE.

P14. Firms with female owners and managers are more likely to have a relatively higher level of SPE.

P15. Firms with highly educated owners and managers are more to have a relatively higher level of SPE.

13 **Sustainability and SME firm size implications:** Firm size has been highlighted in the literature as a critical factor influencing the level of SPE. Normally, the size of a firm represents its available resources (Lepoutre and Heene, 2006). As compared to their larger counterparts, smaller firms are usually recognized to have scarce resources, particularly concerning time, information, financial resources and scale of operations (McKeiver and Gadenne, 2005; Udayasankar, 2008). Such limitations may hinder smaller firms from doing more than larger firms which are required by either law or stakeholders to be more proactive regarding sustainability activities. However, little is known about whether smaller firms are incapable of pursuing a more proactive SPE amid resource scarcity. Based on this argument, this study explores the following proposition:

P16. Larger firms are more likely to have a relatively higher level of SPE.

14 **Sustainability and SME firm age implications:** A firm's age normally represents the accumulated experience in business operations that may be associated with the level of SPE. Arguably, firms learn over time and build a specific set of capabilities that enable them to undertake sustainability initiatives (Hoogendoorn, Guerra and van der Zwan, 2015; Panwar *et al*, 2017). According to Roxas and Chadee (2012), in the early phases of business operations, firms are more likely to be in survival mode and start to engage in sustainability activities only when they overcome the minimum survival threshold. However, a recent study of 478 small US firms noted that firm age was not associated with social engagement (Panwar *et al*, 2017). Therefore, little is known about how a firm's age influences the level of SPE in Vietnamese SMMEs. Based on this argument, this study explores the following proposition.

P17. Firms that have been established for longer are more likely to have a relatively higher level of SPE.

Methodology

The first step in the study involved a literature review to explore relevant concepts and measurements that were closely related to sustainability practice in SMMEs. Then, we developed the measurement construct as follows:

- **Dependent variables**: As this study employed the TBL concept to address SPE, the items constructed for each aspect of sustainability were developed accordingly. We selected items for the economic practices related to SME sustainability development (Mabhungu and Van Der Poll, 2017) as well as items related to financial performance (Joung *et al*, 2013; Feil, de Quevedo and Schreiber, 2015; Tan *et al*, 2015).
- **Independent variables**: Independent variables including various factors categorized as groups, namely external influences, internal influences, internal moderating variables, benefits, and moderating external variables (firm size).

The second step was reviewing and validating the list of items by conducting a pilot study before distributing the questionnaire. The pilot study aimed to eliminate potential problems such as wording, ordering and layout. Accordingly, a draft of the survey questionnaire was reviewed by five people, including two academic scholars and three SMME owners and managers (they are included in the final survey phase) who were familiar with sustainability activities. Consequently, the revised questionnaire was more refined, ensuring a consistent experience for all respondents in which there was no difficulty in answering the questions. The third step was the refinement of the questionnaire to follow a logical sequence, including the four following sections:

- **General information**: This section included six items related to the respondent and firm (gender, age, education, years of experience in the manufacturing sector, firm age, firm size).
- **Sustainability practices**: This section included three aspects of sustainability, including economic, social and environmental.
- **Internal influences**: This section included internal influence, internal moderating influences, and benefits.
- **External influences**: This section included four items, covering the external factors.

Figure 9.1 illustrates the four theoretical constructs of external factors, internal factors, moderating variables and level of SPE.

There is no consensus on the definition of an SME in different countries because criteria can vary from country to country and may vary according to the source. For example, in the European Union, companies with fewer

Figure 9.1 A research model of the influence of internal and external factors on the level of SPE

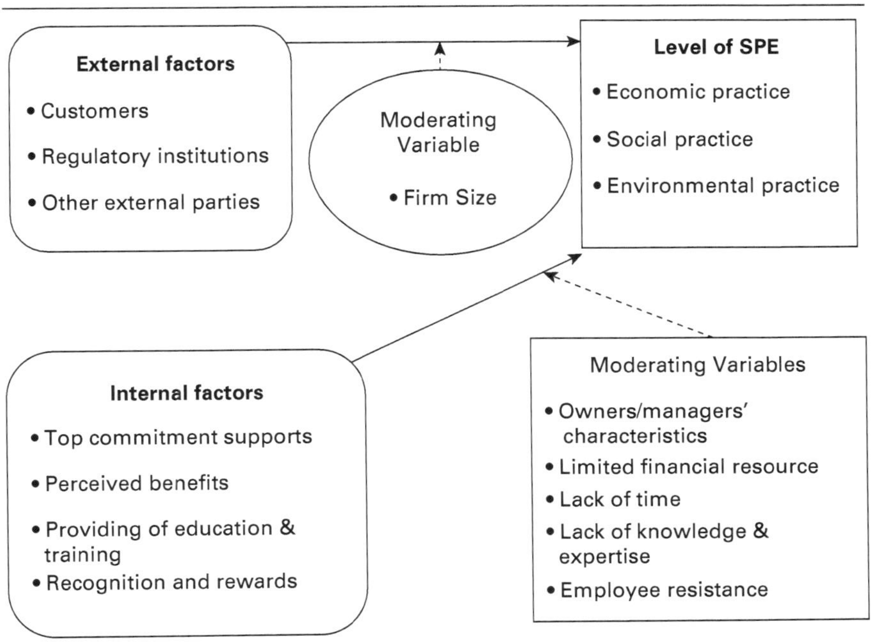

than 250 employees are classified as SMEs (European Commission, 2003). However, this paper focuses on SMMEs in Vietnam; therefore, we employed the definition proposed by the Vietnamese government which designates firms with fewer than 300 employees as SMEs (Government of Vietnam, 2001: Decree No. 90/2001/ND-CP). In the context of developing countries, sustainability development is in its infancy in terms of both government policies and company strategies (Azmat, 2010; Agyemang and Ansong, 2017; Jamali, Lund-Thomsen and Jeppesen, 2017). Furthermore, we integrated multiple informants' responses because their knowledge and critical roles assured the provision of valuable insights regarding their firms' sustainability practices (Moore and Manring, 2009; Bourlakis *et al*, 2014). Between one and three critical respondents in each firm were targeted in this study, depending on the firm size (Bourlakis *et al*, 2014). We applied a convenience sampling approach to study SMMEs in Ho Chi Minh City, Vietnam and its surrounding rural districts, focusing on localities with large industrial areas and a high concentration of the manufacturing sector.

SMME profile: A total of 500 printed questionnaires were distributed, 232 of which were returned. After carefully checking and discarding those with missing values and incomplete questionnaires, 157 (31.4%) valid questionnaires were used for final analysis. Table 9.1 shows the descriptive statistics of the profile summary of 157 respondents.

Table 9.1 Profile summary of respondents

Variables	Frequency	Percentage (%)
Gender		
Male	95	60.5
Female	62	39.5
Total	157	100.0
Age		
18–25	19	12.1
26–34 □	75	47.8
35–40	37	23.6
41–45 □	13	8.3

(continued)

Table 9.1 (Continued)

Variables	Frequency	Percentage (%)
46–50 □	7	4.5
<50	6	3.8
Total	157	100
Respondent profile (position)		
Owner-manager	9	5.7
Owner	15	9.6
Director	16	10.2
Senior manager	41	26.1
Junior manager	48	30.6
Staff	28	17.8
Total	157	100.0
Level of education		
Incomplete high school education	1	.6
Complete high school education	6	3.8
Undergraduate degree	125	79.6
Master's degree and above	25	15.9
Total	157	100.0
Year (s) in the manufacturing sector		
<1 □	3	1.9
1–5 □	43	27.4
6–10 □	67	42.7
11–15 □	25	15.9
<15	19	12.1
Total	157	100.0

Table 9.2 Firms classified according to firm size and firm age

Variables	Frequency	Percentage (%)
Size (no of personnel employed)		
Micro-sized (fewer than 10 employees)	4	2.5
Small-sized (from 10 to 49 employees)	15	9.6
Medium-sized (from 50 to 300 employees)	138	87.9
Total	157	100.0
Firm age		
Less than 5 years	6	3.8
5–9 years	25	15.9
10–15 years	55	35.0
Over 15	71	45.2
Total	157	100.0

Table 9.2 illustrates the respondents' demographic profiles. As indicated, most manufacturing SMEs (87.9%) were classed as medium-sized, having between 50 and 300 employees, and 9.6 per cent were classed as small-sized (between 10 and 49 employees).

Results and discussions of factors affecting sustainability in Vietnamese SMMEs

Questions related to the level of SPE are shown in descending order (see Table 9.3). *Having a clear plan to achieve the target revenue* (3.89 out of a possible 4) ranked highest for economic sustainability practice. This result was not surprising as nearly all SMMEs set a clear plan to achieve target revenue to survive and generate profit. *Tax payment (M = 3.88)* was defined as compliance with mandatory legislative requirements. The least frequent economic sustainability activity was *innovation investments (M = 3.50)*,

Table 9.3 Construct items of sustainability practices and descriptives

Dependent construct	Mean	SD
Questions on economic sustainability practices		
1. Having a clear plan to achieve the target revenue	3.89	.320
2. Tax payment	3.88	.346
3. Having a clear plan to achieve the target profit	3.85	.355
4. Minimizing operational expenses	3.79	.453
5. Innovation investments	3.50	.595
Questions on social sustainability practices		
1. Maintaining interactive two-way communication with customers	3.55	.614
2. Paying competitive salaries	3.46	.615
3. Involvement of customers, suppliers in socially responsible activities	3.34	.789
4. Having regular staff appraisal meetings to respond to staff needs	3.06	.753
5. Allowing staff to work flexible hours to fit their family circumstances	3.21	.809
6. Dealing with socially and environmentally responsible suppliers	3.18	.772
7. Donation and involvement in philanthropy and charity activities	3.08	.716
8. Contribution, involvement in community development	2.93	.777
Questions on environment sustainability practices		
1. Using energy efficiently	3.75	.517
2. Finding feasible solutions to reduce waste	3.71	.624
3. Using products/service friendly to the environment	3.22	.696
4. Recycling of raw material, damaged products, packaging, paper	3.14	.868
5. Using external services for waste treatments	3.03	.837

indicating that nearly half of firms probably overlooked the importance of innovation investments. As widely suggested in previous studies, innovation investments, in terms of entrepreneurial skills, processes and technologies, are essential elements that contribute to the success and sustainability of SMMEs (Bos-brouwers, 2009; Urban and Naidoo, 2012).

The most prevalent sustainability practice, maintaining interactive two-way communication with customers (M = 3.55) scored highest. This result was in line with a recent study by Caldera *et al* (2019), which confirmed that customers are playing a key role in enabling SMMEs to achieve sustainable business practices. Interestingly, paying competitive salaries scored second highest (M = 3.46), with 52.2 per cent responding frequently and 42.7 per cent sometimes. Such a result shows that slightly over half of SMMEs positively addressed the issue of insufficient salaries, which still shows a lack of social responsibilities in the context of Vietnamese SMMEs, as mentioned by Hải and Mai (2014). The most frequently reported environmental sustainability practice, using energy efficiently (M = 3.75), scored highest. The findings were in line with findings in a recent study by Yacob *et al* (2019), which found that SMMEs could gain economic and environmental benefits by using energy efficiently. Conversely, using external services for waste treatments (M = 3.03) scored lowest for environmental sustainability practices, with 6 per cent of respondents reporting never and 29 per cent of respondents choosing seldom. It would be logical to expect that some SMEs generate less toxic waste or hazardous liquid in their manufacturing process, meaning external services for waste treatment may not be a necessary business activity.

Perceived benefits of sustainable practices in Vietnamese SMMEs

The benefit with the highest mean (M = 4.37) was the corporate image and reputation enhancement, with 42 per cent of respondents strongly agreeing and 52.9 per cent agreeing. This finding indicates that a significant proportion of respondents were aware that engagement with sustainability could enhance their corporate image and reputation. This finding is in line with previous research, which has found that engaging in sustainability entails responsible activities and ethical actions, resulting in a positive corporate image of products or services (Jahanshahi and Brem, 2017; Maldonado-Guzman, Pinzón-Castro and Leana-Morales, 2017; de Jesus Pacheco *et al*, 2018). Table 9.4 lists the benefits, in descending order of importance, as perceived by the respondents.

Table 9.4 Benefits of an SPE

Benefits	Mean
1. Corporate image and reputation enhancement	4.37
2. Better working environment	4.32
3. Resource efficiency	4.31
4. Cost reduction	4.26
5. Waste and discharge reduction	4.25
6. Partnership strengthening and potential customer attraction	4.19
7. Employee satisfaction and retention	4.18

Table 9.5 Multivariate tests

Factor	Wilks' Lamda	F	Significance
Gender	.949	1.402b	.249
Age	.850	.873	.595
Level of education	.924	.694	.714
Experience	.874	.899	.549
Position	.823	1.049	.406
Firm age	.855	1.407	.187
Firm size	.612	7.226b	**.000**
Management support	.937	.866b	.522
Education and training	.893	1.513b	.177
Recognition and rewards	.868	1.908b	.083
Lack of time	.949	.348	.979
Lack of financial resource	.815	1.380	.177
Lack of knowledge and expertise	.903	1.363b	.233

(continued)

Table 9.5 (Continued)

Factor	Wilks' Lamda	F	Significance
Employees' resistance	.754	1.943	**.031**
Intricate tax systems	.778	2.293	**.018**
Legislation	.889	1.044	.406
Cost-conscious customers	.769	1.797	**.050**
External support	.924	1.045b	.398
Benefits of engagement	.535	1.516	**.037**

Results of proposition testing

Table 9.5 shows the multivariate effect on the level of economic, social and environmental practices. The multivariate tests demonstrate that the variables showed a significant relationship between the level of SPE and firm size (p = .000), employee resistance (p = 0.031), intricate tax systems (p = .018), benefits of engagement (p = .037) and cost-conscious customers (p = .050; at 95% confidence interval).

Of the variables that had a significant impact on the multivariate tests (Table 9.6), the results illustrate that the level of economic sustainability practice was significantly influenced by firm size *(p = .000)*, employee resistance *(p = 0.01)*, and intricate tax systems *(p = 0.016)*. The level of social sustainability practice was significantly influenced by cost-conscious customers *(p = 0.046)*. Intricate tax systems, employee resistance and firm size were identified as being significantly associated with the level of economic SPE; thus, propositions 1, 3, 10 and 16 are supported. Proposition 1 predicted that firms with owners and managers who believe that intricate tax systems constrain their businesses are more likely to have a relatively lower level of SPE, supporting the fact that intricate tax systems were significantly associated with the level of SPE. This finding is in accord with recent studies (Nguyen *et al*, 2015; Silvestre, 2015), indicating that in emerging or developing economies, complicated taxation and financial policies hinder the ability of SMEs to understand the tax system. Such institutional barriers consume firms' time and human resources, which are frequently limited in

Table 9.6 Tests of between-subject effects

Source	Dependent variable	F	Sig.
Corrected model	Level of economic practice engagement	2.531	.000
	Level of social practice engagement	1.324	.108
	Level of environment practice engagement	1.168	.246
Intercept	Level of economic practice engagement	646.833	.000
	Level of social practice engagement	93.978	.000
	Level of environment practice engagement	66.559	.000
Firm size	Level of economic practice engagement	20.192	**.000**
	Level of social practice engagement	1.399	.253
	Level of environment practice engagement	.766	.468
Employees' resistance	Level of economic practice engagement	3.584	**.010**
	Level of social practice engagement	.558	.694
	Level of environment practice engagement	.858	.493
Intricate tax systems	Level of economic practice engagement	3.674	**.016**
	Level of social practice engagement	1.455	.233
	Level of environment practice engagement	.368	.776
Cost-conscious customers	Level of economic practice engagement	1.503	.209
	Level of social practice engagement	2.539	**.046**

(continued)

Table 9.6 (Continued)

Source	Dependent variable	F	Sig.
	Level of environment practice engagement	1.126	.350
Benefits of engagement	Level of economic practice engagement	1.644	.096
	Level of social practice engagement	1.433	.168
	Level of environment practice engagement	.869	.580

SMEs. Accordingly, this barrier may discourage the growth of SMMEs and their ability to engage effectively with sustainability activities (Table 9.6).

Proposition 3 was supported for the social SPE dependent variable; thus, cost-conscious customers were found to be significantly correlated with the level of social SPE. Proposition 3 predicted that firms with owners and managers who believe that cheaper product prices, rather than sustainability issues, affect customers' buying decisions are more likely to have a relatively lower level of SPE. The result is in agreement with Hasan's (2016) findings which showed that SMME owners and managers did not seriously consider social responsibilities because buyers only ask for the lowest price, rather than the firm's positive social performance.

Proposition 10 predicted that firms with owners and managers who believe that there is employee resistance to addressing sustainability issues are more likely to have a relatively lower level of SPE. The result corroborates the finding of Wiesner, Chadee and Best (2018) that employee resistance in SMEs frequently results from limited to no awareness of the benefits of sustainability activities. The present results indicate that perceived benefits did not have a significant influence. A lack of influence of perceived benefits may, in turn, suggest that sustainability targets were not well established or effectively communicated to reduce employee resistance (Mabhungu and Van Der Poll, 2017). At an organizational level, employee resistance tends to portend a less sustainable culture (Sroufe *et al*, 2010) or a low level of internal readiness to change (Shevchenko, Lévesque and Pagell, 2016), both of which could be barriers to firms achieving true sustainability.

The results also support proposition 16 regarding the level of economic sustainability practice; larger firms are more likely to have a relatively higher level of SPE. The results reveal that firm size did not have a significant influence on social and environmental sustainability practices. However, this finding may indicate that SMEs focus primarily on economic performance to ensure adequate revenue, profit and return on investment, but they also consider the social and environmental implications of their actions (Peña-Vinces and Delgado-Márquez, 2013).

Conclusion

This study investigated the main factors that facilitate or deter SMMEs in Vietnam in their efforts to effectively engage in sustainability practice. The results indicate that intricate tax systems, cost-conscious customers, employee resistance and firm size are all factors significantly associated with the level of SPE:

- **Intricate tax systems**, a significant institutional deterrent, has been suggested as a driver of external influence. Based on the studied sample in Vietnam and existing literature, it is reasonably logical to comment that SMMEs may have to deal with more challenges in developing countries than in developed countries. One possible explanation is that the existence of intricate tax systems, which cause a higher degree of complexity in the institutional environment under which SMMEs operate, inhibit the level of SPE.
- **Cost-conscious customers** indicate that customers are vital external stakeholders and can affect whether SMMEs take action on sustainability. It is evident that customers have put less pressure on the sustainability of SMMEs, particularly concerning social responsibilities. Arguably, this finding is because customers seem to be more concerned with the price of products and services and their quality than with the sustainability performance of SMMEs.
- **Employee resistance** hinders the level of engagement in economic sustainability practices. This finding is crucial as it could assist the owners and managers to improve firms' sustainability performance. For example, the owners and managers should determine ways that match the organizational context and culture to motivate employees with the appropriate type of commitment required to enhance superior sustainability performance

(Raziq and Wiesner, 2016). In doing so, each individual's values would align with the organizational values and principles (Jenkins, 2009).

- **Firm size** influences economic sustainability practice, implying that, generally, small firms may experience more difficulties than their larger counterparts when engaging in sustainability practices. This finding is in line with the view of Mabhungu and Van Der Poll (2017), who highlighted common inhibitors for small businesses, including lack of skills for business planning, difficulties in managing revenue, profit and cost, and hesitancy in investing in innovation.
- **Lack of time and lack of financial resources** were not confirmed in this current study as internal influences on the SPE of SMMEs. However, it should not be ignored that McKeiver and Gadenne (2005) highlighted that larger businesses frequently have more available resources than their smaller counterparts. These resources are mainly time and financial resources, making larger companies more accountable. Therefore, the result of our critical assessment helps to identify solutions for small business owners and managers and their constituents to overcome the barriers they encounter in the context of economic sustainability practice.

Sustainability initiatives can only be embedded in SMMEs through a change of internal processes, namely, changing employee attitudes and perceptions by increasing awareness and education throughout the organizational structure.

Learning outcomes

- From the perspective of SMME owners and managers, the Vietnamese government's role is critical in providing clear, updated and detailed guidance on financial and tax policies.
- External stakeholders can affect whether Vietnamese SMMEs take action on sustainability.
- Employee resistance can hinder the level of SMMEs' engagement in economic sustainability practices.
- SMMEs have fewer available resources than their larger businesses counterparts.

Questions

1. What are the main factors impacting sustainability for Vietnamese SMEs?
2. Discuss the importance of internal and external stakeholders in achieving a sustainable SME.
3. Are the consumers, who may have a preference for a firm's socially responsible products, willing to pay a premium for them? Critically discuss.

References

Abdalla, Y A and Siti-Nabiha (2015) Pressures for sustainability practices in an oil and gas company: evidence from Sudan, *Qualitative Research in Accounting & Management*, **12** (3), pp 256–86

Adams, C A and Frost, G R (2008) Integrating sustainability reporting into management practices, *Accounting Forum*, **32** (4), pp 288–302

Agyemang, O S and Ansong, A (2017) Corporate social responsibility and firm performance of Ghanaian SMEs, *Journal of Global Responsibility*, **8** (1), pp 47–62

Ahi, P and Searcy, C (2013) A comparative literature analysis of definitions for green and sustainable supply chain management, *Journal of Cleaner Production*, **52**, pp 329–41

Amini, M and Bienstock, C C (2014) Corporate sustainability: an integrative definition and framework to evaluate corporate practice and guide academic research, *Journal of Cleaner Production*, **76**, pp 12–19

Anisul Huq, F, Stevenson, M and Zorzini, M (2014) Social sustainability in developing country suppliers, *International Journal of Operations & Production Management*, **34** (5), pp 610–38

Aragón-Correa, J A *et al* (2008) Environmental strategy and performance in small firms: a resource-based perspective, *Journal of Environmental Management*, **86** (1), pp 88–103

Assaf, A G, Josiassen, A and Cvelbar, L K (2012) Does triple bottom line reporting improve hotel performance?, *International Journal of Hospitality Management*, **31** (2), pp 596–600

Azapagic, A (2003) Systems approach to corporate sustainability: a general management framework, *Process Safety and Environmental Protection*, **81** (5), pp 303–16

Azmat, F (2010) Exploring social responsibility of immigrant entrepreneurs: do home country contextual factors play a role?, *European Management Journal*, **28** (5), pp 377–86

Bansal, P (2005) Evolving sustainably: a longitudinal study of corporate sustainable development, *Strategic Management Journal*, **26** (3), pp 197–218

Barkemeyer, R (2011) Corporate perceptions of sustainability challenges in developed and developing countries: constituting a CSR divide?, *Social Responsibility Journal*, **7** (2), pp 257–81

Benzin, C, Chu, M H and Callanan, G (2005) A regional comparision of the motivation and problems of Vietnamese entrepreneurs, *World Scientific*, **10** (1), pp 2–27

Bond, A J *et al* (2010) Informal knowledge processes: the underpinning for sustainability outcomes in EIA?, *Journal of Cleaner Production*, **18** (1), pp 6–13

Bos-brouwers, H E J (2009) Corporate sustainability and innovation in SMEs: evidence of themes and activities in practice, *Business Strategy and the Environment*, **19**, pp 417–35

Bourlakis, M *et al* (2014) Firm size and sustainable performance in food supply chains: insights from Greek SMEs, *International Journal of Production Economics*, **152**, pp 112–30

Caldera, H T S, Desha, C and Dawes, L (2019) Evaluating the enablers and barriers for successful implementation of sustainable business practice in lean SMEs, *Journal of Cleaner Production*, **218**, pp 575–90

Caloghirou, Y, Kastelli, I and Tsakanikas, A (2004) Internal capabilities and external knowledge sources: complements or substitutes for innovative performance?, *Technovation*, **24** (1), pp 29–39

Chen, D *et al* (2014) A holistic and rapid sustainability assessment tool for manufacturing SMEs, *CIRP annals*, **63** (1), pp 437–40

Cordano, M, Marshall, R S and Silverman, M (2010) How do small and medium enterprises go 'green'? A study of environmental management programs in the US wine industry, *Journal of Business Ethics*, **92** (3), pp 463–78

Crals, E and Vereeck, L (2005) The affordability of sustainable entrepreneurship certification for SMEs, *International Journal of Sustainable Development and World Ecology*, **12** (2), pp 173–83

Cui, Z, Liang, X and Lu, X (2015) Prize or price? Corporate social responsibility commitment and sales performance in the Chinese private sector, *Management and Organization Review*, **11** (1), pp 25–44

Darcy, C *et al* (2014) A consideration of organisational sustainability in the SME context: a resource-based view and composite model, *European Journal of Training and Development*, **38** (5), pp 398–414

De Giovanni, P (2012) Do internal and external environmental management contribute to the triple bottom line?, *International Journal of Operations & Production Management*, **32** (3), pp 265–90

Dissanayake, D, Tilt, C and Xydias-Lobo, M (2016) Sustainability reporting by publicly listed companies in Sri Lanka, *Journal of Cleaner Production*, **129**, pp 169–82

Dobers, P and Halme, M (2009) Corporate social responsibility and developing countries, *Corporate Social Responsibility and Environmental Management*, **16** (5), pp 237–49

Elkington, J (1997) Partnerships from cannibals with forks: the triple bottom line of 21st century business, *Environmental Quality Management*, Autumn, pp 37–51

Elkington, J (2001) Enter the triple bottom line, in *The Triple Bottom Line: Does it all add up?*, ed A Henriques and J Richardson, ch 1 (1986), pp 1–16

European Commission (2003) Definition of a Small & Medium Sized Enterprise (SME) in Force at the European Space Agency, May, pp 2–3

Feil, A A, de Quevedo, D M and Schreiber, D (2015) Selection and identification of the indicators for quickly measuring sustainability in micro and small furniture industries, *Sustainable Production and Consumption*, **3** (June), pp 34–44

Fuller, T and Lewis, J (2002) Relationships mean everything: a typology of small-business relationship strategies in a reflexive context, *British Journal of Management*, **13** (4), pp 317–36

Gadenne, D L, Kennedy, J and McKeiver, C (2009) An empirical study of environmental awareness and practices in SMEs, *Journal of Business Ethics*, **84** (1), pp 45–63

Garengo, P, Biazzo, S and Bititci, U S (2005) Performance measurement systems in SMEs: a review for a research agenda, *International Journal of Management Reviews*, 7 (1), pp 25–47

Ghazilla, R A R *et al* (2015) Drivers and barriers analysis for green manufacturing practices in Malaysian SMEs: a preliminary findings, *Procedia Cirp*, **26**, pp 658–63

Gimenez, C, Sierra, V and Rodon, J (2012) Sustainable operations: their impact on the triple bottom line, *International Journal of Production Economics*, **140** (1), pp 149–59

Government of Vietnam (2001) *Decree Number 90/2001/ND-CP issued 23 November 2001 on SME development support*, Vietnamese Government, Hanoi

Govindan, K, Khodaverdi, R and Jafarian, A (2013) A fuzzy multi criteria approach for measuring sustainability performance of a supplier based on triple bottom line approach, *Journal of Cleaner Production*, **47**, pp 345–54

Hải, H V and Mai, N P (2014) An exploratory study of the relationship between lean production and corporate social responsibility in Vietnamese SMEs, *VNU Journal of Science: Economics and Business*, **30** (2)

Hák, T, Janoušková, S and Moldan, B (2016) Sustainable development goals: a need for relevant indicators, *Ecological Indicators*, **60**, pp 565–73

Harding, R (2006) Ecologically sustainable development: origins, implementation and challenges, *Desalination*, **187** (1–3), pp 229–39

Hasan, M N (2016) Measuring and understanding the engagement of Bangladeshi SMEs with sustainable and socially responsible business practices: an ISO 26000 perspective, *Social Responsibility Journal*, **12** (3), pp 584–610

Hassini, E, Surti, C and Searcy, C (2012) A literature review and a case study of sustainable supply chains with a focus on metrics, *International Journal of Production Economics*, **140** (1), pp 69–82

Hilson, G (2012) Corporate social responsibility in the extractive industries: experiences from developing countries, *Resources Policy*, **37** (2), pp 131–37

Høgevold, N M *et al* (2015) A triple bottom line construct and reasons for implementing sustainable business practices in companies and their business networks, *Corporate Governance*, **15** (4), pp 427–43

Hoogendoorn, B, Guerra, D and van der Zwan, P (2015) What drives environmental practices of SMEs?, *Small Business Economics*, **44** (4), pp 759–81

Horisch, J, Johnson, M P and Schaltegger, S (2015) Implementation of sustainability management and company size: a knowledge-based view, *Business Strategy and the Environment*, **24** (8), pp 765–79

Hsu, C H, Chang, A Y and Luo, W (2017) Identifying key performance factors for sustainability development of SMEs – integrating QFD and fuzzy MADM methods, *Journal of Cleaner Production*, **161**, pp 629–45

Jahanshahi, A A and Brem, A (2017) Sustainability in SMEs: top management teams behavioral integration as source of innovativeness, *Sustainability (Switzerland)*, **9** (10), pp 1–16

Jamali, D, Lund-Thomsen, P and Jeppesen, S (2017) SMEs and CSR in developing countries, *Business & Society*, **56** (1), pp 11–22

Jamali, D, Lund-Thomsen, P and Khara, N (2017) CSR institutionalized myths in developing countries: an imminent threat of selective decoupling, *Business & Society*, **56** (3), pp 454–86

Jamali, D and Mirshak, R (2007) Corporate social responsibility (CSR): theory and practice in a developing country context, *Journal of Business Ethics*, **72** (3), pp 243–62

Jenkins, H (2006) Small business champions for corporate social responsibility, *Journal of Business Ethics*, **67** (3), pp 241–56

Jenkins, H (2009) A business opportunity model of corporate social responsibility for small- and medium-sized enterprises, *Business Ethics: A European Review*, **18** (1), pp 21–36

Johnson, M P (2017) Knowledge acquisition and development in sustainability-oriented small and medium-sized enterprises: exploring the practices, capabilities and cooperation, *Journal of Cleaner Production*, **142**, pp 3769–81

Johnson, M P and Schaltegger, S (2016) Two decades of sustainability management tools for SMEs: how far have we come?, *Journal of Small Business Management*, **54** (2), pp 481–505

Jones, J and Corral de Zubielqui, G (2015) Doing well by doing good: a study of university-industry interactions, innovationess and firm performance in sustainability-oriented Australian SMEs, *Technological Forecasting and Social Change*, **123**, pp 262–70

Joung, C B *et al* (2013) Categorization of indicators for sustainable manufacturing, *Ecological Indicators*, **24**, pp 148–57

Kallmuenzer, A *et al* (2017) Trade-offs between dimensions of sustainability: exploratory evidence from family firms in rural tourism regions, *Journal of Sustainable Tourism*, **26** (7), pp 1204–21

Kerr, I R (2006) Leadership strategies for sustainable SME operation, *Business Strategy and the Environment*, **15** (1), pp 30–39

Khurana, S, Haleem, A and Mannan, B (2019) Determinants for integration of sustainability with innovation for Indian manufacturing enterprises: empirical evidence in MSMEs, *Journal of Cleaner Production*, **229**, pp 374–86

Lee, K (2009) Why and how to adopt green management into business organizations?, *Management Decision*, **47** (7), pp 1101–21

Lee, K H, Herold, D M and Yu, A L (2016) Small and medium enterprises and corporate social responsibility practice: a Swedish perspective, *Corporate Social Responsibility and Environmental Management*, **23** (2), pp 88–99

Lee, S Y and Klassen, R D (2008) Drivers and enablers that foster environmental management capabilities in small- and medium-sized suppliers in supply chains, *Production and Operations Management*, **17** (6), pp 573–86

Leonidou, L C *et al* (2017) Internal drivers and performance consequences of small firm green business strategy: the moderating role of external forces, *Journal of Business Ethics*, **140** (3), pp 585–606

Lepoutre, J and Heene, A (2006) Investigating the impact of firm size on small business social responsibility: a critical review, *Journal of Business Ethics*, **67** (3), pp 257–73

Lucas, T, Cunningham, R and Lamberton, G (2009) Small business engagement with sustainability in regional Australia, *Journal of Economic & Social Policy*, **13** (1), pp 40–56

Mabhungu, I and Van Der Poll, B (2017) A review of critical success factors which drives the performance of micro, small and medium enterprises, *International Journal of Business and Management*, **12** (6), p 151

Maldonado-Guzman, G, Pinzón-Castro, S Y and Leana-Morales, C (2017) Corporate social responsibility, brand image and firm reputation in Mexican small business, *Journal of Management and Sustainability*, **7** (3), p 38

Markley, M J and Davis, L (2007) Exploring future competitive advantage through sustainable supply chains, *International Journal of Physical Distribution & Logistics Management*, **37** (9), pp 763–74

Marrewijk, M Van and Werre, M (2002) Multiple levels of corporate sustainability, *Journal of Business Ethics* (October), pp 1–12

Massa, L, Farneti, F and Scappini, B (2015) Developing a sustainability report in a small to medium enterprise: process and consequences, *Meditari Accountancy Research*, **23** (1), pp 62–91

Masurel, E (2007) Why SMEs invest in environmental measures: sustainability evidence from small and medium-sized printing firms, *Business Strategy and the Environment*, **16** (3), pp 190–201

McKeiver, C and Gadenne, D (2005) Environmental management systems in small and medium businesses, *International Small Business Journal*, **23** (5), pp 513–37

McMurray, A J *et al* (2014) Sustainable procurement in Malaysian organizations: practices, barriers and opportunities, *Journal of Purchasing and Supply Management*, **20** (3), pp 195–207

Montiel, I (2008) Corporate social responsibility and corporate sustainability: separate pasts, common futures, *Organization & Environment*, **21** (3), pp 245–69

Moore, S B and Manring, S L (2009) Strategy development in small and medium sized enterprises for sustainability and increased value creation, *Journal of Cleaner Production*, **17** (2), pp 276–82

Nejati, M, Amran, A and Hazlina Ahmad, N (2014) Examining stakeholders influence on environmental responsibility of micro, small and medium-sized enterprises and its outcomes, *Management Decision*, **52** (10), pp 2021–43

Nguyen, Q A, Sullivan Mort, G and D'Souza, C (2015) Vietnam in transition: SMEs and the necessitating environment for entrepreneurship development, *Entrepreneurship and Regional Development*, **27** (3–4), pp 154–80

Nichter, S and Goldmark, L (2009) Small firm growth in developing countries, *World Development*, **37** (9), pp 1453–64

Organisation for Economic Co-operation and Development (2019) [accessed 7 July 2021] G20 contribution to the 2030 agenda progress and way forward, OECD [Online] www.oecd.org/publications/g20-contribution-to-the-2030-agenda-db84dfca-en.htm (archived at https://perma.cc/PAY9-G6H9)

Orji, I J (2019) Examining barriers to organizational change for sustainability and drivers of sustainable performance in the metal manufacturing industry, *Resources, Conservation and Recycling*, **140**, pp 102–14

de Jesus Pacheco, D A *et al* (2018) Eco-innovation determinants in manufacturing SMEs from emerging markets: systematic literature review and challenges, *Journal of Engineering and Technology Management*, **48**, pp 44–63

Palmer, J, Russell, S and McIntosh, M (2012, December) Organizational change for sustainability: an agenda for cultural research, in *Managing for Volatility and Instability: 26th Annual Australian and New Zealand Academy of Management Conference*, Perth, Australia

Panwar, R *et al* (2017) Does the business case matter? The effect of a perceived business case on small firms social engagement, *Journal of Business Ethics*, **144** (3), pp 597–608

Pedersen, E R (2009) The many and the few: rounding up the SMEs that manage CSR in the supply chain, *Supply Chain Management,* **14** (2), pp 109–16

Peña-Vinces, J C and Delgado-Márquez, B L (2013) Are entrepreneurial foreign activities of Peruvian SMNEs influenced by international certifications, corporate social responsibility and green management?, *International Entrepreneurship and Management Journal*, **9** (4), pp 603–18

Perrini, F and Tencati, A (2006) Sustainability and stakeholder management: the need for new corporate performance evaluation and reporting systems, *Business Strategy and the Environment*, **15** (5), pp 296–308

Petts, J, Herd, A and O'Heocha, M (1998) Environmental responsiveness, individuals and organizational learning: SME experience, *Journal of Environmental Planning and Management*, **41** (6), pp 711–30

Phan, U H *et al* (2015) Key determinants of SMEs in Vietnam: combining quantitative and qualitative studies, *Review of European Studies*, **7**, p 359

Polonsky, M J (1995) A stakeholder theory approach to designing environmental marketing strategy, *Journal of Business & Industrial Marketing*, **10** (3), pp 29–46

Preuss, L and Perschke, J (2010) Slipstreaming the larger boats: social responsibility in medium-sized businesses, *Journal of Business Ethics*, **92** (4), pp 531–51

Rachuri, S, Sriram, R D and Sarkar, P (2009) Metrics, standards and industry best practices for sustainable manufacturing systems, *2009 IEEE International Conference on Automation Science and Engineering*, pp 472–77

Rao, P *et al* (2006) Environmental indicators for small and medium enterprises in the Philippines: an empirical research, *Journal of Cleaner Production*, **14** (5), pp 505–15

Raziq, A and Wiesner, R (2016) High performance management practices and sustainability of SMEs: evidence from manufacturing and services-based industries in Pakistan, *Journal of Management Sciences*, **3** (2), pp 83–107

Rettab, B *et al* (2009) A study of management perceptions of the impact of corporate social responsibility on organisational performance in emerging economies: the case of Dubai, *Journal of Business Ethics*, **89** (3), pp 371–90

Revell, A and Blackburn, R (2007) The business case for sustainability? An examination of small firms in the UK's construction and restaurant sectors, *Business Strategy and the Environment*, **16** (6), pp 404–20

Roxas, B and Chadee, D (2012) Environmental sustainability orientation and financial resources of small manufacturing firms in the Philippines, *Social Responsibility Journal*, **8** (2), pp 208–26

Russo, A and Perrini, F (2010) Investigating stakeholder theory and social capital: CSR in large firms and SMEs, *Journal of Business Ethics*, **91** (2), pp 207–21

Russo, A and Tencati, A (2009) Formal vs. informal CSR strategies: evidence from Italian micro, small, medium-sized, and large firms, *Journal of Business Ethics*, **85** (Suppl 2), pp 339–53

Schaper, M (2002) Small firms and environmental management: predictors of green purchasing in Western Australian pharmacies, *International Small Business Journal*, **20** (3), pp 235–49

Searcy, C (2012) Corporate sustainability performance measurement systems: a review and research agenda, *Journal of Business Ethics*, **107** (3), pp 239–53

Shevchenko, A, Lévesque, M and Pagell, M (2016) Why firms delay reaching true sustainability, *Journal of Management Studies*, **53** (5), pp 911–35

Silvestre, B S (2015) Sustainable supply chain management in emerging economies: environmental turbulence, institutional voids and sustainability trajectories, *International Journal of Production Economics*, **167**, pp 156–69

Singh, S, Olugu, E U and Musa, S N (2016) Development of sustainable manufacturing performance evaluation expert system for small and medium enterprises, *Procedia CIRP*, **40**, pp 609–14

Slaper, T F and Hall, T J (2011) The triple bottom line: what is it and how does it work?, *Indiana Business Review*, **86** (1), pp 4–8

Spence, L J and Schmidpeter, R (2003) SMEs, social capital and the common good, *Journal of Business Ethics*, **45** (1), pp 93–108

Sroufe, R *et al* (2010) Are you a leader or a laggard? *HR's role in creating a sustainability culture, People & Strategy*, 33 (1), pp 34–42

Tan, H X *et al* (2015) A sustainability indicator framework for Singapore small and medium-sized manufacturing enterprises, *Procedia Cirp*, **29**, pp 132–37

Tilleman, S (2012) Is employee organizational commitment related to firm environmental sustainability?, *Journal of Small Business & Entrepreneurship*, **25** (4), pp 417–31

Tran, A N and Jeppesen, S (2016) SMEs in their own right: the views of managers and workers in Vietnamese textiles, garment, and footwear companies, *Journal of Business Ethics*, **137** (3), pp 589–608

Tsalis, T A *et al* (2013) A framework development to evaluate the needs of SMEs in order to adopt a sustainability-balanced scorecard, *Journal of Integrative Environmental Sciences*, **10** (3–4), pp 179–97

Udayasankar, K (2008) Corporate social responsibility and firm size, *Journal of Business Ethics*, **83** (2), pp 167–75

Urban, B and Naidoo, R (2012) Business sustainability: empirical evidence on operational skills in SMEs in South Africa, *Journal of Small Business and Enterprise Development*, **19** (1), pp 146–63

Wiengarten, F *et al* (2017) Complexity and the triple bottom line: an information-processing perspective, *International Journal of Operations & Production Management*, **37** (9), pp 1142–63

Wiesner, R, Chadee, D and Best, P (2018) Managing change toward environmental sustainability: a conceptual model in small and medium enterprises, *Organization & Environment*, **31** (2), pp 152–77

World Commission on Economic Development (1987) *Report of the World Commission on Environment and Development: Our common future*, Oxford University Press, Oxford

Yacob, P, Wong, L S and Khor, S C (2019) An empirical investigation of green initiatives and environmental sustainability for manufacturing SMEs, *Journal of Manufacturing Technology Management*, **30** (1), pp 2–25

Zhu, Q *et al* (2008) Firm-level correlates of emergent green supply chain management practices in the Chinese context, *Omega*, **36** (4), pp 577–591

Zorpas, A (2010) Environmental management systems as sustainable tools in the way of life for the SMEs and VSMEs, *Bioresource Technology*, **101** (6), pp 1544–57

10 The circular economy in manufacturing and service solutions

An air compressor company's 'air as a service'

MIRA VALKJÄRVI, UNIVERSITY OF TURKU, FINLAND

DR WEIMU YOU, BRUNEL BUSINESS SCHOOL, BRUNEL UNIVERSITY LONDON, UK

Introduction

The following case study highlights the integral elements of the circular economy concept and details the issues within the field of manufacturing and specifically air compressors. This case study focuses on a company whose founders have long-standing experience in the field of air compressor technology. The founders of the case company set out to solve the issues within the field and to alleviate the environmental impacts caused by traditional air compressors that utilize oil. To achieve this goal, the founders started by *rethinking* how air compressors are designed to *refuse* the use of fossil fuels and to *reduce* the usage of energy. To enable a swift transition towards the circular economy, this case study aims to provide the reader with a practical example of how the circular economy and service-dominant logic can be applied in the manufacturing sector, which in many ways can be regarded as a traditional field resistant to change. Overall, this case study will discuss the themes of circular economy, sustainability and services.

The circular economy and the role of service-dominant logic

Sustainability and the environment are on everyone's lips, from consumers to companies and academics alike. The plethora of topics and terms within the discussion are varied, but when considering the field of manufacturing and the economy in general, the topics are rather limited. The circular economy in this sense is seen as a larger concept to explain the systematic change that needs to take place in the economy to achieve the sustainability goals set as well as tackle the bigger issues faced by the environment. Circular economy is a term for an economic system that *reduces*, *reuses*, *recycles* and *recovers* materials in different business operations as well as consumption processes (Kirchherr, Reike and Hekkert, 2017). While often attributed to the four previously mentioned key components, others have suggested as many as nine: *rethink/refuse*, *reduce*, *reuse*, *repair*, *refurbish*, *remanufacture*, *repurpose*, *recycle* and *recover* (van Buren *et al*, 2016). Now while these describe the many ways in which companies or models can be adapted, they fail to bring the environment into the discourse.

Nature and natural processes are the foundation on which the circular economy is built, as the key logic stems from observing natural processes and how everything has its own place and time (Pearce and Turner, 1990). Some have even adapted how scavengers and decomposers act in nature as a metaphor to indicate and propose how companies should potentially act (Geng and Côté, 2002). This natural discourse has led to the circular economy being defined as a regenerative system (Geissdoerfer *et al*, 2017), based on three basic key principles:

1. design out waste and pollution;
2. keep materials and products in use, and;
3. regenerate natural systems (Ellen MacArthur Foundation, 2017).

Thus, the circular economy operates on the micro level, meso level and macro level as a means to achieve sustainable development which preserves the environment, creates economic prosperity and achieves social equity

(Kirchherr *et al*, 2017). This also highlights the importance of governments in supporting companies in the adoption of CE (Gong *et al*, 2020). This can be achieved by the previously mentioned steps but also by focusing on improved planning and design (Bocken *et al*, 2016), services (Iung and Levrat, 2014) and digital solutions (Ranta, Aarikka-Stenroos and Väisänen, 2021), to mention a few.

As a means to achieve the circular economy with its different principles and components in hand, the entire system needs to be viewed not only from the technologies being utilized and the products being manufactured, but also the life cycle of products, their design (Ghisellini, Cialani and Ulgiati, 2016) and where ownership lies. Thus, adapting a service-oriented logic is a crucial step for companies and service-dominant logic then comes into play. Service-dominant logic was introduced first within the field of marketing as a means to describe the current trends within the field. The concept points out several important phenomena: (1) services as the method of exchange, (2) production processes as a whole service rather than a means to produce products, and (3) that customers are an integral part of the creation of value, also known as value co-creation (Lusch and Vargo, 2014).

In this perspective, some researchers note that instead of viewing selling products and offering maintenance as an after-sales service, maintenance should be an integral property of the product (Iung and Levrat, 2014). Therefore, the logic is that if the producer of a product retains ownership of the product, they will design their products to be of the highest quality (Lusch and Vargo, 2014). In addition, to some extent the current economy already utilizes services as the dominant logic, if we consider consumption of commodities such as electricity and water or services like haircuts, meals and different types of experience-related activities. The existence of services within our current economic model reveals that there will be no need to transition towards a service economy, but rather that current services are a natural development within the economy which will further evolve to utilize service-dominant logic and value creation together with one's customers (Lusch and Vargo, 2014). Yet some academics argue that despite the economy having some service-oriented focus, the natural next step from the circular economy is towards a performance economy with a focus on services (Stahel, 2010).

While there are differing views on the role of services and whether or not it will become a large systematic change, it is clear that to achieve a circular economy, services will be in the centre of it all. The service focus will also require more open cooperation between companies, other entities and customers.

To catalyse the transition towards a circular economy, this case study aims to provide the reader with a practical example of how the circular economy and service-dominant logic can be applied in business activities in the manufacturing sector, which in many aspects is regarded as a traditional field resistant to change. The objective of this chapter is to describe the field of manufacturing and a case company operating in business-to-business sales within the field. In addition, this case study will discuss the themes of circular economy, sustainability and services.

The manufacturing field

The modern manufacturing field, which utilized assembly lines such as those in the factory of Henry Ford, is the norm in achieving mass production and economies of scale to *reduce* costs. When we consider manufacturing, what comes to mind is often large facilities filled with machinery, assembly lines and workers hurrying along. Yet we do not often consider the materials that are flowing through the process and the environmental impact that they have on the manufacturing process. The environmental impact can range from use of virgin materials, materials wasted during the process, maintaining the machines within the factory, the energy and other commodities used within the factory and all the additional steps undertaken after the product leaves the factory premises. The manufacturing processes to some extent are unified, although of course different products may have some specialities in what the manufacturing process may entail and/or the machinery/equipment used. Yet the majority of the process is quite unified and one of the most shared and common aspects is the use of compressed air. Air compressors act in the process as a means of converting power to energy, and to achieve this goal the machine often requires fossil fuels to operate. The use of fossil fuels is commonly known to contribute to CO_2 emissions and climate change, not to mention that in certain manufacturing fields, such as food processing and packaging, the risk of the oil reaching the final product is too high and poses a risk to human health (Tamturbo, 2021).

Manufacturing activities also aim to achieve profitability by scaling production up, which means that the amounts of oil used are substantially higher than in small-scale business activities or private usage. In addition, air compressors used in manufacturing activities are often large and use up large amounts of energy. Of the air compressors in manufacturing, about 80 per cent use oil and 20 per cent are mostly oil-less (Tamturbo, 2021). Yet these mostly oil-less compressors still use oil to lubricate certain components and the bearings, and eventually this oil does leak into the factory setting, possibly to the final products and, worst of all, perhaps the local environment. These oil-less air compressors use a technology that is 50 years old, which highlights the outdated status of the field. Most air compressors using this old technology last up to 10 years, and in some cases minor *remanufacturing* practices can add up to an additional five years according to research (Zanghelini *et al*, 2014). Both types of air compressors, due to the nature of the machinery, oil usage and general wear and tear, lead to air compressor manufacturers gaining large profits through constant maintenance, which is not included in the purchase of an air compressor. In addition, these traditional technologies are known to substantially lose energy efficiency after a few years in use (Tamturbo, 2021). Furthermore, research has found that the use and maintenance phase of the life cycle of air compressors comprises 97 per cent of the emissions; this phase excludes the production phase as well as the disposal phase (Zanghelini *et al*, 2014). The same research found also that another phase in which the environmental impact is large is in the beginning, when new raw materials are being taken on, and that a substantial amount of the materials ends up in landfills, even though some recycling of usable parts is mandatory under EU regulations (Zanghelini *et al*, 2014).

The case company

With all these factors and long-standing experience in the field of air compressor technology, the founders of the case company set out to solve the issues of the field and alleviate the environmental impacts caused by these compressors. They set out to rethink how air compressors are designed to *refuse* the use of fossil fuels and to *reduce* the usage of energy. The case company uses a turbo compressor technology with magnetic bearing technology that enables them to be truly oil-free and has 15 per cent better energy efficiency than traditional air compressors. If utilized globally, the energy efficiency alone would have a considerable impact on the world's energy production, where the change towards green energy could be sustained. Compared to traditional air compressors, the case company's air compressors require 90 per cent less maintenance, which in turn means 90 per cent fewer materials used, saving natural resources during the life cycle of the machine. As the maintenance requirements are low in comparison, the company is able to monitor its functions remotely and, in emergencies, support their customers in *repairing* the machine. The compressor's life cycle is twice those of traditional compressors and can utilize energy that traditional compressors lose while operating. When considering the costs of the entire life cycle of the air compressor, the case company's customers are saving up to 30 per cent as well as having a far superior choice in regard to the environment. Now, while the technological aspects of the air compressors the case company produces are regarded as a significant improvement for their customers from an economic aspect as well as an environmental aspect, they are just at the beginning.

In the field of manufacturing this can be seen from the thought process that the manufacturing industry will slowly shift to accept that there are four commodities that they purchase rather than three. Traditionally in the manufacturing industry there are three types of commodity: electricity, water and heat. Instead of buying machinery to produce these commodities, manufacturing companies often purchase only the service or utility they provide. Compressed air, in the eyes of the case company, should be no different, and that is the service they wish to provide: 'Air as a service'. While considering this aspect from the viewpoint of the manufacturing companies, it also makes sense that they do not wish to know what types of machine are producing the air, or how much maintenance they require and so forth; they just need the compressed air. The service aspect of providing customers with a commodity they need as a service is a logical one and creates value for the customers. Now, if a company decides to purchase air as a service, this simply means that the case company will place their machine in their customer's facility for them to use, and once they do not require the machine anymore, the case company will take it back and resell the machine forward, which is one of the principles of the circular economy. The service logic also means that the machine's ownership stays with the case company, which motivates them to keep their machines up to date and as long-lasting as possible.

To recap the actions that the case company took in regard to the circular economy framework:

- The case company started out by rethinking what types of air compressor are being produced and designed out fossil fuels and, as such, *refused* to use them.
- The case company's technology *reduces* the amount of energy being used, and by retaining ownership they are able to *reuse* parts and *repair* and *refurbish* the machinery they provide to their customers; then, when the compressor reaches the end of its life span, the parts can be reused to manufacture another compressor.

- The parts of the machinery that are not used are then *recycled* by the case company appropriately, so that nothing is wasted.

On a general level, if we consider the benefits and concerns of a company retaining ownership of their products and materials, we arrive at the list shown in Figure 10.1.

Conclusion

With the case company's solution, we feel as if all the problems of the manufacturing industry are solved, but it is, after all, only one solution to one issue within the larger domain of manufacturing. Yet it proves that a small change can make a big difference and perhaps act as a catalyst to others to develop their business towards the circular economy and service logic in an attempt to *reduce* humankind's impact on the environment. While the discussion on how to make an impact is often divided between consumers' actions and companies' actions, the part that is neglected is considering the role of consumers in their professional roles and how a positive impact can be made internally within companies, not only in their private roles (Teerikangas *et al*, 2020).

The discussion on how actors and agents behave within companies is an important one to consider, as often the reason behind why circular economy business models are not adapted is reluctance. One study found that the reluctance in the manufacturing field to adopt circular economy business models was due to perceptions and that commonplace challenges could be

Figure 10.1 General advantages and disadvantages of retaining ownership for a company

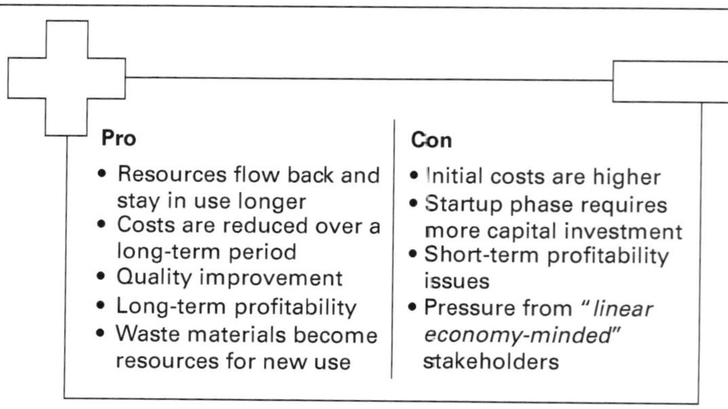

overcome in practice (Linder and Williander, 2017). In addition, academic research within the manufacturing field in regard to the circular economy is often focused either on the technologies used or the different ways companies can measure or model their activities (Acerbi and Taisch, 2020). It has been found that there is little theoretical discussion on the circular economy and that more research into the human aspects of the transition is needed (Sarja, Onkila and Mäkelä, 2020).

After studying the case, the reader will be able to remember what types of air compressor there are in the manufacturing field and their differences. Furthermore, the reader will be able to understand and explain the concepts of the circular economy and service thinking. With the given 9Rs of the circular economy (*rethink/refuse*, *reduce*, *reuse*, *repair*, *refurbish*, *remanufacture*, *repurpose*, *recycle* and *recover*), the reader will be able to apply these principles to other scenarios and functions of business. With the detailed example combined with relevant terms, the reader will be able to analyse new situations and the connections they have with the case. With the given concepts, the reader will be able to apply, analyse and more importantly evaluate new situations that they will encounter in different domains of business. With the introduced principles and supporting questions, the reader will be able to apply and create their own solutions, aligned with their personal environmental goals.

Learning outcomes

- This case has highlighted the importance of revisioning already existing processes or products and how they can be provided to customers.
- The case provides an example of how the shift in ownership can prove to be a solution that brings a company long-lasting business and profit while their customers enjoy improved service solutions.
- The case provides a detailed explanation of how the manufacturing field works in relation to air compressors, what problems the field has and how they could be solved with a new paradigm.
- The case helps the reader to recognize and appreciate the importance of long-term decision making; the circular economy and service solutions focus on achieving long-term profitability instead of short-term benefits. This means achieving a more stable base of profit.

- The case highlights the potential for service thinking. When a traditional manufacturing product can logically be changed into a commodity that is purchased as a service, it opens up possibilities in different fields.
- The case highlights the environmental benefits in retaining ownership of a company's products/materials, as when a company is invested in keeping its own materials in circulation, it gains monetary benefits while the negative impacts on the environment are *reduced*.

Questions

With these thoughts in mind, we have compiled a list of questions to contemplate:

1 What are the advantages and disadvantages of products as a service?
2 What are the next steps for the company, in regard to strategy and sustainability?
3 Consider everyday items that you own. Which of these could actually be purchased as a service? Do you actually need the item or just the function it accomplishes?
4 Consider the different circular economy principles (eg *rethink, reduce, reuse*, etc) outlined in the case. Are they all fulfilled by the case company's business activities?

References

Acerbi, F and Taisch, M (2020) A literature review on circular economy adoption in the manufacturing sector, *Journal of Cleaner Production*, **273**, article 123086

Bocken, N M *et al* (2016) Product design and business model strategies for a circular economy, *Journal of Industrial and Production Engineering*, **33** (5), pp 308–20

Ellen MacArthur Foundation (2017) [accessed 7 July 2021] *What is the* Circular Economy? *Ellen MacArthur Foundation* [Online] www.ellenmacarthurfoundation.org/circular-economy/what-is-the-circular-economy (archived at https://perma.cc/LH7X-X49G)

Geissdoerfer, M *et al* (2017) The circular economy–a new sustainability paradigm?, *Journal of Cleaner Production*, **143**, pp 757–68

Geng, Y and Côté, R P (2002) Scavengers and decomposers in an eco-industrial park, *The International Journal of Sustainable Development & World Ecology*, **9** (4), pp 333–40

Ghisellini, P, Cialani, C and Ulgiati, S (2016) A review on circular economy: the expected transition to a balanced interplay of environmental and economic systems, *Journal of Cleaner Production*, **114**, pp 11–32

Gong, Y *et al* (2020) Investigation into circular economy of plastics: the case of the UK fast moving consumer goods industry, *Journal of Cleaner Production*, **244**, article 118941

Iung, B and Levrat, E (2014) Advanced maintenance services for promoting sustainability, *Procedia CIRP*, **22**, pp 15–22

Kirchherr, J, Reike, D and Hekkert, M (2017) Conceptualizing the circular economy: an analysis of 114 definitions, *Resources, Conservation and Recycling*, **127**, pp 221–32

Linder, M and Williander, M (2017) Circular business model innovation: inherent uncertainties, *Business Strategy and the Environment*, **26** (2), pp 182–96

Lusch, R F and Vargo, S L (2014) *Service-Dominant Logic: Premises, perspectives, possibilities*, Cambridge University Press, Cambridge

Pearce, D W and Turner, R K (1990) *Economics of Natural Resources and the Environment*, JHU Press, Baltimore

Ranta, V, Aarikka-Stenroos, L and Väisänen, J M (2021) Digital technologies catalyzing business model innovation for circular economy – multiple case study, *Resources, Conservation and Recycling*, **164**, article 105155

Sarja, M, Onkila, T and Mäkelä, M (2020) A systematic literature review of the transition to the circular economy in business organizations: obstacles, catalysts and ambivalences, *Journal of Cleaner Production*, **286**, article 125492

Stahel, W R (2010) *The Performance Economy*, 2nd edn, Palgrave Macmillan, New York

Tamturbo (2021) [accessed 7 July 2021] Industry and Market, *Tamturbo* [Online] www.tamturbo.com/industry-and-market/ (archived at https://perma.cc/4GHF-QR38)

Teerikangas, S *et al* (2020) [accessed 7 July 2021] Policy Brief: Invitation: Join the Circular Economy Celebration! *CICAT2025* [Online] https://cicat2025.turkuamk.fi/uploads/2020/09/8af5175f-cicat2025_policy_brief_2.pdf (archived at https://perma.cc/3RS9-5RTY)

Van Buren, N *et al* (2016) Towards a circular economy: the role of Dutch logistics industries and governments, *Sustainability*, **8** (7), p 647

Zanghelini, G M *et al* (2014) Waste management life cycle assessment: the case of a reciprocating air compressor in Brazil, *Journal of Cleaner Production*, **70**, pp 164–74

11 Sustainable supplier management at Coca-Cola India

Creating a green ecosystem

DR TOM MCNAMARA, RENNES SCHOOL OF BUSINESS, FRANCE

DR IRENA DESCUBES, RENNES SCHOOL OF BUSINESS, FRANCE

Introduction

While the company might not do much to promote it today, Coca-Cola started out as a cocaine-based tonic in 1886, the brainchild of a former Confederate colonel named John Pemberton, in the town of Atlanta, Georgia. From its humble beginnings the company wanted to differentiate itself as a luxury product, and put great emphasis on marketing, branding and growth strategies. These efforts paid off early. By the 1920s the brand was easily identified by people as far away as Shanghai looking to quench their thirst (Feloni, 2016). Today, Coca-Cola (NYSE: KO) is a global behemoth, with almost $38 billion in net operating revenue (fiscal year 2019) and a presence in over 200 countries. The company claims its products are served to customers 1.9 billion times a day, capturing roughly $1 out of every $4 that consumers spend on non-alcoholic beverages (coca-colacompany.com).

In 1950, Coca-Cola opened its first bottling plant in India, in the city of New Delhi. But by 1977 the company would be forced to leave due to the country's odious Foreign Exchange Act, a law which placed limits on how much a foreign company could invest in India. However, in 1991 the Indian economy started to liberalize once more and in 1993 Coca-Cola returned, opening a production facility just outside the city of Agra (coca-colaindia.com; Panchal, 2014).

Today, with 54 plants, Coca-Cola is one of the premier beverage companies in India, providing a complete range of soft drinks, juices, teas, coffees, water and energy drinks. Its brands are beloved by millions of local consumers, and with a network of more than 2.6 million retail outlets, the company is a vital force in the Indian economy. Coke says that, as of 2011, it had invested $2 billion in India, and that by the end of 2020 it planned to invest another $5 billion (Krishna, 2020; coca-colaindia.com). Almost 25,000 people are directly employed by the company, with an estimated 1.5 million more employed indirectly through Coke's 'ecosystem' of purchasing, production, and supply chain and logistics activities. At every step of its value chain, Coke tries to integrate local producers, adopting a 'farm to fork' strategy that benefits Indian society. As a result, 95 per cent of the ingredients used to make Coca-Cola products are sourced locally (Krishna, 2020; coca-colaindia.com).

The challenge for Coca-Cola, however, is to make sure that this above-mentioned high economic impact does not leave a comparable carbon footprint on the Indian environment.

The environmental challenge facing Coca-Cola

Concerns about climate change, the depletion of resources and increasing levels of pollution have given companies an incentive to figure out ways to reduce the environmental impact of their operations (Jia *et al*, 2015). Increasingly, beverage companies are recognized as a source of a disturbing amount of pollution. By 2021 it is expected that more than half a trillion plastic bottles will be produced every year – this equates into almost 16,000 bottles manufactured every second. Unfortunately, many of these bottles are carelessly discarded, ending up in the ocean (Laville and Taylor, 2017). Recycling rates for bottles vary widely, with some countries reportedly recovering over 90 per cent of their plastic bottles, while others achieve a rate of only 10 per cent (Lucas, 2019). However, the use of plastic bottles would appear to have some environmental benefits. According to the British Plastics Federation (BPF), admittedly a plastics lobbying group, producing bottles from 100 per cent recycled plastic uses 75 per cent less energy than making them from new plastic. Furthermore, using plastic bottles means using less fuel in transport and logistics, resulting in savings of up to 40 per cent (bpf.co.uk).

That said, plastic bottles are increasingly being seen as a menace to the environment. And for many people, Coca-Cola is Public Enemy # 1. For two years in a row (2018 and 2019), Coca-Cola had the dubious honour of being named the world's most polluting brand in a global audit carried out by a group known as 'Break Free From Plastic'. It was reported that Coke was responsible for generating more plastic waste than the next top three polluters combined. Perhaps not exactly scientific, the 'audit' consisted of 72,000 volunteers combing beaches, waterways and neighbourhoods near where they lived and worked, picking up all forms of discarded waste in a one-day clean-up exercise held in September 2019. Over 475,000 pieces of plastic waste were collected, with the number-one brand being Coca-Cola, which was responsible for 11,732 pieces of plastic rubbish. More precisely, Coke was found to be the number-one source for plastic waste in Europe and Africa, and the second-largest source in Asia and South America. Surprisingly, Coca-Cola, based in the United States, ranked only fifth among all companies responsible for plastic debris in North America (Lerner, 2019; Nace, 2019).

Sustainable supply chain management (SSCM) – a possible solution?

More and more, companies face pressure to take responsibility for the social, economic and environmental aspects of their operations (Hartmann and Moeller, 2014). Coca-Cola would be no exception. One way for companies to behave as good corporate citizens is through sustainable supply chain management (SSCM). Historically, supply chain management has been defined as the coordination of the traditional business activities of a given company across all of the associated businesses for a given supply chain, with the goal being to improve the overall performance of each individual company and the supply chain as a whole (Mentzer *et al*, 2001). SSCM would advance this concept by addressing the integration of social, economic and environmental objectives across a given firm's supply chain operations, with the goal being to improve the sustainability of the processes that are responsible for producing goods or services (Carter and

Rogers, 2008; Seuring and Müller, 2008). SSCM encompasses several practices, including the sustainable design of products, sustainable production of goods and services, evaluation and selection of suppliers according to their sustainable capabilities, and sustainable logistics, to name just a few (Sarkis and Dhavale, 2015; Hofstetter, 2018). However, of all of these elements, sustainable supplier selection perhaps is the most important. Since suppliers are located upstream in a company's supply chain, any disruptions with a given supplier could have a dramatic effect on downstream operations. Therefore, effective supplier selection, in terms of sustainability, is critical (Li *et al*, 2019).

To summarize, SSCM is the practice of making traditional supply chain management more sustainable (Kuik *et al*, 2010), and it is being seen increasingly by companies as a priority in strategic terms of their operations (Song *et al*, 2017a, 2017b). For its part, Coca-Cola realizes that it needs to adapt its supply chain to be more sustainable, and to its credit, the company has already taken major steps towards that goal.

Environmental responsibility at Coca-Cola

Mr James Quincey, Chairman and Chief Executive Officer at Coca-Cola, says that the company is committed to promoting sustainability. 'We have a track record of setting ambitious sustainability goals, and going after them. In the end, there is only one planet, and we all want to live on it, and we want to be able to do so with a good quality of life. That requires us to hit our sustainability goals' (Bursztynsky, 2019).

For Coke, this is a daunting task. The company produced an astounding 110 billion plastic bottles in 2016 alone (Bursztynsky, 2019). Realizing its responsibility to reclaim and dispose of this waste in an environmentally proper manner, in December of 2018 Coke announced that it was investing in technology that would make it easier to use recycled plastic in the manufacturing of its bottles, and that by 2030 the company hoped that 50 per cent of the bottles that it produced would contain recycled plastic (Bursztynsky, 2019). As distasteful as plastic might be to many consumers, Mr Quincy insists that the plastic used in its bottles, polyethylene terephthalate (more commonly referred to as PET), produces less carbon dioxide than aluminium cans or glass bottles (Lucas, 2019). Coca-Cola says that it needs to reduce its carbon footprint and is already looking beyond recycling efforts. As proof of his commitment to sustainability, Mr Quincey highlights the fact that in 2016 Coca-Cola became 'water neutral'; that is, all of the water that is used in its finished products gets replenished back to nature (Bursztynsky, 2019).

In its 2019 Business and Sustainability Report (Coca-Cola, 2020), the company makes clear its intentions to reduce greenhouse gas (GHG) emissions throughout its supply chain, with the eventual goal being the reduction of GHG emissions by 25 per cent by the year 2030 (from what they were in 2015). The decisions taken in Atlanta with respect to improving the health of the planet and its inhabitants would be applied to practically all of the countries that Coca-Cola operates in, and India would be no exception.

Coca-Cola's sustainability efforts in India

Coca-Cola India is committed to having a green supply chain, as well as improving its SSCM capabilities. Coke's framework for sustainability employs a 'multi-level, multi-stakeholder approach', which is in accordance with the UN Sustainable Development Goals. It is based on a partnership between the Indian government, the private sector and the local community.

In 2018, Coca-Cola India carried out a detailed analysis to determine what the company's sustainability priorities should be in terms of their possible impact on business operations and the issues that stakeholders were most concerned with, based on the internal and external sustainability priorities.

Coke determined that its internal sustainability priorities were:

- Water stewardship
- Ethics and governance
- Product and ingredient safety
- Responsible supply chain management
- Manufacturing waste
- Sustainable agriculture
- Sustainable packaging
- Low calorie and no sugar portfolio
- Climate change

In terms of external stakeholders, the sustainability priorities were determined to be:

- Transparent nutrition information
- Community engagement
- Occupational Health & Safety (OHS)
- Human and workplace rights
- Diversity and equal opportunity
- Women's empowerment
- Post-consumer recycling
- Employee wellness, development & engagement
- Retailer capability development
- Responsible marketing
- Data security and privacy
- Sanitation and hygiene (CCIPL Sustainability Update 2018–19).

Truth be told, Coke has no shortage of achievements that it can point to in order to show its green credentials and ambitions. The company is proud of the fact that 50 per cent of the energy that it uses comes from renewable sources (coca-colaindia.com). Other ways Coke is reducing its energy usage and pollution generation is through LED lights, energy-efficient motors, pumps, compressors and refrigeration systems, roof-top solar panels, and boilers that use compressed natural gas (CNG) and biomass (CCIPL Sustainability Update 2018–19). All of these efforts will, in turn, help the Indian government achieve its goal of reducing the country's GHG emissions to the levels that they were in 2005 by the year 2030 (coca-colaindia.com).

As a further sign of Coke's commitment to India's environment, the company announced in June 2018 a recycling programme designed to 'recover and recycle one package for every single one that we put out in the market' by the year 2030 (Financial Express, 2018). In addition, Coke has a system in place to buy offsetting credits from people who recycle PET bottles. The company intends to spend almost $150 million to develop a country-wide green ecosystem for the sustainable management of plastic waste. Plans call for the creation of what are known as material recovery and segregation facilities (MRFs), which will promote the collection and separation of waste at the source in the cities of Delhi, Chennai, Andhra Pradesh, Uttar Pradesh and Karnataka. The goal is to have no recyclable material sent to landfill by 2025 (Balaji, 2019; Krishna, 2020).

Perhaps no one can speak with more authority about Coke's sustainability efforts in India than Mr Ishteyaque Amjad, Vice President of Sustainability and Public Affairs, Coca-Cola India and South West Asia. Mr Amjad highlights the fact that Coke identifies as being 'local', citing the example that for their juice brand Maaza, mangoes known as Neelam are used when the product is sold in Tamil Nadu; however, when the same product is sold in the north of India, Coke uses Kesar mangoes (Krishna, 2020). In terms of supply chain management, it doesn't get more local than that.

But Coke's ambitions with regard to its farmers and local suppliers go way beyond mangoes. The company wants to improve the way Indian agriculture works, providing higher-quality fruit and better-tasting products. To do this, Coke talks of having a closed loop between consumers and farmers. Mr Amjad says that this will be achieved by the company's ambitious Fruit Circular Economy initiative. The $1.7 billion project's immediate goal is to rectify the many inefficiencies seen in Indian farming. By providing training and improved agricultural methods, higher-quality fruit will be produced, with Coca-Cola providing the demand for this increased output through new fruit-based product offerings. This will, in effect, create a symbiotic relationship between Coca-Cola and its local farmers. Not only will the company's supply chain become more sustainable, quality will also improve thanks to having control over all the operations needed to produce beverages from 'grove to glass'. In an added benefit to the local community, Coca-Cola believes that farmers' incomes will double by 2022. As one executive explained, Coke is about providing consumers with choices, adding, 'In India, we will localize these choices' (IANS, 2019; Krishna, 2020; The Economic Times, 2017; The Wharton School, 2017).

For Coca-Cola, local also means 'sustainably sourced', that is, that any ingredients supplied adhere to the company's high standards with regard to human and worker rights, respect for the environment, and using sustainable agricultural methods. All of these can be found in Coca-Cola's Sustainable Agriculture Guiding Principles (SAGP). When a supplier becomes part of Coke's ecosystem, they must agree to abide by the SAGP, ensuring that the company will have a green supply chain (coca-colaindia.com).

Another sustainability concern for Coca-Cola is water. From the start, even as a curious elixir in the Atlanta area of America's deep South, the company had the ingenious idea to keep distribution costs low by using locally sourced water in the production process. Unfortunately, by the 2000s Coca-Cola was receiving a great deal of criticism from farmers in regions where water was a scarce commodity. In 2007 Coke was the target of a boycott orchestrated by US college students in solidarity with Indian farmers who were accusing the company of stealing their resources and endangering their incomes. As a result of this public protest, in that same year the company announced that it would dedicate itself to being more responsible with regard to the way it managed its water use. Coke's CEO at the time, E Neville Isdell, announced that 'the Coca-Cola Company pledges to replace every drop of water we use in our beverages and their production to achieve balance in communities and in nature with the water we use' (MacDonald, 2018).

In India, Mr Amjad explains that Coke uses 1.7 litres of water for each litre of beverage that it produces. As a result, the company believes that, in order to be sustainable, it has an obligation to replenish the India aquifer with over three times the volume of beverages that it produces. Over the past 10 years, Coca-Cola India has set up initiatives to replenish the water it uses. The company utilizes a '3R' approach to water stewardship: Reduce, Recycle and Replenish. Mr Amjad boasts that as a result of using cutting-edge technology, combined with coordination with bottling partners to recycle and reuse water whenever possible, the company has seen a 30 per cent improvement in a key sustainability metric – Water Usage Ratio (WUR). Presently, a reported 200 per cent of the water that Coca-Cola India uses in its operations gets restored to nature (coca-colaindia.com; Krishna, 2020).

Perhaps one of the most encouraging aspects of Coke's focus on sustainability, as well as one of its most ambitious, is the stated objective of empowering women. The company says that it is making deliberate efforts to integrate small businesses that are owned by women throughout its supply chain. By providing access to relevant training programmes, as well as financial services, Coca-Cola believes that it will provide women with the skills and confidence they need to create successful businesses (coca-colacompany.com).

To accelerate this desire to empower women, Coca-Cola India plans on installing 1,000 solar-powered coolers in small shops that are owned by women, primarily in rural parts of India. The novelty of these devices is that they do not just cool beverages. They also have built-in chargers for mobile phones, as well as a rechargeable solar lantern. Remote Indian villages usually have an intermittent supply of electricity (if any at all). The rechargeable lantern allows shops to stay open after sunset, meaning more business from customers who want to enjoy a cool drink in the evening, and the mobile charger allows shop owners to gain a nominal fee for its use. Plus, the solar-powered coolers help shop owners reduce their electricity bills (coca-colaindia.com).

Maintaining SSCM in challenging times

A key element of successful SSCM, in the context of a global supply chain, would be clear governance mechanisms (Koberg and Longoni, 2019). These can be referred to as any 'practices and initiatives' that a company uses in order to better manage its relationship with the members of its supply chain, as well as any relevant stakeholders, with the goal being to improve operating results in terms of sustainability (Formentini and Taticchi, 2016). At Coke, sustainability governance would take the form of a Policy and Sustainability Committee. Its job is to assist the Board of Directors in 'overseeing the company's policies and programs and related risks to the company that concern regulatory, public policy and corporate social responsibility matters, including progress against the company's sustainability goals' (Coca-Cola, 2020).

Another tool that Coca-Cola India would use to manage its sustainable supply chain would be something known as an Enterprise Risk Management (ERM) structure. This allows the company to 'identify, assess and manage existing and new risks in a planned and coordinated manner with minimum disruption and cost, to protect and preserve our human, physical and financial assets'. This ERM structure would be reinforced by a system of internal audits.

In addition to the previously discussed SAGP for farmers, the company has a list of Supplier Guiding Principles (SGP) for suppliers. All qualified suppliers are contractually obligated to adhere to the SGP. Suppliers are expected to have appropriate controls and systems in place to ensure that members of Coca-Cola's supply chain in India adhere to the SGP. To verify this, Coke systematically uses independent third-party auditors to review the operations of their suppliers. Substandard performance is expected to be swiftly corrected. If a supplier fails to respect the SGP, they risk having their contract terminated. This additional layer of control is a way to ensure that when you do business with Coca-Cola you respect certain fundamental rights and principles with regard to good conduct. The company says that the SGP is based upon the notion that:

> good corporate citizenship is essential to our long-term business success and must be reflected in our relationships and actions in our workplaces and the workplaces of those who are authorized to directly supply to our business. The Supplier Guiding Principles communicate our values and expectations and emphasize the importance of responsible workplace policies and practices that comply, at a minimum, with applicable environmental/labor laws and regulations. (CCIPL Sustainability Update 2018–19)

More recently, Coca-Cola, like all companies, has had to face the challenges of the viral pandemic known as Covid-19. Here, once again, maintaining high standards with regard to sustainability (as well as health and safety) is at the forefront. Mr Amjad says that Coca-Cola has been coordinating with local farmers and suppliers, reassuring them of their importance and the company's commitment to sustainability, even during this global crisis (Krishna, 2020).

Using SSCM to gain a competitive advantage?

The Indian non-alcoholic beverage market is an extremely competitive one. Not only does Coca-Cola have to compete with its arch nemesis Pepsi, it must also compete with hundreds of local brands. While Coke is still by far the industry leader in India, having an almost 50 per cent market share, it still is underrepresented in rural markets, where 'hyper-localized' flavours would be the preference. In 2019, Coke saw its market share grow by an anaemic 0.05 per cent, which was much better than Pepsi's 2.2 per cent decline. But the segment known as 'regional brands' saw its market share grow by 1.2 per cent. This, Coke believes, is where the future lies (Bhushan, 2020).

Coca-Cola's SSCM efforts and know-how have served the company well until now. The hope is that SSCM will make the company even more local and more sustainable, helping it to continue its journey of bringing refreshing drinks to thirsty Indian consumers.

Learning outcomes

- This case has highlighted the importance of considering the web of interconnected stakeholders for effective decision making in a circular economy.
- The case provides an example of multi-criteria decision making, where the criteria stem from the agendas and objectives of the stakeholders involved.
- The case helps to appreciate the importance of open loop supply chains within the sustainability transition.
- The case highlights the potential of biomethanization and the supply chain that supports this renewable energy.

Questions

1 What would be some of the governance mechanisms that Coca-Cola uses to ensure that its sustainability efforts in India succeed? Can you think of any others? Explain.

2 If you were designing an updated list of Supplier Guiding Principles (SGP) for Coca-Cola in India, what would it look like? What support would you offer for a company wish ng to do business with Coca-Cola India?

3 Coca-Cola has several sustainable priorities for its internal operations and external stakeholders. Which dc you think are the most important and why? Which do you think are the least important and why? Be sure to explain your answers.

References

Balaji, R (2019) [accessed 7 July 2021] From Planting Trees to Promoting Waste Segregation, Here's How These Companies Are Helping the Environment, *YourStory*, 5 June [Online] https://yourstory.com/socialstory/2019/06/world-environment-day-companies-csr (archived at https://perma.cc/A8UC-H9S8)

Bhushan, R (2020) [accessed 7 July 2021] Regional Drink Brands Grow at Twice the Rate of Pepsi, Coca-Cola, *The Economic Times*, 20 February [Online] https://economictimes.indiatimes.com/industry/cons-products/fmcg/regional-drink-brands-grew-at-twice-the-rate-of-pepsi-coca-cola/articleshow/74218961.cms?utm_source=contentofinterest&utm_medium=text&utm_campaign=cppst (archived at https://perma.cc/UU9Z-45GX)

British Plastics Federation (BFP): bpf.co.uk (archived at

Bursztynsky, J (2019) [accessed 7 July 2021] Coca-Cola CEO: Wall Street Plays Catch-up Rewarding Firms for Socially Responsible Investments, *CNBC*, 9 December [Online] www.cnbc.com/2019/12/09/coca-cola-ceo-james-quincey-wall-street-catching-up-on-esg-investing.html (archived at https://perma.cc/M4MU-8CJM)

Carter, C R and Rogers, D S (2008) A framework of sustainable supply chain management: moving toward new theory, *International Journal of Physical Distribution & Logistics Management*, **38** (5), pp 360–87

Coca-Cola (2020) [accessed 7 July 2021] 2019 Business and Sustainability Report, *Coca-Cola*, April [Online] www.coca-colacompany.com/content/dam/journey/us/en/reports/coca-cola-business-and-sustainability-report-2019.pdf (archived at https://perma.cc/7GBQ-RKF4)

Coca-Cola India Private Limited (CCIPL) [accessed 08 July 2021] Sustainability Update 2018-19 Online Supplementary Report, *CCIPL* [Online] www.google.com/url?sa=t&rct=j&q=&esrc=s&source=web&cd=&ved=2ahUKEwiuuIbI-9PxAhWvy4UKHc6-DjQQFnoECAIQAA&url=https%3A%2F%2Fwww.coca-colaindia.com%2Fcontent%2Fdam%2Fjourney%2Fin%2Fen%2Fprivate%2Fhero-story%2FCCIPL-Online-Supplement_2018-19_Final.pdf&usg=AOvVaw2kWRWRYacMScEs3UQ0qlqq (archived at https://perma.cc/JZ6J-H6VM)

Feloni, R (2016) [accessed 7 July 2021] 7 Strategies Coca-Cola Used to Become One of the World's Most Recognizable Brands, *Business Insider*, 19 February [Online] www.businessinsider.fr/us/strategies-coca-cola-used-to-become-an-iconic-brand-2016-2 (archived at https://perma.cc/JP78-AV3U)

Financial Express (2018) [accessed 7 July 2021] Coca-Cola, Infosys, Others Pledge to Beat Plastic Pollution in India, 2 June [Online] www.financialexpress.com/industry/coca-cola-infosys-others-pledge-to-beat-plastic-pollution-in-india/1191193/ (archived at https://perma.cc/JM4C-NCQU)

Formentini, M and Taticchi, P (2016) Corporate sustainability approaches and governance mechanisms in sustainable supply chain management, *Journal of Cleaner Production*, **112**, pp 1920–33

Hartmann, J and Moeller, S (2014) Chain liability in multitier supply chains? Responsibility attributions for unsustainable supplier behavior, *Journal of Operations Management*, **32** (5), pp 281–94

Hofstetter, J S (2018) Extending management upstream in supply chains beyond direct suppliers, *IEEE Engineering Management Review*, **46** (1), pp 106–16

IANS (2019) [accessed 7 July 2021] Coke to Complete $1.7 bn Investment in 'Fruit Circular Economy', *IANS*, 10 November [Online] www.outlookindia.com/newsscroll/coke-to-complete-17-bn-investment-in-fruit-circular-economy/1659376 (archived at https://perma.cc/8WJA-A33N)

Jia, P, Diabat, A and Mathiyazhagan, K (2015) Analyzing the SSCM practices in the mining and mineral industry by ISM approach, *Resources Policy*, **46**, pp 76–85

Koberg, E and Longoni, A (2019) A systematic review of sustainable supply chain management in global supply chains, *Journal of Cleaner Production*, **207**, pp 1084–98

Krishna, V (2020) [accessed 7 July 2021] Sustainability during COVID-19: Coca-Cola India VP on how the Company is Adopting Best Practices, *YourStory*, 19 August [Online] https://yourstory.com/2020/08/sustainability-covid-19-coca-cola-india-ishteyaque-amjad (archived at https://perma.cc/JU5S-8RFU)

Kuik, S S, Nagalingam, S V and Amer, Y (2010) Challenges in implementing sustainable supply chain within a collaborative manufacturing network, *Proceedings of the 8th International Conference on Supply Chain Management and Information Systems*, Hong Kong, pp 1–8

Laville, S and Taylor, M (2017) [accessed 7 July 2021] A Million Bottles a Minute: World's Plastic Binge 'as Dangerous as Climate Change', *The Guardian*, 28 June [Online] www.theguardian.com/environment/2017/jun/28/a-million-a-minute-worlds-plastic-bottle-binge-as-dangerous-as-climate-change (archived at https://perma.cc/DKG5-FQZN)

Lerner, S (2019) [accessed 7 July 2021] Coca-Cola Named Most Polluting Brand in Global Audit of Plastic Waste, *The Intercept*, 23 October [Online] https://theintercept.com/2019/10/23/coca-cola-plastic-waste-pollution/ (archived at https://perma.cc/H9SM-XJ8J)

Li, J, Fang, H and Song, W (2019) Sustainable supplier selection based on SSCM practices: a rough cloud TOPSIS approach, *Journal of Cleaner Production*, **222**, pp 606–21

Lucas, A (2019) [accessed 7 July 2021] Coca-Cola and Pepsi Agree Plastic Waste is a Problem, but the Solution is More Complicated, *CNBC*, 24 January [Online] www.cnbc.com/2019/01/24/coca-cola-and-pepsi-agree-on-the-plastic-waste-problem-but-the-solution-is-more-complicated.html (archived at https://perma.cc/FX4L-CXP3)

MacDonald, C (2018) [accessed 7 July 2021] Coke Claims to Give Back as Much Water as it Uses: An Investigation Shows it Isn't Even Close, *The Verge*, 31 May [Online] www.theverge.com/2018/5/31/17377964/coca-cola-water-sustainability-recycling-controversy-investigation (archived at https://perma.cc/J4GC-FNHE)

Mentzer, J T *et al* (2001) Defining supply chain management, *Journal of Business Logistics,* **22** (2), pp 1—25

Nace, T (2019) [accessed 7 July 2021] Coca-Cola Named The World's Most Polluting Brand in Plastic Waste Audit, *Forbes*, 29 October 29 [Online] www.forbes.com/sites/trevornace/2019/10/29/coca-cola-named-the-worlds-most-polluting-brand-in-plastic-waste-audit/#3321937674e0 (archived at https://perma.cc/4DNX-AVLW)

Panchal, S (2014) [accessed 7 July 2021] Economic Milestone: Exit of the MNCs (1977), *Forbes India*, 14 August [Online] www.forbesindia.com/article/independence-day-special/economic-milestone-exit-of-the-mncs-(1977)/38431/1 (archived at https://perma.cc/DUW5-MXW2)

Sarkis, J and Dhavale, DG (2015) Supplier selection for sustainable operations: a triple bottom-line approach using a Bayesian framework, *International Journal of Production Economics*, **166**, pp 177–91

Seuring, S and Müller, M (2008) From a literature review to a conceptual framework for sustainable supply chain management, *Journal of Cleaner Production*, **16** (15), pp 1699–710

Song, W, Ming, X and Liu, H C (2017a) Identifying critical risk factors of sustainable supply chain management: a rough strength-relation analysis method, *Journal of Cleaner Production*, **143**, pp 100–15

Song, W, Xu, Z and Liu, H C (2017b) Developing sustainable supplier selection criteria for solar air-conditioner manufacturer: an integrated approach, *Renewable and Sustainable Energy Reviews*, **79**, pp 1461–71

The Economic Times (2017) [accessed 7 July 2021] Coca-Cola, Partners to Spend $1.7 Billion on Indian Agri Ecosystem, *The Economic Times*, 5 June [Online] https://economictimes.indiatimes.com/industry/cons-products/food/coca-cola-partners-to-spend-1-7-billion-on-indian-agri-ecosystem/articleshow/59002204.cms (archived at https://perma.cc/2VAZ-8R63)

The Wharton School (2017) [accessed 7 July 2021] Will Coca-Cola's New India Strategy Have Fizz or Go Flat?, *Knowledge@Wharton*, University of Pennsylvania, 17 November [Online] https://knowledge.wharton.upenn.edu/article/will-coca-colas-new-india-strategy-fizz-go-flat/ (archived at https://perma.cc/UW7V-VNXX)

Small and sustainable 12

The challenges of a small business in the Global South competing in domestic and international markets

DR DAIANE MÜLLING NEUTZLING, UNIVERSITY OF FORTALEZA, FORTALEZA, BRAZIL[1]

FREDIANO DA SILVA JALES, UNIVERSITY OF FORTALEZA, FORTALEZA, BRAZIL

BRENO MOTA FERNANDES, BERLIN SCHOOL OF ECONOMICS AND LAW, GERMANY

Introduction

This chapter aims to address the case of a small company and SME in the food sector located in the Northeast region of Brazil. The study shows the company's main practices, difficulties, challenges and motivations to manage its business using a sustainability orientation in the context of a sustainable supply chain. This case study includes a descriptive in-depth account of the focal company and its supply chain members were interviewed, including representatives of the focal company, raw material suppliers, exporters, brokers and its clients.

Sustainable supply chain management and its impact on SMEs

Over the years, the concept of sustainability based on Elkington's (1997) triple bottom line (TBL), focusing on environmental, social and economic sustainability, has spread in the business through the adoption of strategies and practices that, in conjunction with social and environmental principles, would help companies to develop more responsible and sustainable practices while being more competitive (Saeed and Kersten, 2019). Thus, it is observed that companies develop sustainability initiatives within and outside their organizational limits when stimuli exist through collaborative relationships with stakeholders and supply chain members (Neutzling *et al*, 2018). The academic literature in the area of sustainable supply chain management (SSCM) indicates a predominance of studies discussing large companies' strategies and relationships with their partners; however, it is notable that other perspectives are also important and must be explored empirically, for instance small and medium enterprises (SMEs) (Ashby *et al*, 2012; Touboulic and Walker, 2015). Toubolic and Walker (2015) emphasize that the focus on large corporations brings a top-down approach to studies of sustainability in supply chains, whose practices and tools do not always apply to SMEs, for example. Therefore, studies in SMEs are becoming increasingly important, due to the relevance that such companies have in economies worldwide (Kot, 2018) and to the potential for environmental impact as well (Kasim and Ismail, 2012).

SMEs are usually addressed as those that have a low level of knowledge in sustainability (Williams and O'Donovan, 2015) and a limited capacity to implement sustainable practices (Caldera *et al*, 2018). However, they can receive significant benefits from adopting sustainable practices, through waste reduction, energy savings, employee retention and, along the supply chain, the potential for innovation and new market opportunities (Kot, 2018). According to the study of the main sustainable practices carried out by Johnson and Schaltegger (2015), a difference can be observed between the sustainable management methods used by large companies and by SMEs. Thus, it is interesting that the practices used by SMEs are studied and explored empirically for a greater understanding of sustainability management in companies of all sizes (Walker and Jones, 2012). The barriers and motivations of companies in adopting these practices can be essential assets for their elaboration in such a way that they are better suited to the companies' profiles.

Another empirical gap is related to the origin of SMEs. According to Jia *et al* (2018), although there is an abundance of work in the area of SMEs, they are still mostly focused in countries at the Global North. Specific questions about SMEs in countries in the Global South are still underexplored (Khalid *et al*, 2015).

SMEs are usually addressed as those that use data collection techniques such as semi-structured interviews, direct observation and documentary research. The interviews, once one of the most important pieces of information for a case study (Yin, 2018), were used as a primary source in the collection of research data following a semi-structured interview script. Direct observation was used to explore SME SSCM, because it allows the observation of some notable behaviours and/or conditions in the organizational environment, in order to contribute additional information on the issues studied (Yin, 2018). The documentary survey was used to corroborate and increase the evidence from other sources, in order to complement them (Yin, 2018).

The company: Natvita

Founded in 1999, Natvita is a small company that produces clarified and pulpful tropical fruits such as cashew, pineapple, acerola, banana, watermelon and melon (Figure 12.1). The company trades in both the B2B and B2C markets. Natvita has a competitive advantage in the cashew juice market through the use of tubular membrane for the juice clarification process, thus allowing for higher efficiency and conservation of some of the natural

Figure 12.1 Natvita (some of the product range)

characteristics of the juice, such as taste and smell. Moreover, the company ensures the product is free from any contact with animal flesh in the clarification process in fruits because it is all done through gelatin.

In 2018, in partnership with another private company and a public company engaged in research in agriculture (EMBRAPA), Natvita developed the first organic, canned, clarified cashew juice. This extended the product's longevity and conserved its vitamin C content. Cashew is a fruit with high vitamin C content (up to six times more than orange). The production of cashew and cashew nuts is concentrated in the Northeast region of Brazil.

Natvita primarily serves the domestic market, but at the end of 2018 it made its first direct export. This was done through cooperation with the regional food union and an international business centre from the federation of local industries. The company is the first brand to commercialize canned cashew juice, by extending the product's life, preserving the product's natural characteristics and having fully recyclable material.

Sustainability orientation

In the initial reports of the interviewees linked to the focal company, there was the notion that the company was founded aiming at using sustainability as a competitive factor in the market. However, because it is a small company it suffers from some limitations imposed by the market. The company works with organic products as its core business and a secondary line of conventional products. With regard to sustainable production, it uses organic certification (third-party Institute of Brewing and Distilling (IBD) certification) for pulps and clarified juices. Regarding quality and food safety, it follows the Hazard Analysis and Critical Control Point (HACCP) standards and a third specific certification for the rules that govern the orthodox Jewish diet, the Kosher Certification.

For a small company that has limited resources specializing in sustainability, certifications serve as essential guidelines in the processes of adaptation, better understanding of practices and risk management. External audits are perceived as important because they are assessments proving that the processes are in accordance with what is expected, such as in the procedural aspects, the product and even in its work with collaborators. As a way of mitigating the impact of the manufacturing processes, the company adopts practices such as a water treatment station and emissions of atmospheric gases, not using certain chemicals in the cleaning process and waste management. With regard to the latter, it is mainly linked to the remains of peels and fruit pomace. The company allocates these by-products to the manufacture of animal feed distributed to partner farms in the region. The quality manager at the focal company noted that:

> We always challenge ourselves in pursuing excellence, to have a much cleaner, leaner process, in order to give a very nice destination both for this bagasse and for the entire production process of our company. And this is a personal motivation, to leave this process very lean, so to speak.

With regard to external processes, which apply to the supply chain, the demands imposed on suppliers are closely linked to what customers demand. That leads us to the seminal works of sustainability in supply chains, those of Seuring and Müller (2008) and Beske and Seuring (2014), where they state that companies usually pass on the demands of customers to their suppliers, in which several processes can be imposed, but mainly in search of collaboration and development of suppliers.

In the case of Natvita, the company seeks to adopt different strategies. The company has distinct groups of suppliers, both organic and conventional. With regard to organic suppliers, there is a greater security due to the required certifications. In addition, HACCP focuses on quality control and sanitary surveillance issues. Moreover, there are also social criteria, such as not using child labour or working conditions that constitute modern slavery. It is still common today in the inner cities of Brazil to find farms working irregularly with respect to the formalization of workers' labour contracts. For this reason, this issue is reinforced in the relationship with suppliers. Currently, the company has been looking for Fair Trade certified suppliers, but it has difficulties in the tropical fruit sector, as all interviewees noted:

> If it is an organic product, we demand IBD certification, if it has it (the supplier), in order to certify that this product is in fact organic in nature, and we can have all our traceability, since the traceability of our product starts from the suppliers to the final product on the shelves. (Supply chain manager)
>
> In addition to organic certification, there are desirable ones, such as fair trade, which has been requested by customers as well, but it is more complicated to obtain [...]. (Company founder and CEO)

In order to collaborate with suppliers, the company offers technical assistance with the required quality standards, from purchasing some supplies and even in processes required by the certification:

> They are being trained by a specialized agronomist who will guide them to conduct and manage the culture so that they have a satisfactory result, achieving productivity and quality that is interesting for the company and ultimately for everyone. By offering quality, it will help the company to find its sustainability, because it will be able to deliver a higher-quality product to the customer, which is what the customer wants. [...] (Company founder and CEO)

However, a weakness was identified with regard to the traceability processes when suppliers are not organic. In order to have greater control over its supply chain, the focal company is developing a process to monitor suppliers regarding compliance with social and environmental practices, but argues that it has difficulties in traceability. According to the managers, a point that weighs in their favour is the fact that the company works very strongly on trust relationships with them. This is important from the perspective of risk management and the possibility of collaborating on any identified problems:

> Regarding our conventional product, we don't ask for a certification so much, but if he used some type of pesticide or similar, we ask to be able to have a list, because whether we want it or not, it can influence the final product and the process, especially on the issue of allergens, that someone might have some type of intolerance, then this may end up having an impact. [...] (We ask for an) invoice, and sometimes we ask for a record of the map to find out if it is registered, because we need to have this traceability in a certain way. (Supply chain manager)
>
> We have our suppliers who are very loyal to us; in addition to the basic prerequisites, they work with ethics, responsibility and seriousness. When one of them deviates from these principles, it is disconnected from the company's operations. (Business director)

Regarding this issue, Natvita considered FSSC 22000 (Food Safety System Certification) certification as an internal challenge that offers a complete certification programme, including ISO 22000 and industry-specific PRP (Pre-Requisite Programme) and HACCP (Hazard Analysis and Critical Control Point). This also extends to the entire supply chain, encompassing a detailed approach to supplier operations. For the director, risk management in the company can only be done in a more in-depth way through the realization of this certification:

> We are seeking to create a process for monitoring suppliers. We already have a written process, all outlined, with approval of suppliers, an operational procedure, which we did here. And we are trying to make this implementation, because we have an organic product, but we do not have a follow-up that the supplier is also sending an organic product, as it may even have an organic certificate, but if it is not doing the procedure correctly, we have no way of knowing. (…) We are trying to obtain the FSSC (Food Safety System Certification), which is one that encompasses food security, and for that we will have to have this procedure complete and working, and the future expectation that we have is complete monitoring of suppliers, to carry out audits with them too, to have an inspection of documents that we end up not having now. (Quality manager)

Incentives and potentials

The incentives of the focal company in adopting sustainable practices come mainly from customers. According to the quality manager, innovation in the company's production process is one of the main reasons why customers, especially business-to-business (B2B) customers, work with the company. With respect to business-to-customers (B2C), it is known that in the international market there is an ever-increasing appreciation organic products. Therefore, there is great potential to increase the domestic consumer market. Certifications were essential to access these markets and seek competitiveness:

> Our customers are very concerned with all of our certifications, especially in the matter of traceability, to know if what we are selling matches with what they are buying. So, they always look for this information. [...] I think that this would be a question focused a little on transparency, because they are fully aware of our process and we are aware of their process, so it is a very safe thing to do, it is very transparent. We were able to exchange information without many restrictions, and this makes the whole process much easier. (Quality manager)

The good communication with the company's top management is corroborated with its international partners. In addition, the company's flexibility, given its structure, allows the exploration of several products/markets that larger companies do not serve because they are too big. Based on the approach to its customers, this flexibility allows the company to explore product innovation based on their demand. The company started to test the development of pulps with a higher concentration of vitamin C, for example, using organic acerola, which is a fruit with good adaptation to the region and which has a good potential for the international market:

> We started to work, started to get to know each other, there was a demand for a product there, then we went there to visit, to meet them. There was this matter of proximity, we saw that we could do the processes and we also had affinity, we get along, all of that. They were more focused on cashews and we were more focused on acerola, then there was the market possibility, the possibility of working nearby, developing processes, we did a lot of tests with (E1), who likes tests a lot, developed a product along with it, with the pulp like this, already controlling the vitamin C content so it doesn't lose it during production. The proximity helped to develop a method, and then make the project feasible. (Exporter company representative)

Another initiative is related to the processing of fruits in order to use all the potential that the fruit can offer. The opportunity to develop a cashew burger, for example, was observed in the cashew bagasse. The focal company would take full advantage of the fruit and align itself with a market trend that aims at the consumption of plant-based products, mainly by the vegan consumer. The product, which is developed in partnership with EMBRAPA, is undergoing a feasibility study process which verifies the production process. Although it is expected to be a strong product in the food market, it is still undergoing experimentation:

> An advantage for Natvita is that this is a family business and is very flexible in terms of needs, that is, they could respond to many different needs in terms of quality, in terms of service, so this is an advantage. Companies that do the same thing as Natvita, but with a large structure, are not as flexible as Natvita. This is an advantage. (Broker representative)
>
> They bring us some demands, some needs and we go after them… Some specific things, which are difficult to do, but sometimes we do it even with losses. But to be able to serve the customer, to try the product, and then, we imagine that it can go on to a larger scale. (Company founder and CEO)
>
> We always try to see how the market is reacting, and from that, we are innovating our product. We have some new opportunities that are emerging in the mix of fruits, for example, carrots with cashews, beetroots with cashews, and we are starting to migrate to this market as well, to meet an emerging demand. (Supply chain manager)

Challenges for the business sustainability

When asked about the main barriers and challenges for a sustainable business, the interviewees point out the high costs of organic production and the difficulty of having gains in scale due to industrial capacity, both of which consequently affect competitiveness. Certification, despite giving business advantages, increases costs due to the need for both an external audit and internal human resources for this to be achieved. In addition, it also affects the product's attractiveness in the domestic market:

> Our biggest barrier is the issue of cost. We are in the juice business, there are big companies here in the region. We have a high cost [...] the industrial installation of a company like Natvita, in structure, is not as efficient as one from a large company. Furthermore, we have the certification that brings us higher costs, audit costs and internal human resources to monitor and achieve the certification. Therefore, as it is an organic product, it does not come out very cheap to make such a product, and it ends up impacting our product when it arrives on the shelves. There are also added taxes. The final product arrives with a slightly higher value, unlike some competitors that manage to lower the cost a little more. So, this becomes a barrier to us for not having a much larger market, due to the cost of our final product. (Supply chain manager)

The broker who represents the company's international customers agrees with this limitation, which is the high cost of certification:

> I think the main problem is the certification, because these small, small and medium-sized companies already have social engagement, have a good relationship with their suppliers and partners. But in order to gain international credibility, they need to contact the certification institute in order to conduct an audit and be registered as [using] good practice. (Broker representative)

In addition, some processes, such as waste management, depend on the local government. The quality manager points out that the company, due to the amount of waste produced, does not need a private waste disposal company. Therefore, they depend on public collection that occurs twice a week, often generating garbage accumulation in the company. Another aspect highlighted is that there are no businesses related to selective collection and recycling that could be added as partners in the company's disposal chain.

Due to the limited production structure, Natvita merged with another company in 2019. According to the manager, this decision was strategic since there was the possibility of continuing with the brand, but at the same time expanding production capacity and increasing market competitiveness:

> The company is currently undergoing a major change and is [undertaking] the merger of three industries, forming one. [...] Today, our capacity has a limitation and is aiming for bigger things, so it was necessary to move in this direction to expand our operating capacity. So, our motivation is always to meet what our market is demanding, looking for. Not only in terms of products, but also in production capacity. (Business director)

Certifications such as FSSC and HACCP were remembered by the quality manager, with their adoption linked to greater recognition, better accreditation, market expansion, knowledge and quality of work. The interviewee, however, reiterates that this type of certification is mainly a demand from international customers, due to the concern with product quality:

> Everything is very connected to this, and as we need to have better recognition, better accreditation, in order to have a market (larger market share), to have knowledge, I believe that your greatest motivation, as a manager, as a company owner, is to receive greater certification and thus have a better quality of work and be able to arrive at an international fair, for example, and be able to say 'I have a product that is certified in such a standard and is here ready to sell to you'. [...] We are highly demanded by customers, including this FSSC audit, which is a step further than the HACCP, which we did in July of this year, [and] was a requirement from a customer. (Quality manager)

For the business director, the market is demanding responsibility with sustainability. In relation to the national territory, there is still a lack of demand, with more incidence in Europe. He cites the case of French clients who wanted to meet a cashew producer and who were strongly interested in the social work of a school supported by the farmers:

> The market is demanding this (responsibility with sustainability), there is no escape from this reality. In Brazil it is still little (the attention), but in Europe it is basic. I already have clients who arrived here from France that I took to visit a cashew farm, where a school operated, for example, supported by the farm staff. The client spent more time observing social work than the farm itself. (Business director)

For the representative of the exporting company and the broker, as players in the international market, international customers seek to invest in their suppliers. International companies, such as Suntory, use this tool to check the quality and supply chain of their supplier, in order to ensure the consistency of these aspects and adapt it to their code of conduct. Certifications such as Fair Trade are used as a way to ensure partnership between customers and suppliers and to ensure a long-lasting relationship. However, this depends on the supplier's ability to gain trust with its customers:

> More and more companies, which I was talking about before, are interested in having a firm, strong and secure partnership with the organization that produces the products. So now it is starting to return this Fair Trade certification, these things. There is interest, not from everyone, but from many. However, the company's ability to gain trust with the buyer is always linked to it, which is the most difficult. (Exporter company representative)
>
> I think they are interested in investing in suppliers, because this is the way to check quality, check the supply chain and this is very important for customers to have a better understanding and a better supply chain management. [...] Customers here take care of this, because it ensures consistency in the supply chain. I mean, if you have a strong supplier, you can do business for longer than if you have a weaker supplier. This social responsibility is very important for large companies like Suntory and, if you want to work with these companies, you need to be involved in a type of code of conduct and you must take this policy into account in your relationship with Suntory and with your suppliers, partners. (Broker representative)

Discussion

As already highlighted in the introduction of this case, companies seek to adopt sustainability practices in the internal environment and throughout their supply chains, seeking, above all, to improve performance and risk management (Seuring and Müller, 2008). Understanding the barriers and motivations for implementing sustainable practices also allows a better understanding of the challenges for the implementation of new processes. In this context the notion of sustainability is linked to the company's core business, which, because it is often organic processing, needs to meet the specific requirements of the legislation governing it. However, we can observe an orientation towards sustainability coming from the company's employees, either from senior management or from those responsible for the supply chain and quality.

Within the context of the case study it is observed that the pressure for the development of sustainable practices comes in great part from the clients, mainly the international ones. Although there is this external pressure, the company sees its suitability for certifications spontaneously, so that there is no need to educate the company in order to meet clients' demands for sustainability. Thus, although there is an orientation towards sustainability from the focal company, the implementation of sustainable practices comes mainly from the external environment of the company through the demand for certifications. We saw that the orientation towards sustainability is very much linked to the pursuit of certifications.

The relationship of the focal company with its suppliers is transparent and reliable. The support given to suppliers takes place with technical assistance, in the form of investment, training, and even with commodities. The company aims at a long-term relationship with its suppliers by enabling processes that are not ideal for them so that a supplier can develop. Thus, despite the fact that the focal company is involved in assessing suppliers in risk and performance evaluation, there is a priority for the company in its supply chain management for sustainable products. This is largely due to its development of sustainable practices internally. However, through certification, the company is concerned with ensuring the safety of its suppliers in its supply chain.

It was not possible to observe de-commoditization processes, incentives and rewards to suppliers that comply with sustainability policies, or regulations in their activities. Also, this study did not find any assistance to suppliers that are developing socio-environmental initiatives with their upstream suppliers or assistance to improve the capacities of suppliers generally, not just to benefit a single firm.

Regarding barriers and difficulties, they are the physical structure of the company, its productivity, the high production costs and the limitation of human and financial resources. Because the focal company's products have a high added value, care in the internal and external environment is highly important. The high costs of production and adaptation to certifications make the company's product more expensive, and the need to monitor professionals in the area is essential for the development of these activities. As a small company, the physical structure of the company did not allow an increase in production, which led it to merge with another company with a better production structure in 2019. Government barriers were pointed out in different ways in the company: first, in relation to the legislation that the company needs to comply with for its own maintenance, and second, in relation to public garbage collection, with accumulation of waste due to the insufficient weekly service. These results are consistent with what Johnson and Schaltegger (2015) found in their research.

Regarding motivations, complying with the legislation places the company in a positive light in relation to its customers. It is also observed that certification is seen as a factor that is costly, so there are complaints from managers regarding financial difficulties, and it is even recognized by customers. At the same time, it is an excellent risk management mechanism for operations' internal processes, as well as in the selection of suppliers and in their relationship with them. In addition, it is a determining factor for access to markets.

In the food sector especially, international buyers have demanded certifications as a governance mechanism to ensure the quality and transparency of their sustainable practices (Alvarez *et al*, 2010; Hajjar *et al*, 2019). However, we can also see that small companies are more limited in terms of qualified human resources and of technical and financial resources, which increases the challenges in adopting sustainable practices (Del Río *et al*, 2010). The main strategy to overcome those challenges and develop competences to sustainability is through collaboration with stakeholders such as research centres, universities and non-governmental organizations (NGOs) (Bustos and Moors, 2018; Hajjar *et al*, 2019). These partnerships are relevant to the implementation of certification and to learning and competitiveness in sustainability (Hajjar *et al*, 2019).

Learning outcomes

- This case has highlighted the challenges for a small company operating as a sustainable business seeking competitiveness in international markets.
- The case shows the importance of certifications for companies in the Global South to access international markets.
- The case highlights the relevance of partnership with non-traditional members in supply chains for sustainability purposes.

Questions

1 Does company size matter in introducing sustainability practices? Discuss.

2 Based on the case study of Natvita, what are the challenges as well as advantages for an SME implementing sustainable practices?

3 Discuss the inherent role of stakeholders in implementing sustainable practices. To what extent did it shape Natvita's sustainability practices?

Endnote

1 The authors acknowledge the financial support given by CNPq in the conduct of the research.

References

Alvarez, G, Pilbeam, C and Wilding, R (2010) Nestlé Nespresso AAA sustainable quality program: an investigation into the governance dynamics in a multi-stakeholder supply chain network, *Supply Chain Management,* **15** (2), pp 165–82

Ashby, A, Leat, M and Hudson-Smith, M (2012) Making connections: a review of supply chain management and sustainability literature, *Supply Chain Management*, **17** (5), pp 497–516

Beske, P and Seuring, S (2014) Putting sustainability into supply chain management, *Supply Chain Management*, **19** (3), pp 322–31

Bustos, C A and Moors, E H (2018) Reducing post-harvest food losses through innovative collaboration: insights from the Colombian and Mexican avocado supply chains, *Journal of Cleaner Production*, **199** (1), pp 1020–34

Caldera, H T S, Desha, C and Dawes, L (2018) Exploring the characteristics of sustainable business practice in small and medium-sized enterprises: experiences from the Australian manufacturing industry, *Journal of Cleaner Production*, **177**, pp 338–49

Del Río, P, Carrillo-Hermosilla, J and Könnölä, T (2010) Policy strategies to promote eco-innovation: an integrated framework, *Journal of Industrial Ecology*, **14** (4), pp 541–57

Elkington, J (1997) Partnerships from cannibals with forks: the triple bottom line of 21st-century business, *Environmental Quality Management*, **6**, pp 37–51

Hajjar, R *et al* (2019) Scaling up sustainability in commodity agriculture: transferability of governance mechanisms across the coffee and cattle sectors in Brazil. *Journal of Cleaner Production*, **206**, pp 124–32

Jia, F *et al* (2018) Sustainable supply chain management in developing countries: an analysis of the literature, *Journal of Cleaner Production*, **189**, pp 263–78

Johnson, M P and Schaltegger, S (2015) Two decades of sustainability management tools for SMEs: how far have we come?, *Journal of Small Business Management*, **54** (2), pp 481–505

Kasim, A and Ismail, A (2012) Environmentally friendly practices among restaurants: drivers and barriers to change, *Journal of Sustainable Tourism*, **20** (4), pp 551–70

Khalid, R U *et al* (2015) Putting sustainable supply chain management into base of the pyramid research, *Supply Chain Management*, **20** (6), pp 681–96

Kot, S (2018) Sustainable supply chain management in small and medium enterprises, *Sustainability*, **10** (4), p 1143

Neutzling, D M *et al* (2018) Linking sustainability-oriented innovation to supply chain relationship integration, *Journal of Cleaner Production*, **172**, pp 3448–58

Saeed, A M and Kersten, W (2019) Drivers of sustainable supply chain management: identification and classification, *Sustainability*, **11** (4), pp 1–23

Seuring, S and Müller, M (2008) From a literature review to a conceptual framework for sustainable supply chain management, *Journal of Cleaner Production*, **16** (15), pp 1699–710

Touboulic, A and Walker, H (2015) Theories in sustainable supply chain management: a structured literature review, *International Journal of Physical Distribution & Logistics Management*, **45** (1), pp 16–42

Walker, H and Jones, N (2012) Sustainable supply chain management across the UK private sector, *Supply Chain Management*, **17** (1), pp 15–28

Williams, B R and O'Donovan, G (2015) The accountants' perspective on sustainable business practices in SMEs, *Social Responsibility Journal*, **29** (1), pp 3–10

Yin, R K (2018) *Case Study Research: Design and methods*, 6th edn, SAGE, Thousand Oaks, CA

The circular supply chain 13

Study of a cross-industry collaboration

ANNE RATSIMANDRESY, ESCP BUSINESS SCHOOL, FRANCE

PROFESSOR JOE MIEMCZYK, ESCP BUSINESS SCHOOL, UK

Background

Human activities have been the main drivers of global environmental change since the Industrial Revolution. They have led to the breach of four of the nine planetary limits (stratospheric ozone depletion; loss of biosphere integrity; chemical pollution; the release of novel entities; climate change; ocean acidification; freshwater consumption and the global hydrological cycle; land system change; nitrogen and phosphorus flows to the biosphere and oceans) that allow the survival of most of the living beings of our era, including humans (Rockström *et al*, 2009).The planetary limits are the thresholds that humanity must not exceed in order not to compromise the favourable conditions in which it has been able to develop and to be able to live in a safe ecosystem. The four breached limits are the climate crisis, ocean acidification, ozone depletion and biodiversity loss. The scientific community considers that the crossing of these limits implies major risks that could be brutal, non-linear, potentially catastrophic, systemic and partly unpredictable (Rockström *et al*, 2009).

To address this situation, it is now indispensable to integrate the three pillars of sustainable development (also known as the triple bottom line) to our way of living: people, profit and planet. The challenge of sustainable development is to reconcile these three tenets for a better balance. Hence, the definition of sustainable development is a development that meets the needs of the present without compromising the ability of future generations to meet their own needs (Brundtland, 1987). It consists of economic performance (profit) guaranteeing along the way social (people) and environmental (planet) capital protection and restoration (Elkington, 1998). The achievement of this objective has been divided into 17 Sustainable Development Goals (SDG): no poverty; zero hunger; good health and well-being; quality education; gender equality; clean water and sanitation; affordable and clean energy; decent work and economic growth; industry, innovation and infrastructure; reducing inequality; sustainable cities and communities; responsible consumption and production; climate action; life below water; life on land; peace, justice, and strong institutions; partnerships for the Goals. These link to the 'millennium goal' defined by the United Nations in 2015, to be reached by 2030 (UN, 2021). With 10 years remaining, the issues raised by the three components of sustainable development are far from being resolved.

To reach this ambitious but necessary goal, all actors have a contribution to make and firms are now held more and more responsible by their stakeholders to take part in the transition towards a sustainably viable future (De Angelis *et al*, 2018) and these stakeholders can act in a number of different areas. In this chapter, we will focus on supply chain actors. The examples provided below give some insight into the various actions that can be managed by supply chain management (SCM) to address the three dimensions of sustainable development.

- **People**: This refers to the social dimension of sustainable development where companies' supply chains should ensure, for example, ethical management of their suppliers, addressing issues such as health and safety, decent working conditions, fair representation of the interests of the workers and other areas affecting people along their supply chains.
- **Profit**: The sustainable supply chain should be efficient and secure, allowing the company to create sustainable revenue. The economic benefit could range from the global value created, including for the different stakeholders of the company, to sustainable profit streams along the supply chains.
- **Planet**: This refers to the environmental dimension of sustainable development, where the supply chain should take into consideration the different impacts that it generates and try to limit the pressure on the environment. This can be achieved, for example, through purchasing sustainable resources (such as renewable, bio-degradable materials), using eco-design for their products (for example, taking into account the

product life cycle when designing for reparability, and responsible disposal of the product). The environmental management of the logistics of the firm can also take into account the fuel consumed and the carbon generated during inbound/outbound transportation.

We have seen how sustainable supply chains in general can be levers to reach the sustainable development of firms and organizations. We will now focus on the subcategory of circular supply chains. Our current way of consuming is linear as it follows an extract–use–dispose pattern, where resources are obtained, transformed, consumed, and thrown away when no more utility is found in the products. In this context the notion of a circular economy (CE) brings a new angle, wherein the circular economy proposes a model where the circulation of resources and energy would be retained in a closed loop (here, closed loop considers the reverse logistics after the item has reached end of its life cycle), allowing the need for the inclusion of new inputs/raw materials into production systems to be reduced. Currently there is less consensus on a unified or official definition for the circular economy, as it integrates different dimensions related to:

- **green economy**: environmentally friendly growth;
- **performance or service economy**: focusing on selling services rather than products; and
- **industrial ecology**: the study of material and energy flows through industrial systems.

The Ellen MacArthur Foundation (EMF) has driven the CE agenda as a charity working with governments, businesses and educators to facilitate the transition from a linear to a circular economy (Ellen MacArthur Foundation, 2021). The EMF summarizes a CE in three pillars:

(a) designing out waste and pollution;

(b) keeping products and material in use; and

(c) regenerating natural systems.

The circular economy implies different principles, such as using circular inputs (for example, resources that are safe, renewable, recycled) and using circular processes and designs. This means that products should be designed to allow their lives to be extended; they should also be reused or dissembled at the end of their lives, so they no longer become waste and maintain their highest value at all times. Circular flows – to recapture the value of the products through reuse, remanufacture, redistributing or recycling options – use systems-thinking, considering all the stakeholders of the firm, looking for connections between ideas, people and resources belonging to the company network to design solutions. In this context, companies can contribute to embedding circularity to their own supply chains. There are very diverse forms and patterns for circular supply chains; some of the most common are briefly described as follows:

- Reverse logistics or closed-loop supply chains (CLSC), which recover value and avoid waste through activities such as return processes, product repair and refurbishment.
- Eco-industrial parks (EIP, sometimes called 'industrial symbiosis'), based on the famous example of Kalundborg in Denmark (Wikipedia, 2021), which is a form of transversal supply chain dedicated to closing the resource flows between different organizations by grouping together within an industrial area to gain competitive advantage by material exchange, energy exchange, information exchange etc.
- By-product synergies are innovative methods to dispose of waste and create value from waste supplied by a partner. According to the consultancy International Synergies, which specializes in industrial symbiosis, 80% of industrial symbiosis and by-product synergy opportunities are outside the boundaries of the industrial sector.

This first theoretical section of the chapter aimed at presenting the basic knowledge related to sustainable supply chains, with a highlight on circular supply chains. The following section develops a practical case study involving these concepts. The case presented here is a by-product synergy set up between two leading global companies belonging to two different industrial sectors, with established supply chain policies and environmental objectives, which they decided to pursue further in their sustainability efforts and practices by partnering.

The Heinz–Ford case

This case is based on a real collaboration that started in 2012 between two companies: Ford Motor Company and H. J. Heinz. The details reported here are taken from the press releases put out by the two companies (Ford Media Centre, 2021) as well as from the details given by Dr Vidhu Nagpal, R&D director of H. J. Heinz and at the start of the partnership.

The first case company, Ford Motor Company, is a US automaker founded in 1903 (Ford Motor Company, 2021). The company designs, manufactures, markets and services cars, trucks and SUVs worldwide. Ford is the second-largest US-based automaker and the sixth largest in the world based on 2019 vehicle production. Ford's sustainable initiatives include responsible material sourcing, reducing greenhouse gas emissions from vehicles and protecting human rights throughout the supply chain. The second case company, H. J. Heinz, is a US food processing company founded in 1869 specializing in ketchups, sauces and meals (Heinz, 2021). Heinz manufactures thousands of food products in plants on six continents and markets these products in more than 200 countries and territories. The company claims to have 150 number-one or number-two brands worldwide. Heinz ranked first in ketchup in the United States with a market share of more than 50 per cent. Sustainable measures taken by H. J Heinz include greenhouse gas reduction targets, reduced energy consumption, sustainable use of palm oil and control of relevant suppliers on the issue of animal welfare.

In the early 2010s Heinz, Ford, The Coca-Cola Company, Nike and Procter and Gamble began a technical collaboration to develop sustainable materials. The common idea was to find a way to decrease their negative environmental impact along with decreasing their dependence on petroleum-based plastics currently used at that time. The idea was to innovate in the composition of the PET plastics used in their products by increasing the integration of plant-based materials. These five companies could exchange ideas freely as they were not competitors:

- **Heinz**: The challenge for Heinz at that time was to innovate on their packaging to propose a sustainable offer without increasing costs. Cutting off petroleum and using new materials was very expensive. Dr Vidhu Nagpal was hired to drive packaging innovation through material innovation for Heinz to solve this equation. The objective that Dr Nagpal's teams wanted to reach at that time was to develop a packaging integrating up to 30% of plant-based technologies in the PET plastic used to bottle the brand's best-selling product, Heinz Tomato Ketchup. A significant challenge at that time lay in the origin of the plants that should be integrated in the technology. First, the material used should not originate from plants especially grown for this purpose. The reason at that time was to not add to the 'food vs biofuel/biomaterial criticism' where concern about land availability and the use of crops for biofuel or biomaterial production rather than for food was high during the 2010s. The second challenge lay in the proper use of agricultural waste. Indeed, agricultural waste should preferably be left on the field as the decomposition process is necessary to provide nutrition to the soil. The team of researchers integrated these constraints and ran searches to find alternative sources for the new material. They realized that Heinz was generating a lot of factory waste that could be repurposed: for example, two million tons of tomatoes were used annually to produce Heinz's best-selling product, ketchup. In the process, the coating (the peels) were pulled off the tomatoes during the transformation process. This material, 'pomace', contained a considerable amount of fibres that were thrown away by the factories. This waste generated subsidiary costs related to its treatment. The research teams, in partnership with Coca-Cola R&D scientists, found an innovative way to recycle these natural fibres by using them to replace the polymer fibres used to reinforce plastics (petrol-based fibres used at that time were usually expensive). Unlike other agricultural waste, tomato pomace was an industrial waste that was not intended to provide nutrients for arable land anyway. They turned this industrial waste into valuable components for a plant-based composite material, along with decreasing their costs.

- **Ford**: At the same moment, Ford (also belonging to the same R&D group) was working on a related technology and also facing challenges: their plant-based composite material was well received by their sustainability-sensitive consumers, except for two concerns. First, the composite material was made from agricultural waste (not the ideal source of biomaterial, as explained earlier), and second, this agricultural waste was generating an annoying odour in the finished product. These two points were critical for Ford. During a meeting of the R&D group, Heinz submitted to Ford the idea of a collaboration to find a new application for the pomace-based composite for the automotive industry. Ford was interested in the material and offered to partner to investigate the use of these fibres for composite materials for vehicle manufacturing, using Ford facilities for compounding and extrusion moulding in their laboratories. From 2014, the material was tested in vehicle wiring racks and storage bins. Related patents have been registered for this innovation, which allowed the use of the plastic to be cut by 20%, replaced by tomato fibres.

For Ford, the successful development of such composite material reduces dependence on petrochemicals in vehicle manufacturing. For Heinz, a partner's use of its by-products constitutes a subsidiary revenue stream and reduces its waste volume. The adequate choice of the source of the bioplastic did not negatively impact the crop production destined to food production. It is a case of a collaborative and circular supply initiative having both an environmental and economic positive impact. According to Dr Vidhu Nagpal, this partnership was possible because of the cross-industrial nature of the initiative: the protagonists were able to exchange ideas to create innovative solutions and to put in place this collaboration thanks to the fact that they were not competitors and had complementary knowledge of their industrial sectors.

Table 13.1 briefly summarizes the different aspects of the collaboration for both parties.

Table 13.1 The collaborative process and advantages achieved through the Heinz–Ford collaboration

Context	H. J. Heinz	Ford Motor Company
Initial situation	• Heinz wants to increase its sustainable impact and decrease its dependency on petroleum though the utilization of plant-based composite materials for their packaging. • Heinz wanted to favour factory waste rather than agricultural waste as source for their biomaterial and was doing research in this direction in partnership with The Coca-Cola Company.	• Ford wants to increase its sustainable impact and decrease its dependency on petroleum though the utilization of plant-based composite materials in their vehicle manufacturing.
Opportunity for collaboration	• Heinz releases industrial waste from millions of tons of tomatoes generated by ketchup production in their factories. Treatment of this waste represents a subsidiary cost for the factories.	• Ford was struggling with an agricultural waste-based plastic that also had the inconvenience of generating an annoying odour in their finished products. There was a need for a new material solving these issues.

(continued)

Table 13.1 (continued)

Context	H. J. Heinz	Ford Motor Company
Contribution to collaboration	• Heinz had already made significant R&D progress in the integration of tomato pomace into plastic materials. • Heinz supplies Ford with the tomato pomace.	• Ford offered to adapt Heinz technology with a new application dedicated to automotive manufacturing, thanks to its laboratories and facilities.
Advantages	• Heinz extends its knowledge of the applications of the use of its industrial by-products. • By selling the pomace, Heinz converts an industrial waste and cost into a subsidiary revenue.	• Ford decreases the amount of petroleum in its vehicle wiring racks and storage bins by 20%. • The pomace-based material is significantly cheaper than the polymer fibres previously used.

Learning outcomes

- Circular supply chains are one of the responses that firms can operate to contribute to sustainable development. They can take diverse forms, such as reverse logistics, closed-loop supply chains, eco-industrial parks, by-product synergies…. Circular supply chains can involve, to some extent, collaboration between different organizations.
- Circular supply chains can involve companies belonging to different sectors, wishing to operationalize sustainable development, in a win–win arrangement. Eighty per cent of circular collaboration opportunities are cross-industrial.
- The Heinz–Ford collaboration is a case of cross-sector by-product collaboration: the waste generated by the agrifood industry becomes a raw material for the automotive industry.

Questions

1 What role do supply chains play in corporate sustainability?

2 What do you understand by the term 'circular economy'? How does it relate to 'sustainable development'?

3 What are the main circular supply chain configurations?

4 How does the Heinz–Ford supply partnership integrate the principles of sustainable development and the circular economy?

References

Brundtland, G H (1987) Our Common Future – call for action, *Environmental Conservation*, **14**, pp 291–94

De Angelis, R, Howard, M and Miemczyk, J (2018) Supply chain management and the circular economy: towards the circular supply chain, *Production Planning & Control*, **29**, pp 425–37

Elkington, J (1998) Partnerships from cannibals with forks: the triple bottom line of 21st-century business, *Environmental Quality Management*, **8**, pp 37–51

Ellen MacArthur Foundation (EMF) [accessed 7 July 2021] Our Mission is to Accelerate the Transition to a Circular Economy, *Ellen MacArthur Foundation* [Online] www.ellenmacarthurfoundation.org/ (archived at https://perma.cc/N9YZ-97H4)

Ford Motor Company [accessed 7 July 2021] About Us, *Ford Motor Company* [Online] https://corporate.ford.com/about/history.html (archived at https://perma.cc/669Q-X7MT)

Ford Media Centre [accessed 7 July 2021] Ford Media Centre [Online] https://media.ford.com/content/fordmedia/feu/gb/en.html (archived at https://perma.cc/JG5R-5WRT)

Heinz [accessed 7 July 2021] The Proud History of Heinz, *Heinz* [Online] www.heinz.com/Our-Heritage (archived at https://perma.cc/84DJ-6NMC)

Rockström, J *et al* (2009) A safe operating space for humanity, *Nature*, **461**, pp 472–75

UN [accessed 7 July 2021] Make the SDGs a reality, *UN* [Online] https://sustainabledevelopment.un.org/ (archived at https://perma.cc/Q2FM-N7SL)

Wikipedia (2021) [accessed 7 July 2021] Kalundborg, *Wikipedia* [Online] https://en.wikipedia.org/wiki/Kalundborg (archived at https://perma.cc/ENS5-3LTJ)

The cargo-partner iLogistics Centre 14

A warehouse made completely out of wood

MILAN LANI, CORPORATE DIRECTOR PRODUCT MANAGEMENT CONTRACT LOGISTICS, CARGO-PARTNER GMBH AUSTRIA

ALAN ZALAS, CARGO-PARTNER GMBH AUSTRIA

Introduction

This chapter is provided by cargo-partner as a case study to explore their sustainable SCM practices, focusing on environmental sustainability. Sustainability has become a key component of cargo-partner's strategy, focused on several factors which influence the level of sustainability engagement in cargo-partner's supply chain and its interaction with its partners, such as:

- As sustainability has gained substantial attention in recent years, cargo-partner has focused on sustainability of materials used, sustainable processes applied and selection of their collaboration partners.
- Driving towards green and sustainable practices in third-party (3PL) supply chains such as cargo-partner from a strategy perspective, not only structural changes but also time and financial and human resources. Hence, we see that these efforts are usually driven by companies' vision and supported by top management (Evangelista *et al*, 2017).
- The adoption of green SCM practices in cargo-partner has shown results in terms of emission impact, sustainability of materials utilized, company human resource, amortization on investment and sustainability engagement.

Therefore, this chapter introduces how sustainability is defined and embedded in 3PLs followed by a case study highlighting how environmental sustainability has shaped the choices for cargo-partner's iLogistics Centre Austria.

Understanding how sustainability is embedded in 3PLs

In the 1990s, natural and social capital were considered as unrestrictive and therefore without economic value or a measure of their gain or loss (UNCTAD, 1996), contrary to today's conditions, where the current prognosis on the consumption rate of the earth's natural resources is estimated to be 50 per cent faster than it can be replenished (WWF, 2014). Hence, we can see that the current discussions in the academic literature as well as in business have shifted towards the sustainability agenda. The sustainable agenda entails the triple bottom line (TBL), including:

- **Economic sustainability**, which involves the benefits to economic aspects of a company and its stakeholders (Vachon and Mao, 2008; Steurer and Konrad, 2009; Dyllick and Hockerts, 2002).
- **Environmental sustainability**, which focuses on reducing environmental impact through more efficient use of materials and natural resources and through pollution prevention (Rothenberg *et al*, 2001).
- **Social sustainability**, which involves benefits that have an impact both outside the company (ie benefits that a company may bring to the surrounding society) and inside the company (ie supporting worker health, safety and well-being, encouraging future generations to develop skills and capabilities, and promoting a high quality of life) (Pagell and Wu, 2009).

Sustainable development encourages 'a development that meets the needs of the present without compromising the ability of future generations to meet their own needs' (Brundtland, 1987). When considering sustainability, the long-term perspective is imperative, wherein the life-cycle assessment (LCA, also known as life-cycle analysis, eco balance, and cradle-to-grave analysis) needs to be utilized, which is a technique to assess environmental impacts associated with all the stages of a product's life:

- raw material extraction through materials processing;
- manufacture;

- distribution;
- use;
- repair and maintenance;
- disposal or recycling;
- its impact of production until its recycling.

Evangalista *et al* (2017) noted that 'despite an increasing number of third-party logistics service providers (3PLs) [regarding] environmental sustainability as a key area of management, there is still great uncertainty on how 3PLs implement environmental strategies and on how they translate green efforts into practice'. Therefore, we will see, based on one project of cargo-partner, namely the iLogistics Centre in Fischamend, Austria, how sustainability is planned, executed and translated into cargo-partner's daily operations.

The case company profile: cargo-partner

cargo-partner is a privately run full-service logistics provider with a broad portfolio of air, sea and land transport and logistics services. With over a third of a century of expertise in information technology and supply chain optimization, they develop tailor-made services for a variety of industries in order to create competitive advantage for their clientele around the world. cargo-partner was founded in 1983 and achieved a turnover of €1.05 billion in 2020 with 3,150 employees (Zalas, 2018).

cargo-partner aims to optimize all processes along the supply chain and concentrate on quality assurance and sustainable progress in order to offer fast and efficient solutions and to ensure the long-term success of the company, its customers, its employees and the industry in a sustainable manner. The continuous improvement process is based on their responsibility to their clients, their passion for innovation and their conviction of the importance of economic, ecological and social sustainability. cargo-partner's quality assurance measures are fully integrated into in-house IT systems and are supported by several national and international certificates and memberships.

Building and utilizing the iLogistics Centre

Due to cargo-partner's steady growth, the company is investing heavily in the expansion of its global logistics capacity. At the company's headquarters in Fischamend, right next to Vienna Airport (VIE), it was necessary to expand the warehouse capacity in order to avoid any bottlenecks. cargo-partner is concerned with sustainable operations from the start, hence the decision for the warehouse was in favour of a wooden structure in order to achieve the sustainability goals. The company owner, Mr Stefan Krauter, wanted to show what is technically possible and demonstrate that environmental and economic sustainability can go hand in hand. He set an example with the construction of the sustainable and innovative iLogistics Centre made out of wood. The new warehouse was built within one year, as 365 days passed between the breaking of the ground in June 2017 and the start of operations at the new warehouse. It took 10 weeks to construct the building envelope. The sustainable warehouse offers 24,500 pallet spaces in the high-bay warehouse on 7,800 m^2 as well as storage on 2,000 m^2 in the incoming and outgoing goods area and a small parts warehouse (spare parts logistics) on 1,800 m^2. Some key facts for the warehouse are as follows (Zalas, 2019):

- 12,250 m^2 storage space.
- 24,500 pallet slots.
- 2,000 m^2 operative handling area.
- 17 airtight truck loading docks + 3 docks for other purposes (2 are fully covered with glass to let more natural light into the warehouse (removable) and 1 station has the fixed container with a carpentry workshop).
- Wide and narrow aisle racking systems (induction-based navigation system).
- 32,000 small parts bins (KLT bins).
- Long and heavy goods are stored in the 8-metre-high cantilever rack and moved with a special four-way forklift.
- 8 m long oversized gate for long goods.
- Fully automated Lean-Lift, ideal for the storage of light- and dust-sensitive small parts. The Lean-Lift is connected to cargo-partner's electronic warehouse management software (and with cargo-partner's own supply chain management platform 'SPOT'). It is fully automated and works according to the 'goods-to-picker' principle.
- Carpentry workshop for packaging of oversized parts.

With its innovative timber construction, this warehouse facility is a milestone in sustainable architecture and will hopefully set a new standard in the industry. With the modern iLogistics Centre, cargo-partner makes an active contribution to climate protection and is well equipped for the requirements of a dynamic future. The wood-based construction allows for natural temperature (15–25 °C +/– 2 °C) and humidity (max. 70%) control and thus low operating costs.

The building design combines modern material ecology with energy-efficient and sustainable architecture. The entire building – with the exception of the elevator shafts – is made completely out of wood, from the wall and roof construction to the façade. The construction was completed within only one year. At the end of the building's life cycle after 70–100 years, the construction material (wood) does not require elaborate disposal procedures, but can eventually be used as an environment-friendly energy source. Located at a strategic point right next to the highway, five minutes from Vienna Airport, 20 minutes from the city centre and 40 minutes from Bratislava, the site is ideally situated at a major European distribution hub. The iLogistics Centre offers maximum flexibility and enables late cut-off times in air, sea, road and parcel transport. Some key facts relevant to environmental, social and economic indices included the creation of 35 new jobs and local investment into land, construction and planning costs which totals approximately €17 million.

Building with wood is active climate protection. In order to absorb as much CO_2 from the material cycle for as long as possible, it is worthwhile using as much wood as possible in highly durable products. Wood replaces conventional building materials such as bricks or concrete, whose production is carbon-intensive, thus avoiding additional CO_2 emissions. Furthermore, timber constructions are massive carbon reservoirs.

The timber used is PEFC and FSC certified and was harvested from sustainably cultivated forests in Bavaria and Austria. In addition to modern, energy-efficient lighting technology, 20 thermal-bridge-optimized loading docks enable further energy savings. The lock gates don't open until the truck is hermetically docked. The warehouse is not only temperature and humidity controlled, but also virtually dust-free. In addition to excellent insulation and floor quality, all truck docks have locks installed to ensure temperature stability, humidity limits and cleanliness of the warehouse.

Sustainable environmentally friendly material sourcing and operations entailed the following raw materials (Table 14.1):

- Timber construction.
- Total of 4,200 m^3 timber used = CO_2 reduction of 8,400 t (Every m^3 which replaces other building materials reduces CO_2 emissions by an average of 1.1 t. In addition, timber is a carbon reservoir: 0.9 t of CO_2 stored in every m^3).
- Cost-efficient temperature range between 15 °C and 25 °C (+/– 2 °C).
- Constant humidity of up to 70%.
- Environment-friendly energy source after reaching end of its service life (70–100 years).
- Fire-resistance class of R60 and high earthquake resistance.
- Large-scale photovoltaic plant can be retrofitted onto the roof.

Having discussed the materials and operations that impact the environment and local businesses, cargo-partner is also keen to develop the social and economic aspects of sustainability.

Table 14.1 Emission calculation indices

What does 8,400 t of CO_2 reduction really mean in practice?

cargo-partner calculated the effect of these saved emissions:

- Every cubic metre of wood which replaces other building materials reduces the CO_2 emissions in the atmosphere by an average of 1.1 t. In addition, timber constructions are massive carbon reservoirs: 0.9 t of CO_2 are stored in every cubic metre of wood.
- This makes a total of: 1.1 saved + 0.9 stored = 2 t CO_2 / m^3 wood.
- In the iLogistics Centre, 4,200 m^3 of wood was used = ~4,200 t CO_2 saved + ~4,200 t CO_2 stored.
- This results in a total CO_2 reduction of 8,400 t. Note: Half of this was 'saved' (by replacing other materials), the other half was 'stored' (by acting as a carbon reservoir).
- 8,400 t of stored CO_2 correspond to the yearly power consumption of 1,240 households or
- The average CO_2 emissions of 1,774 people driving their cars for one year.

Sustainability from an economic and social point of view

Nobody can 'save the world on their own' – with this notion cargo-partner intends to contribute and play their role to make it a little better. cargo-partner sees the greatest leverage of our limited resources where they can influence the system and the processes with a change in the right direction. However, having mentioned environmental and process-related projects, cargo-partner also contributes to social sustainability. Hence, with this aim, cargo-partner supports and/or implements selected projects that meet their requirements for sustainability. Some of these are:

- The support of social projects with a number of organizations around the world for over 10 years, including Jugend Eine Welt, Light for the World, SOS Children's Villages and numerous other international and local institutions.
- In the recent past too, cargo-partner has repeatedly joined new initiatives that advocate environmentally friendly technologies in logistics. These include the Council for Sustainable Logistics, which deals with:
  - future-proof city and warehouse logistics;
  - promoting the development of e-trucks;
  - Logistics 2030+ project, which offers solutions to optimize urban freight transport; and
  - contributing to projects which aim to reduce CO_2 in the Vienna and Lower Austria district through design and innovative solutions.

cargo-partner has been operating logistics services in Fischamend for over 35 years, and by expanding its capacities with the new iLogistics Centre it created around 35 new jobs on site – in total there are around 280 employees at the headquarters location The warehouse expansion also strengthens the local community and triggers growth impulses for regional development. The creation of new jobs strengthens purchasing power and quality of life in the entire area and in this way has a direct economic benefit for the common good. For example, the number of residents in the communities around the airport has increased by 12.3 per cent over the past 10 years (Zalas, 2019).

The sustainable supply chain agenda is an integral part of cargo-partner's operations and strategic decision making, albeit the case study only highlighted one project in a selection of interesting projects to follow in the 3PL arena.

Learning outcomes

- This case has highlighted the importance of considering sustainability for effective decision making in 3PL.
- The case provides an example of 3PL decision making during a growth phase where sustainability criteria are involved from inception to execution.
- The case provides a good example of the embedding of a 3PL, especially the environmental sustainability in their strategic planning.

Questions

1. What are the three key sustainability areas that cargo-partner has excelled in?
2. To what extent does strategic planning of a company, in this case cargo-partner GmbH, impact the sustainability agenda of a company?
3. What are the key strengths of cargo-partner in terms of sustainability strategy?

References

Dyllick, T and Hockerts, K (2002) Beyond the business case for corporate sustainability, *Business strategy and the Environment*, **11** (2), pp 130–41

Brundtland, G (ed) (1987) *Our Common Future: The World Commission on Environment and Development*, Oxford University Press, Oxford

Evangelista, P, Colicchia, C and Creazza, A (2017) Is environmental sustainability a strategic priority for logistics service providers?, *Journal of Environmental Management*, **198**, pp 353–62

Pagell, M and Wu, Z (2009) Building a more complete theory of sustainable supply chain management using case studies of 10 exemplars, *Journal of Supply Chain Management*, **45** (2), pp 37–56

Rothenberg, S, Pil, F K and Maxwell, J (2001) Lean, green, and the quest for superior environmental performance, *Production and Operations Management*, **10** (3), pp 228–43

Steurer, R and Konrad, A (2009) Business–society relations in Central-Eastern and Western Europe: how those who lead in sustainability reporting bridge the gap in corporate (social) responsibility, *Scandinavian Journal of Management*, **25** (1), pp 23–36

United Nations Conference on Trade and Development (UNCTAD) (1996) Incentives and Disincentives for the Adoption of Sustainable Development by Transnational Corporations, United Nations, Geneva

Vachon, S and Mao, Z (2008) Linking supply chain strength to sustainable development: a country-level analysis, *Journal of Cleaner Production*, **16** (15), pp 1552–60

WWF (2014) *Living Planet Report: Species and places, people and places*, WWF International, Gland, Switzerland

Zalas, A (2018) Central Eastern European Logistics & SCM Excellence Award Application: cargo-partner iLogistics Centre Austria, cargo-partner presentation

Zalas, A (2019) Einreichung: BVL – Nachhaltigkeitspreis Logistik 2019, cargo-partner iLogistics Centre Fischamend, cargo-partner GmbH, Austria

15 'What is the impact of your company on the world?'

Developing changes towards supply chain sustainability

DR ANA P FERREIRA ALVES, FEDERAL INSTITUTE OF EDUCATION, SCIENCE AND TECHNOLOGY OF RIO GRANDE DO SUL (IFRS), BRAZIL

DR MINELLE E SILVA, EXCELIA BUSINESS SCHOOL, FRANCE

Introduction

This chapter is based on a case study developed with a medium-sized family-owned company (Company Alfa) located in the Rio Grande do Sul state, Southern Brazil. The research was undertaken over years, aiming to understand how this manufacturer of rubber products started to move from a traditional business model to a sustainable one. This is a representative case of a transformative approach of actions within the company as well as sustainability actions disseminated throughout its supply chain.

To understand the case, additional information is necessary on the context where it is placed (Fritz and Silva, 2018). Company Alfa is headquartertered in a city with huge influence from German and Italian immigration that occurred at the beginning of the 20th century. The local culture therefore has some elements from those countries. In addition, the Rio Grande do Sul state has a border with Argentina and Uruguay. This context needs to be considered when discussing the practices of the company.

Our investigation identified that in the past decade the company started to reflect on its influence on society. Thus, from a branding assessment, the managers started to question the positioning of the company in the market as well as the reasons why the company needs to exist. By reflecting on these reasons, several questions emerged, such as:

- What is the company's contribution to and impact on the community in which it is placed, to its supply chain members and to the world in general?
- If the company closed its manufacturing operations, what would happen in the world and in the marketplace?
- Why is the company located in this particular city and region of the country (and not another city, eg São Paulo)?

Based on these reflections, John and Steven – the top managers of the company – began to find answers to these questions and to think about the company's business model. After discussions on how to better manage the business in order to have a positive impact on the world, they decided to develop several changes leading to sustainability and sustainable operations. To this end, it would be necessary to introduce sustainability into its core business once one of the answers found was: 'we want to make a difference in the world'. Therefore, the company started to develop actions to preserve nature, the quality of life of the people and the company's profitability. This was possible by developing sustainable changes in strategy, in human resources, in marketing and in supply chain management.

This case study focuses on the understanding of the real impact of companies shifting their internal actions as a first step towards changing their supply chain actions and operations. Over time, Company Alfa strengthened its business model for sustainability, which reinforced its contribution to make a difference, starting from its direct stakeholders. We emphasize the two central ideas to understand this case: (1) supply chain sustainability refers to 'the specific managerial actions that are taken to make the supply chain more sustainable with an end goal of creating a truly sustainable chain' (Pagell and Wu, 2009: 38), and (2) sustainability is only practised when it becomes a keyword on a company's mission statement and an integral part of its daily operations and activities, which is argued in this case (Silva and Figueiredo, 2020).

The company

Company Alfa is a Brazilian company founded in 1924. The company was the first in the Rio Grande do Sul state to develop products based on rubber. Its initial activities included repair of tyres and the manufacture of waterproof fabrics with rubber, besides the production of rubber components. Over 100 years, Company Alfa has gone through different positions, strategies and management practices, including a centralized model and a decentralized model focusing on strategic business units and a collegiate approach. The company has changed its operating markets several times due to the business opportunities and manufacturing expenses considered, which became uneconomical. In the past, according to Alves and Nascimento (2016), the following items were part of the product portfolio:

- balls and tennis rackets;
- life jackets and inflatable boats;
- professional and children's clothing;
- utensils for hospitals and barracks, among others.

Currently, Company Alfa operates in three segments of the market – (a) education, (b) health and (c) coating – from the manufacturing of diversified items such as erasers, hot/cold water bags, thermal bags, elastic bands, rubber balls and others. This is a family company, with John being the grandson of the first owner. Steven is the general director of the company. Both John and Steven consider themselves facilitators within Company Alfa. According to them, their work as facilitators aims to direct efforts to reflect on different points of view that can bring diverse contributions and solutions to Company Alfa. In other words, their role is to stimulate the whole organization in developing new actions focused on the impact target. They are both sustainability enthusiasts and want sustainability actions to be developed by all stakeholders.

It is also worth mentioning that the company operates throughout Brazil and South American countries, through a network of sales representatives and promoters. To keep pace with production, the company has two industrial units, one located in the centre of the city and another located in the industrial district of the same city. In addition, Company Alfa directly employs approximately 750 employees and has around 1,000 subcontractors, including its direct suppliers (Alievi and Antinarelli, 2015). Nowadays, the company ranks among the most sustainable companies within Brazil.

Changing the strategy: 'turning the key'

The 'turning the key' process (as it is called by John and Steven) began in 2007 with the hiring of an agency to evaluate the brand positioning of Company Alfa.

This evaluation sought to strengthen the company's brand and its positioning. However, this work raised several questions not exclusively linked to the brand. What does the brand stand for in the world? What do we want to do with the brand? How will Company Alfa differentiate itself from other companies? In short, Company Alfa's existence was not clearly defined, nor were its characteristics that define and make it unique as an organization (the company's DNA).

After several questions and reflections, Steven and John realized that if the company stopped its operations, few things would have had to change. Another company would take Company Alfa's place in the marketplace, people would continue to work, and so on. However, that was not what they wanted. They wanted more! They wanted to make a difference in the world. Gradually, Steven and John understood that Company Alfa only exists because there are people who influence, and are influenced by, the company's activities. So, they would have to work with and for people! The answer to all inquiries was to bring people and organizations together to create sustainable solutions. It would then find a new way of thinking about its business scope and context.

John and Steven began to reflect on the management of the company and the best way to do business – considering sustainability and the company's impact upon the world. It is important to realize that the role of top management was essential to consolidate a shift towards more sustainable development. In this case, a company specializing in sustainability and social business was hired to advise Company Alfa on these reflections – a partnership that continues to this day.

In 2008, a new management model based on principles of sustainability started. According to John and Steven, the idea was clear: they could not become a non-governmental organization (NGO) to help the environment and people, and leave the business flowing in parallel, but should seek to integrate sustainability into Company Alfa's core business. Thus, sustainability came to be understood as an opportunity and investment, not just as an organizational expense (Orsato, 2006). The broad concept of sustainability, and the interfaces with supply chain management, strongly suggests that sustainability is indeed a licence for doing business in the 21st century (Carter and Easton, 2011).

In 2009, the 'turning of the key' occurred; the turnaround represents a transformation in the way that the company was managed, including sustainability practices for the benefit of the environment and society as a whole – the triple bottom line (social, economic and environmental aspects) (Elkington, 1997). Thus, the institutional commitment, the drivers (see Table 15.1), the strategic decisions and the restructuring of Company Alfa's organizational chart were reassigned. It was established that the strategic area of action is well-being. To this end, well-being is defined as 'to make the world a good place for everyone', based on the understanding that welfare is part of the individual and the collective.

Table 15.1 Company Alfa's sustainability drivers (Company Alfa, 2016)

Drivers
We act according to the people.
We seek relevant solutions with simplicity.
We are ethical in all our relationships.
We preserve for posterity.
We operate in ethical markets that value life.

Table 15.2 Company Alfa's directions and meanings (adapted from Alievi and Antinarelli, 2015)

Directions	Meaning
Non-renewable inputs	Gradually replace non-renewable inputs used in the production process with renewable inputs in all company activities.
Carbon-neutral company	Reduce emissions of greenhouse gases and offset those that cannot be avoided, to achieve the goal of becoming a carbon-neutral company.
Import substitution	Reduce and gradually replace the imports made by products of the national market, valuing local production.
Occupation and income	Privilege occupation and income in new business models, ensuring the promotion of social and economic development in the region where the company is installed.
Difference between lowest and highest salary	Contribute to the policies of remuneration and performance, positions and salaries to collaborate effectively to better distribute income and reduce social inequalities.
Market with restrictions	Do not engage in business of any kind with industries that impose ill-treatment on animals, employ child or slave labour, or involve operations involving tobacco, war material, gambling, pesticides or alcoholic beverages.

In addition to the sustainability drivers, some sustainable directions were defined by the company. Table 15.2 shows these directions, which represent internal goals and strategic organizational actions. To reach these directions, it is necessary to have a closer relationship with different stakeholders in order to address all actions effectively.

To consolidate the implementation of the sustainable directions, a new organizational structure was set up to monitor changes in strategies, starting with the idea of bringing management closer to a cooperative and collaborative environment. Until 2009, Company Alfa operated through its strategic business units. Each business unit was well defined and well separated, consisting of different departments for each unit. Considering the 'turn of the key', collegiate deliberations were held about a more integrated management, in which collective decisions were sought, respecting internal and external diversity and embedded complexities, as well as involving greater dialogue between the organization members. Managers of the defunct departments were renamed coordinators and directors were appointed by facilitators. That is why John and Steven became the facilitators within Company Alfa.

Colleges are classified based upon their operations comprising supply chain, innovation, customers and production, and support, covering learning spaces, incubator, impact and strategy. The flattening of the hierarchical structure of the organization provided the constitution of new areas, such as the 'Impacts area'. The Impacts area aims to reduce, minimize and/or eliminate the impacts of the company's processes and products on the environment and society, with autonomy to interfere in Company Alfa activities. It should be noted that the power relations within the organization chart did not disappear, but the potential conflicts and tensions were softened by the proposal to cooperate to obtain good results for the organization.

However, in order to consolidate Company Alfa's new way of thinking, it was decided to keep some strategies from the old business model, since the proposal was not to carry out a reengineering process, where one starts from scratch to build something new. The idea was to reflect on Company Alfa's role in society, as John and Steven understood that their company was not fully sustainable. In fact, every sustainability practice relies on particular activities developed internally and throughout the supply chain (Silva and Figueiredo, 2020), which change according to the business model of each organization. Therefore, by analysing their practices, Company Alfa is not a standard to be followed by other organizations since each organization must understand how best to introduce socio-environmental practices in their context.

Advancing changes for sustainability

Table 15.3 illustrates some changes that were defined in the company after 2009 as strategic decisions. These decisions depend on the directions selected and were developed collectively by following the new organizational structure and decisions.

Table 15.3 Sustainable directions and strategic decisions (Alves and Nascimento, 2016)

Directions	Strategic Decisions
Non-renewable inputs	• Introduction of natural rubber in the production process. • Reuse of waste in the production process itself.
Carbon-neutral company	• Inventory of greenhouse gas emissions for all scopes. • Compensation of GHG emissions by planting native trees. • Cancellation of participation with stands at trade fairs.
Import substitution	• Replacement of suppliers from China with companies located in Brazil and Argentina. • Withdrawal of products from the portfolio offered.
Occupation and income	• Permanence of the plants in the city of Santa Cruz do Sul. • Project with rubber tappers from the Amazon to supply rubber. • Project for first employment of young people in social vulnerability. • Partnership with solid waste pickers' cooperative of Santa Cruz do Sul for the correct disposal of recyclable waste.
Difference between lowest and highest salary	• New calculation basis for salary readjustments. • Reduction of working hours to 40 hours per week, increasing the value of each employee's time worked.
Market with restrictions	• Control of suppliers for good work practices. • Cancellation of the production of non-toxic rubber mats for the tobacco industry.

There are also partnerships with educational institutions (eg Federal University of Rio Grande do Sul – UFRGS), SESC (ie representative of commerce), government agencies and non-governmental organizations. In 2013, Company Alfa together with SESI and SENAI (ie governmental bodies) proposed a project for the construction of a social innovation laboratory (lab). This laboratory is a collective and collaborative space that seeks to involve different stakeholders of the company: universities, community, government, suppliers and other organizations. The proposal is that the laboratory fosters support and movement in the areas of learning and incubation of projects and lines of work. This is part of some social sustainability actions developed by the company.

Amid internal changes, the company realized that to practise sustainability further, actions needed to be developed with supply chain members, as there is no sustainable company without a sustainable supply chain (Beske and Seuring, 2014). Currently, the social innovation lab is a space for discoveries and promoting interactions between the company (its structure, products, employees) and the community (people and institutions). The space aims to have significant impact upon teaching and learning and also creating solutions that help to improve people's lives (eg new product development projects).

Translating internal actions into supply chain sustainability

To ensure that strategic decisions were fully achieved, Company Alfa started to develop a set of connections with supply chain members. This integration happened mainly because its orientation towards sustainability started when the company reflected upon its impact on the world. According to Silva *et al* (2020), once a company develops or strengthens its strategic orientation, it is possible for supply chain sustainability to emerge. To this end, these authors point out that actions rely on strategies, which definitely is the case in Company Alfa:

- **Environmental sustainability**: Alves and Nascimento (2016) identified multiple sustainability actions developed by this company in a proactive way. This proactive behaviour demonstrates that the company is oriented for sustainability and engaged in working with stakeholders towards a more sustainable supply chain. For example, concerning environmental sustainability, the company created several programmes and projects (eg reverse logistics, transportation, and organic food consumption).

- **Social sustainability**: To achieve these programmes and projects – and others related to social sustainability – partnerships with suppliers and distributors were needed, aiming to disseminate sustainability practices throughout the supply chain. Facilitators claim that all company actions prioritize transparent dialogue and collaboration with stakeholders. Therefore, Company Alfa keeps in touch with its suppliers and customers to communicate decisions and understand how they are facing everyday situations.
- **Economic sustainability**: By following the new organizational structure, the company targeted developing a closer relationship with its stakeholders, which was clearly observed with the new project, 'natural rubber'. Previously to 'turning the key', the company was focused on cost as the main reason to buy a product, which means the traditional way of doing business. However, new values became part of the company and new actions started to be developed. For example, to increase the use of natural rubber (ie material less impactful to the environment), the company started a new project developed with indigenous communities in Amazonia, which represents another geographical context, but can contribute to its strategy. The project had as its main target to ensure that a fair trade could exist with these groups, which was not the case before. There are many problems of local migration because of low wages in collecting rubber from nature; therefore, the new project renews the connection between indigenous people (ie suppliers) and its locality (ie the forest).

In this context, environmental changes were shared and developed together with transportation companies, among others. During some meetings and annual events, the carriers were required to reduce their emissions. From the first annual event, the company engaged the transport suppliers; in the second year, they had some results that they shared with other suppliers (most competitors). According to John, 'we explained to them [carriers] the way we measure our GHG emissions [...] [and] today we have almost all transport suppliers doing the GHG inventory; now five [out of six] are starting emission reduction'. In a complementary way, using his words, 'we are not forcing anyone to do anything, we just called upon them. Our purpose when we did this was not to force them, it was just to show the things that we were doing'.

In addition, as presented in Table 15.3, the company started to develop some market restrictions, which created some trade-offs in its financial results. For instance, Company Alfa has decided to stop selling its products to tobacco companies, which were one key buyer in the region. The region where the company is located is centrally based on tobacco production. Even having some products specially developed for these buyers, the company understood that maintaining that business connection no longer represented its strategy and how they intend to work as a business. Therefore, they incorporated the financial trade-off because they need to search for new buyers and start new product development projects. This decision made other supply chain members understand that moving towards sustainable operations was not a superficial decision, but in fact sustainability had become part of the core business.

The company has developed multiple actions throughout the supply chain to ensure they apply its orientation towards sustainability as part of the new strategic decisions. Based on this evidence, we assume that Company Alfa's proposal is not to change the world or solve all global problems, but rather to verify that the company's processes can be modified and realized in a more sustainable way and, consequently, practise the strategy and new business model. This perspective has helped the company to increase its positive impact in the world.

Reflections

Facing this trajectory, which includes moments before the turn, during the turn and after the turn of the key, John and Steven have other answers to the initial concerns. They believe Company Alfa has a reason to exist: people. They understand that if Company Alfa disappears today, much will change because the company is seeking to make a difference in the world, contributing to people's quality of life without harming the environment. It also involves supply chain members (eg as the above-mentioned indigenous people) who are sometimes forbidden to stay in their context because of the external pressures, for example with payment of low wages. By focusing on people, Company Alfa understands that they can really make a difference, because by following their strategic decisions they have an impact on society. Some issues that should be addressed were:

1 Supply chain sustainability relies on mindset change, which in this case was well represented by the company's reflection upon its impact on the world.

2 Orientation towards sustainability is essential for the company in moving in a strategic way from reflections to actions while ensuring an effective practice.

3 Strategic decisions cannot remain general, but should be turned into specific actions involving multiple stakeholders.

4 To introduce supply chain sustainability, companies do not need to be born sustainable, because they can change their orientation towards sustainability.

In addition, two reflective questions emerge for your company:

5 What is the contribution of your company to society?

6 How does your company impact the world?

When companies define their strategic decisions and include supply chain members in moving towards supply chain sustainability, there are multiple gains for all involved. It creates trust, information sharing, long-term relationships, risk sharing, competitive advantage and customer satisfaction, which are key things in managing a supply chain (Min *et al*, 2019). As presented by the authors, nowadays companies that do not think about or practise sustainability are not following the needs of the market.

Finally, changes in the way developed by Company Alfa create other elements such as resilience: when facing crisis, a low impact can be identified. For instance, during the Covid-19 pandemic, despite the need for lockdown, few changes were observed in the strategy of the company in its connections with supply chain members (eg maintenance of previous orders and payment) and a strong sustainability practice. The company established dialogues and constant virtual meetings to assess what measures needed to be taken to ensure the well-being of all stakeholders. Facilitators created a work committee to monitor the situation and make it efficient. In this context, a contingency plan was developed, guiding the company's operation with a focus on health and safety.

Learning outcomes

- This case study demonstrates the importance of strategic orientation towards supply chain sustainability. Through describing the shift in processes, the case provides a good example of changes over time. This in turn means that it is not only about saying that the company is sustainable; rather it involves an effective and evolving practice of sustainability.

- The case provides an example of a transformative change from a traditional to a sustainable business model. The transition process relies on strategic decisions and actions developed both internally and externally.
- This case study highlights the need for top management support in introducing supply chain sustainability, which includes taking care of people and creating a clear understanding of companies' contribution in society.
- The case also provides an example of how family companies and medium-sized companies can engage with supply chain sustainability, which is not limited to large and multinational companies as usually presented in the literature.

Questions

1. To what extent are companies and their supply chains responsible for taking sustainability actions? Are they impactful on society?
2. What are the main supply chain sustainability actions within Company Alfa? Please use quotes from the case to justify your answer.
3. What is required to maintain the new sustainable business model in Company Alfa? What happens if your suppliers do not engage with that?
4. Do you believe these strategic decisions can be sustained over time?
5. If you were the manager of Company Alfa, would you have followed the same steps as John and Steven or would you develop a different sustainability strategy? Please justify your answer.
6. As a consumer, do you see the value of these changes for a more sustainable supply chain? What would be the best actions to communicate this to final consumers?

References

Alievi, R M and Antinarelli, A (2015) Construindo a gestão estratégica sustentável: um estudo sobre a empresa Mercur SA, *Revista de Administração da Universidade Federal de Santa Maria*, 8, pp 69–83

Alves, A P F, and Nascimento, L F M (2016) Proatividade de práticas sustentáveis: uma análise das práticas da empresa Mercur SA, *Revista de Administração da Universidade Federal de Santa Maria*, **9**, pp 25–42

Beske, P and Seuring, S (2014) Putting sustainability into supply chain management, *Supply Chain Management*, **19** (3), pp 322–31

Carter, C R and Easton, P L (2011) Sustainable supply chain management: evolution and future directions, *International Journal of Physical Distribution & Logistics Management*, **41** (1), pp 46–62

Elkington, J (1997) *Cannibals with Forks: The triple bottom line of 21st century business*, Capstone, Oxford

Fritz, M M C and Silva, M E (2018) Exploring supply chain sustainability research in Latin America, *International Journal of Physical Distribution & Logistics Management*, **48** (8), pp 818–41

Min, S, Zacharia, Z G and Smith, C D (2019) Defining supply chain management: in the past, present, and future, *Journal of Business Logistics*, **40** (1), pp 44–55

Orsato, R J (2006) Competitive environmental strategies: when does it pay to be green?, *California Management Review*, **48** (2), pp 127–43

Pagell, M and Wu, Z (2009) Building a more complete theory of sustainable supply chain management using case studies of 10 exemplars, *Journal of Supply Chain Management*, **45**, pp 37–56

Silva, M E and Figueiredo, M D (2020) Practicing sustainability for responsible business in supply chains, *Journal of Cleaner Production*, **251**, pp 119621

Silva, M E *et al* (2020) The role of orientation towards sustainability in supply chains: insights from empirical experiences, *Benchmarking*, doi:10.1108/BIJ-07-2017-0184

INDEX

Bold page numbers indicate tables, *italic* numbers indicate figures